John Louis Petit

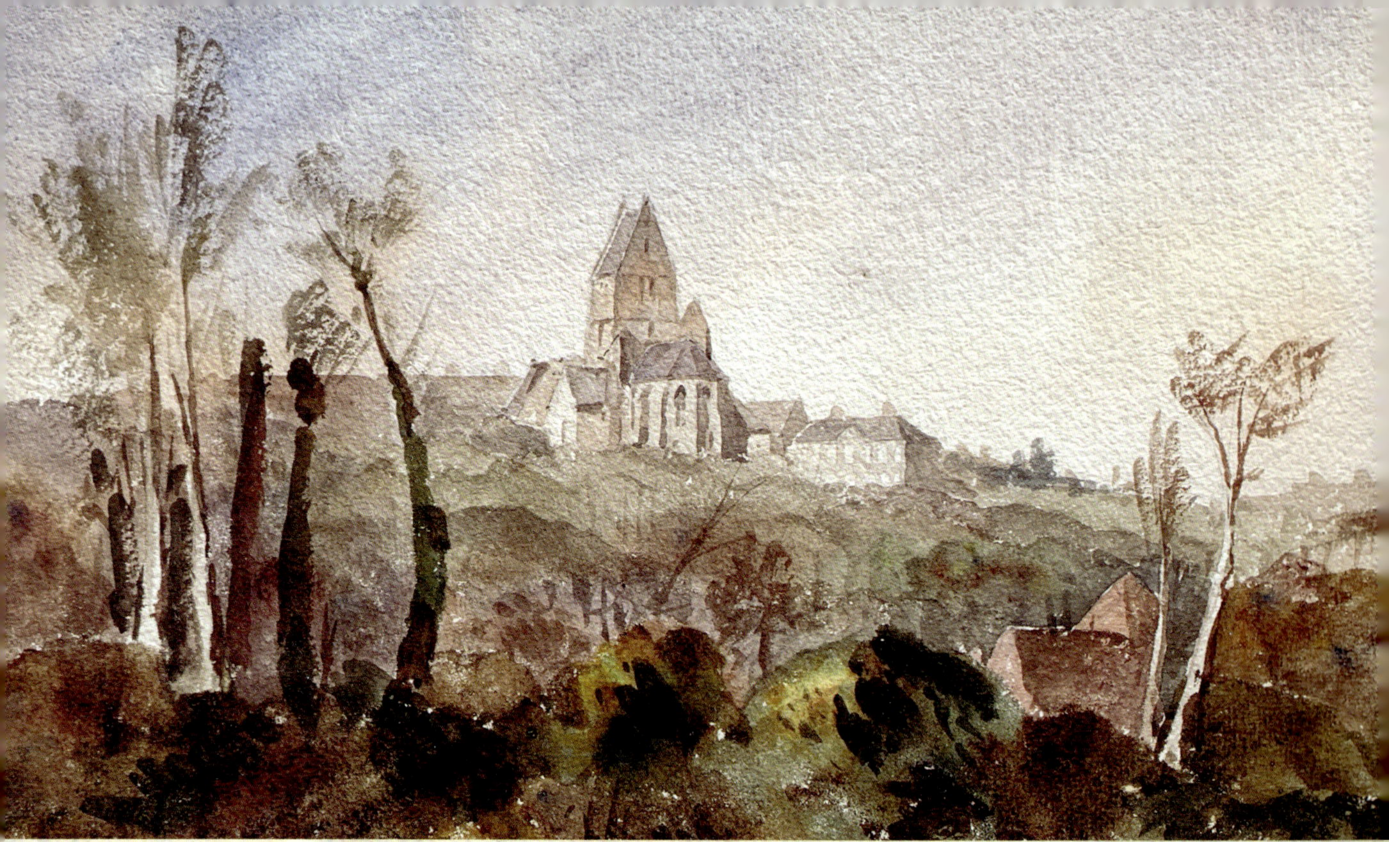

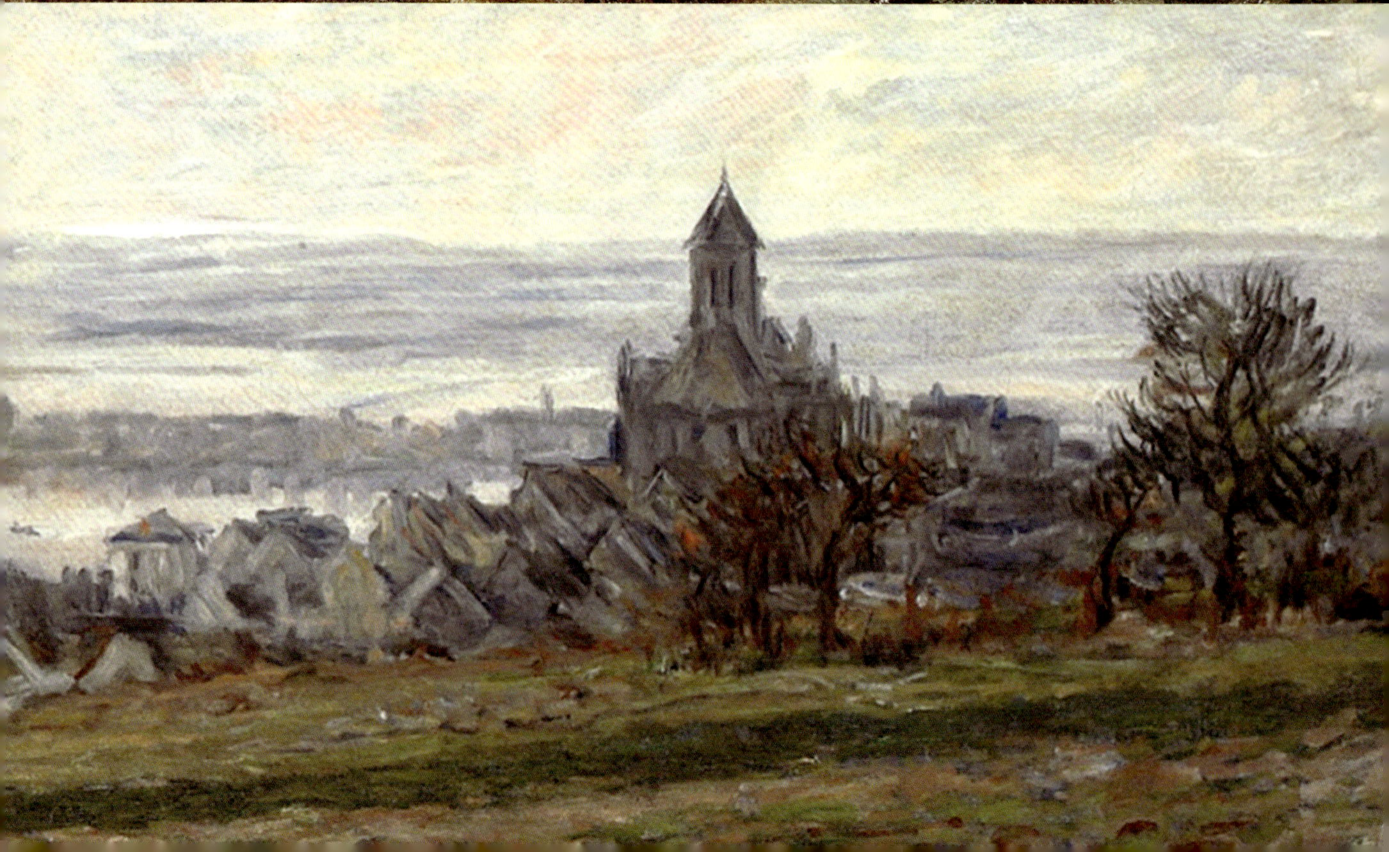

J. L. PETIT

Britain's Lost Pre-Impressionist

2. Frontispiece opposite above: *Orval*, Normandy, 1854
3. Frontispiece opposite below: Claude Monet, *Church at Vétheuil*, 1881
   Public domain image, wikiart, original in private collection

PHILIP MODIANO

RPS PUBLICATIONS

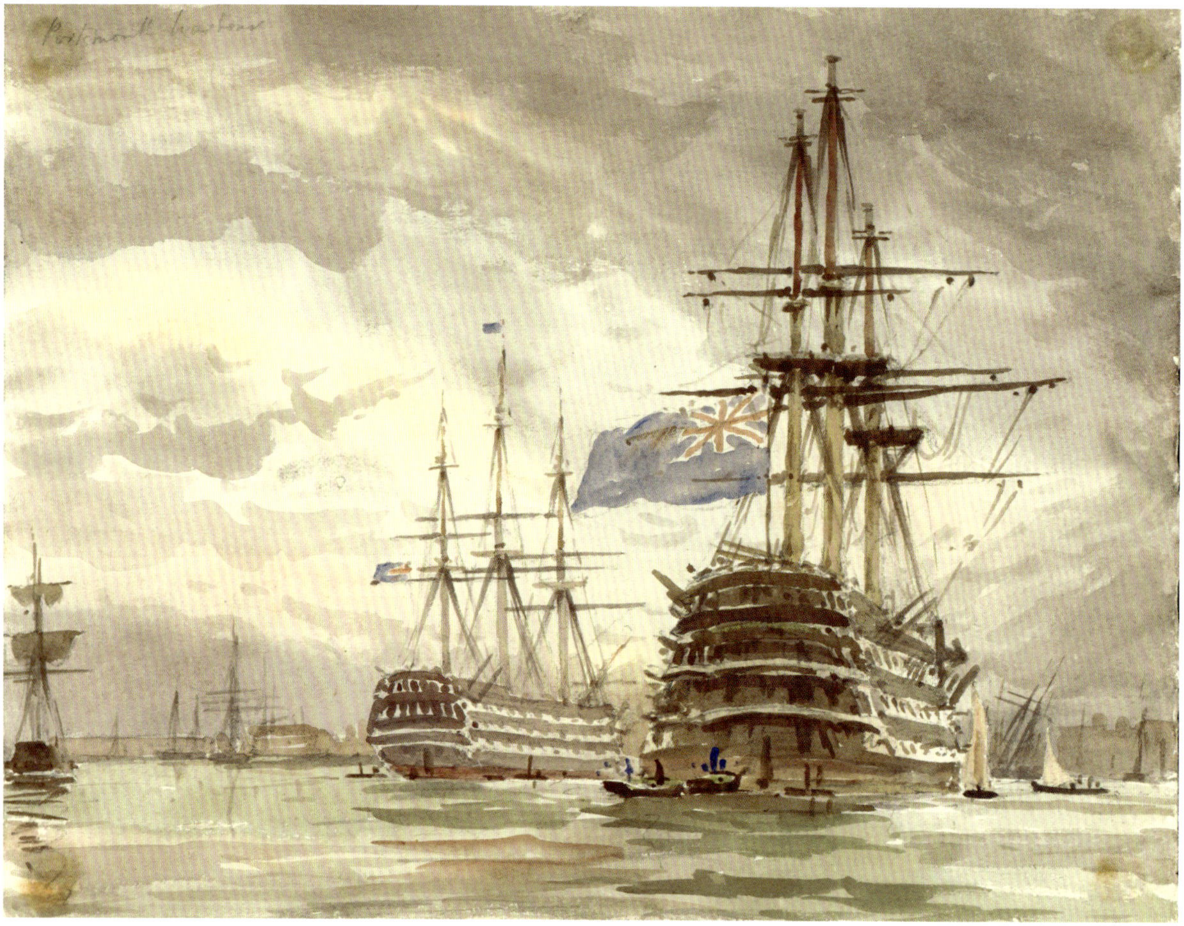

4. *At Portsmouth,* c. 1839 Courtesy Special Collections, Hartley Library, Southampton University (MS283)

Contents

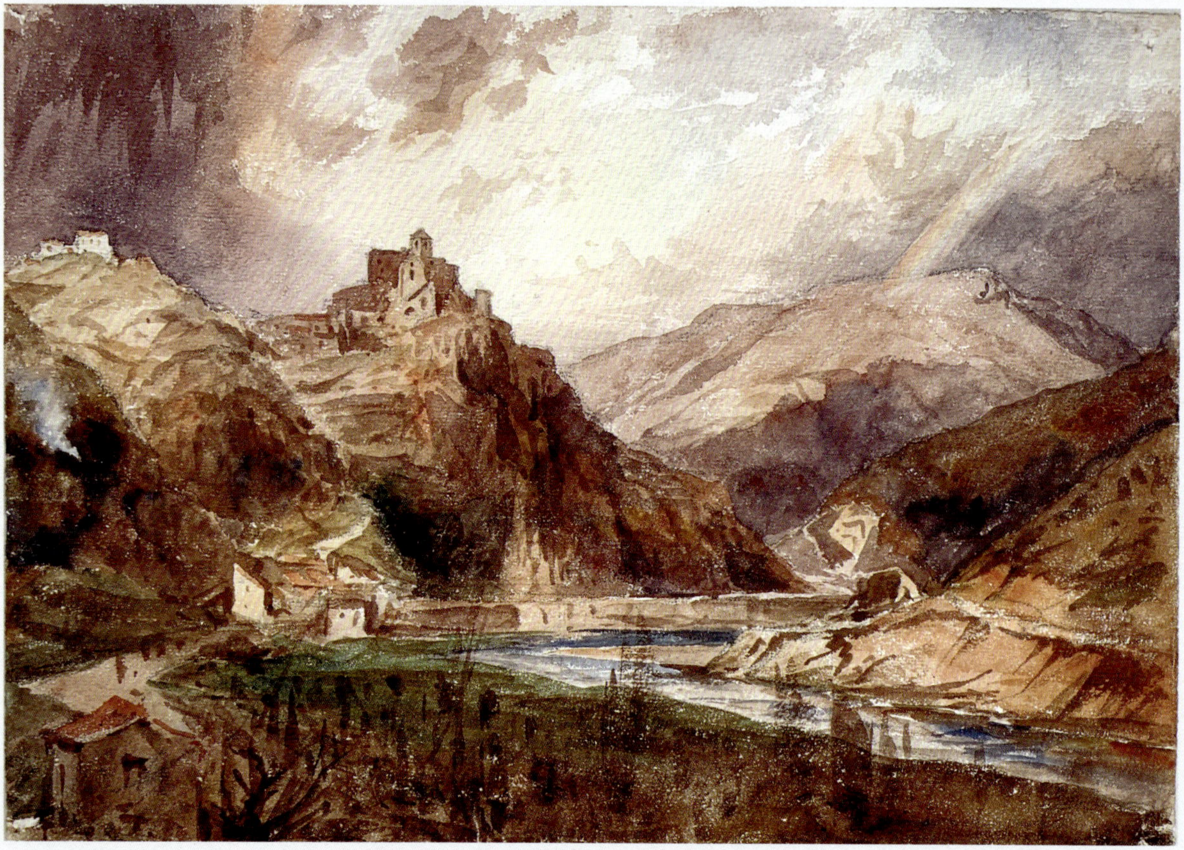

5. *On the Allier,* 10 April 1854

Foreword

by Dr Trevor James

There are many examples of historical figures from all ages being reinterpreted and their reputations rising or in some cases falling. But the story of John Louis Petit is extraordinary even in that context. From national treasure in the 1850s and 1860s, he was almost entirely forgotten by the turn of this century. Now we are starting to see that his contemporaries had the better judgement. While the focus of this book is Petit's art, we must not forget that architecturally he was also important, and has been equally overlooked in recent years.

This is not the easiest time to reintroduce a watercolour artist of the nineteenth century. Modern art has captured the minds and pockets of patrons. Yet, on the other hand, the absence of fashion in this corner of art history allows us to be objective, and assess his significance, completely independently of the unpredictable art market and its hype. In this we can parallel Petit's own disdain for such constraints and influences. We will make hay while the sun shines elsewhere.

I have had the pleasure of watching this research develop over the past three years, and have seen firsthand how Petit's art of locations around Staffordshire can interest and be accessible to school students as well as adults. The authenticity and passion of the artist shines through the 150 years since the pictures were completed. Now with this broader introduction to the artist's accomplishments his importance on many levels becomes more apparent, and we see a uniquely modern artist for the mid-nineteenth century.

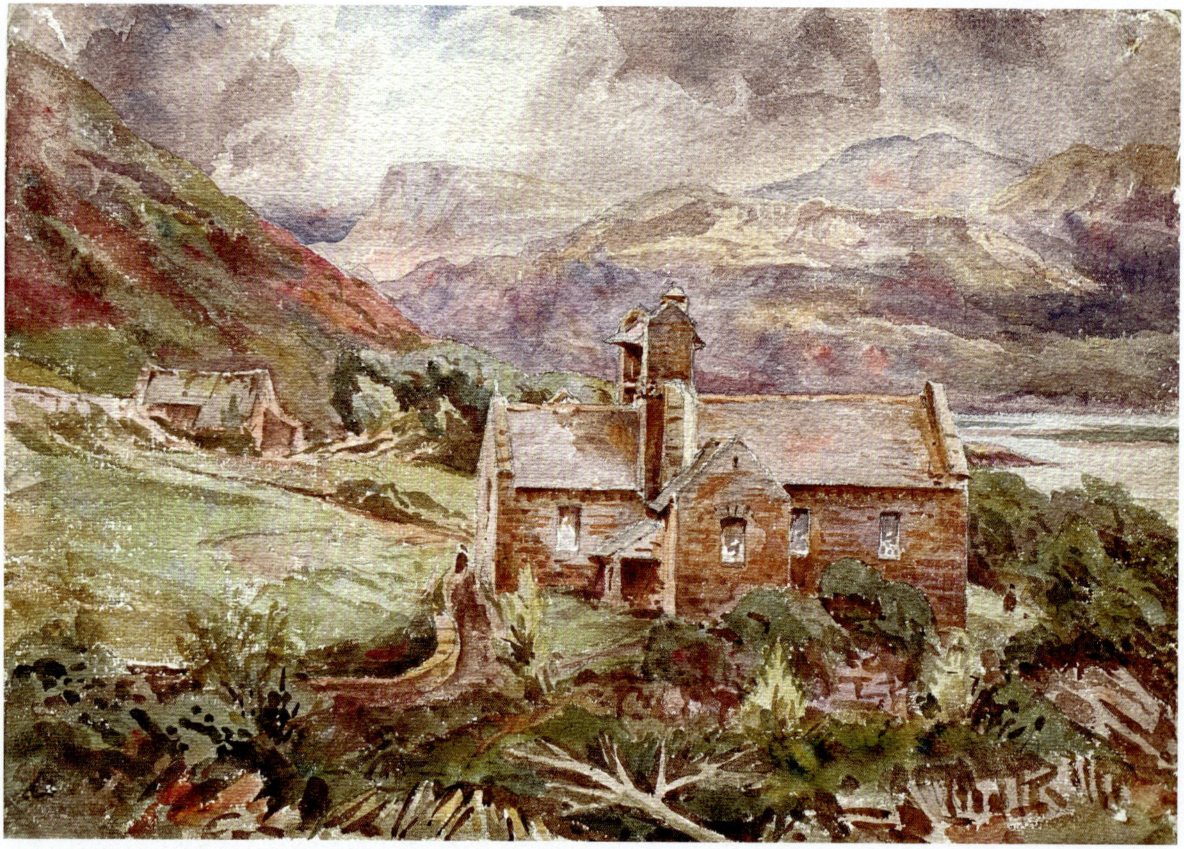

6. *Caerdeon,* 14 September 1866. The building is now under protection of the Friends of Friendless Churches
7. Opposite page, top left: Portrait of Petit as a young man
8. Opposite page, top right: J. L. Petit, photograph in later life
   Likely to have been taken by Philip Delamotte, or by Susannah Petit

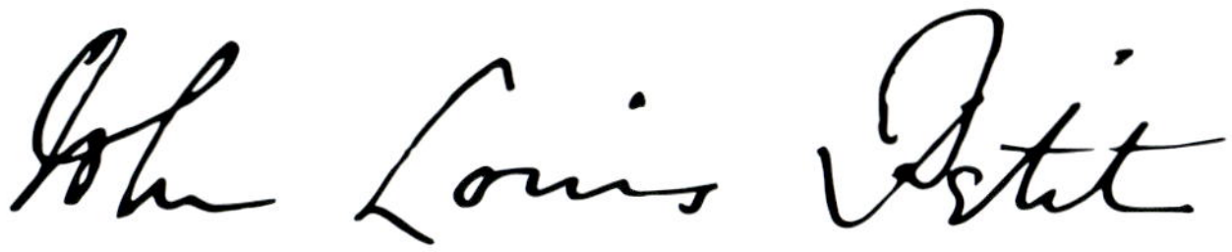

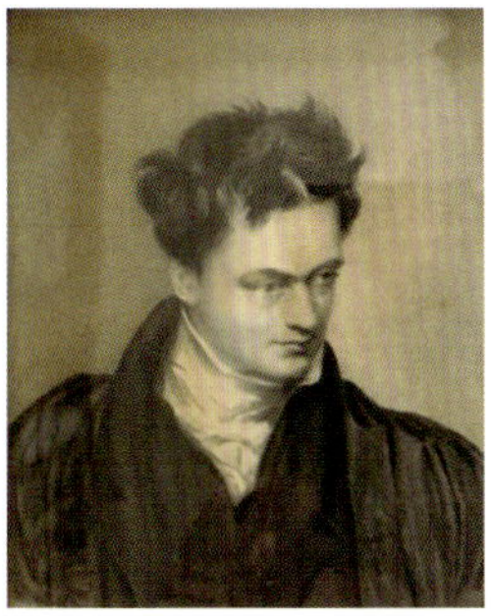

John Louis Petit (1801–68) was highly appreciated as an artist in his day. He was also a leading writer and speaker on architecture, one of the strongest opponents of the Gothic Revival. As an architect he built only one church (see opposite) but he contributed many designs and ideas to others. His art was mainly exhibited at his large public lectures and at the Architectural Exhibitions sponsored by the Royal Institute of British Architects (RIBA) during the 1850s and 1860s.[1] Because he never tried to sell his work, after he died most of his art was lost until the 1990s. As it has been widely dispersed since then, only now is the full breadth of what he achieved gradually being uncovered.

This book is an introduction for those encountering Petit for the first time, or for those who would like an overview of his art.

Petit was not just a very good artist, remarkable even in that well-endowed century of British art, but unusual too. Unusual because he stood apart from contemporaries in Britain after 1850, Pre-Raphaelite or classical, and because the path he chose coincided in some respects with what would become prevalent in France, a little later. Subsequently it would take many decades for art in Britain to catch up.

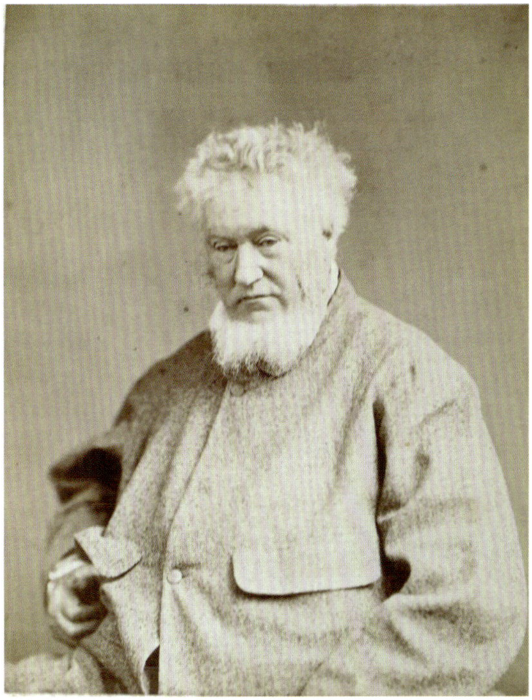

Painting from the 1820s to the 1860s, Petit's activity starts during the 'golden age' of British watercolourists. His early pictures, prior to 1845, were never exhibited. After that date he began to exhibit at public lectures that he gave and this later art becomes more and more distinctive. While the majority of his art was of medieval churches - indeed Petit ranks as one of the greatest historical artists of churches - this book will focus on his other work, where he painted more freely, unconstrained by the market or convention.

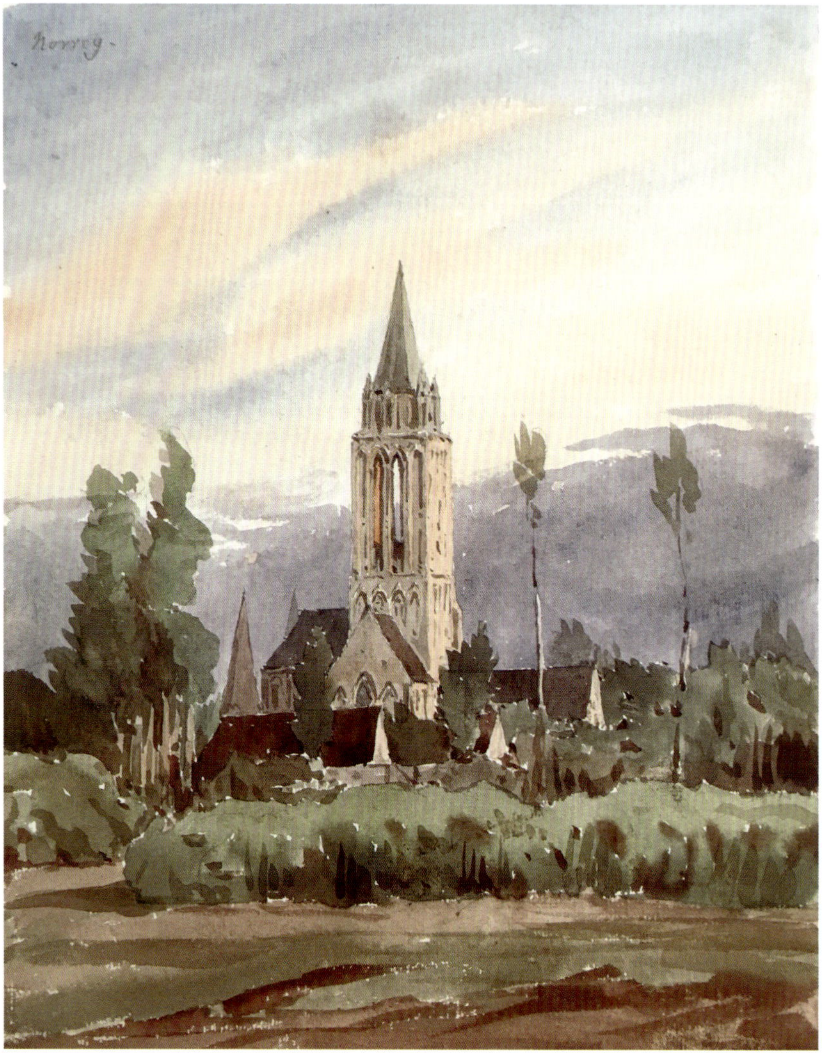

Painting intensively for over 40 years, he was as dedicated as any professional. As we can understand from the long poem he wrote at the end of his life, *The Lesser and the Greater Light,* Petit painted to convey the spiritual beauty of nature and the precious beauty of medieval churches at risk from thoughtless restoration. Working neither for the commercial market nor for patrons, he painted to express his beliefs, his love of nature and to help explain his opposition to the dogmas of the Gothic Revival. Petit's pictures became a significant draw for his public lectures, which continued until his last year.

Following his death in 1868, there was a major exhibition in London of 339 of his pictures.[2] Then the vast majority of Petit's art, over 10,000 works, disappeared for 120 years. Petit had married but died childless. His papers and art went to three sisters who had lived with him for the previous twenty years and who had travelled and painted with

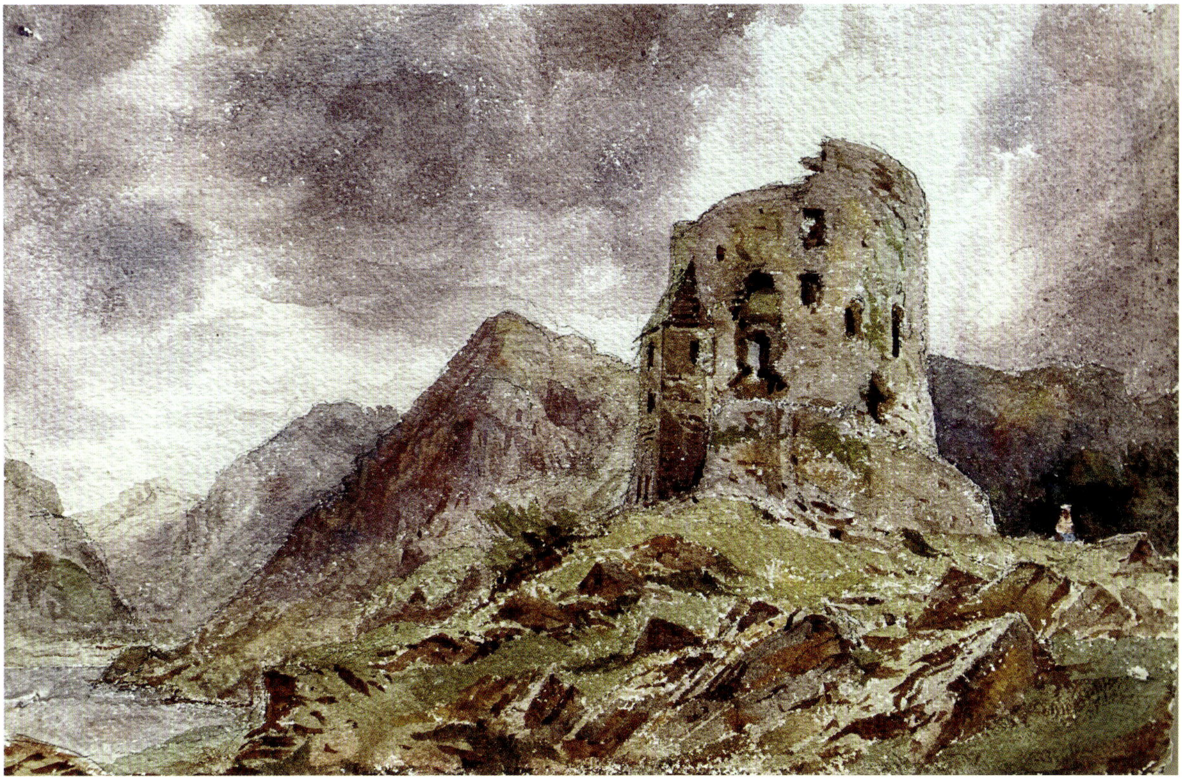

9. *Dolbadarn Castle,* 1 July 1858
10. Opposite: *Norrey,* 1839

him. One in particular, Emma, was his major support, organizing his work into folios, arranging the posthumous exhibition, and publishing the long poem he had written and three articles he had not completed. However, when his sister died everything went to a nephew who appeared to take no interest.

The hoard was discovered in an attic or outbuilding of a house in Surrey that had belonged to Petit's grand-niece. New owners dumped the pictures in auctions during the 1980s and 1990s. They were scattered widely, and never studied as a whole. The research underpinning this book covers only about one third of the total, perhaps representative, but one cannot be certain. Good examples appear, unattributed, most years.

John Ruskin (1819–1900), and his remarkable five-volume analysis of landscape art, *Modern Painters,* can help us understand Petit's work. Significantly, despite the profound differences in their architectural writing and in the style of their watercolours, Petit found new ways to paint what Ruskin advocated, more directly than those artists more closely associated with Ruskin's writing.

The first, introductory, part of this book explores his unusual motivation; how he was different from his contemporaries; and how what we can see now is not quite the same as his contemporaries and family focused on. Then the main sections of the book give examples of the variety of his work during his career.

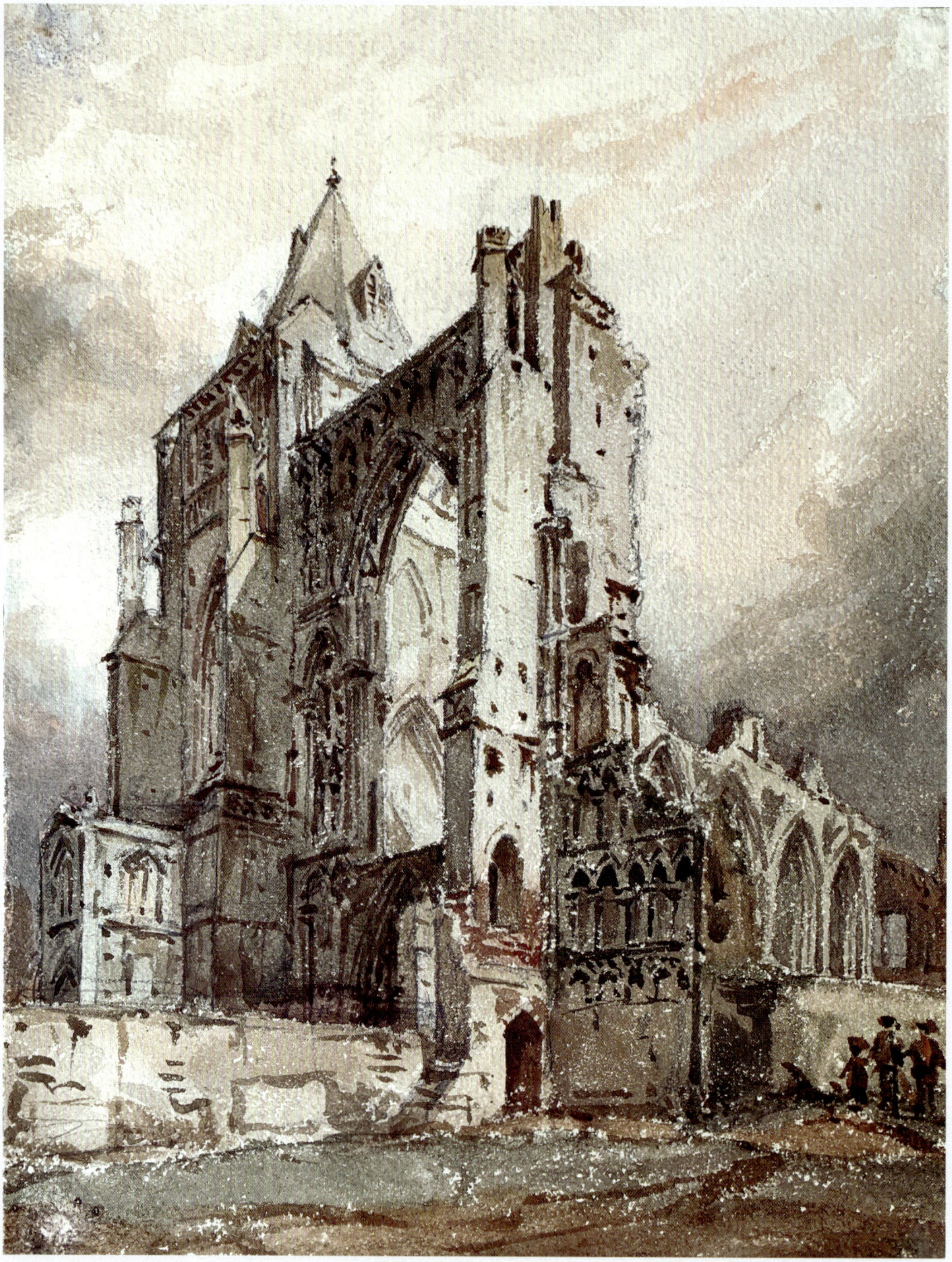

11. *Crowland Abbey*, Lincolnshire, c. 1845

Petit's Motivation and the Role of his Art

The difference between great and mean art lies, not in definable methods of handling, or in styles of representation, or choices of subjects, but wholly in the nobleness of the end to which the effort of the painter is addressed.
John Ruskin, *Modern Painters vol III*[3]

Central to understanding Petit's art is that he never painted for money, and thus escaped the main dilemma for most artists then and now. Petit was fortunate in that he did not need to live from his art. His father, the incumbent vicar of Shareshill, just north of Wolverhampton, had been wealthy, having inherited extensive landholdings in the region. He died in 1822, when Petit was just 21, and the family then moved to Lichfield.

Petit himself took holy orders after graduating from Cambridge in 1825, as did a high proportion of graduates in those days. Unlike most he actually worked as a curate in Lichfield and then at Bradfield in Essex, until 1834, when he resigned parish duties to focus on his twin vocations of art and church architecture for the rest of his life. Invariably he was described as modest, generous and 'noble-hearted'.[4]

Petit became a public figure late, aged forty, with the publication of his first book, *Remarks on Church Architecture (Remarks)*, in 1841. Praised by some as the best architectural work by any living author[5], the book catapulted him to the centre of the heated architectural debates around the revival of Gothic.

The first the public saw of his art were the 290 illustrations completed for *Remarks*. With just a handful of exceptions these were all traced from his own pen and ink drawings, which in turn were based on his own watercolours done on the spot (see 12-13 and the section on drawings on pages 60-65).

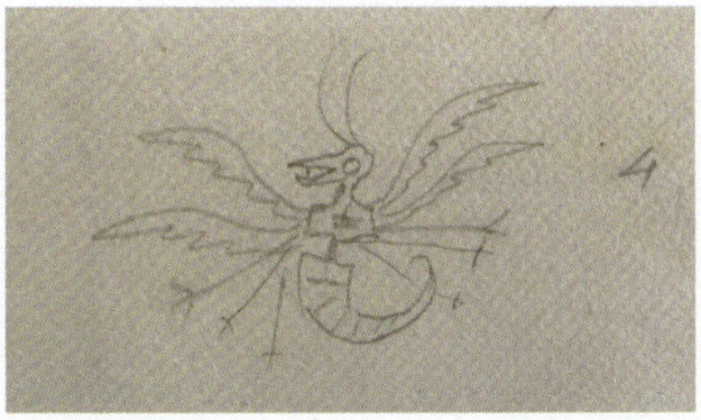

The Doodles

Starting around 1855, with increasing frequency, Petit doodles on the back of his paintings. These are usually significant, often humorous, events of the day. We include a few in no particular order.

D1. 13 October 1855, an annoying insect at Schwarzach

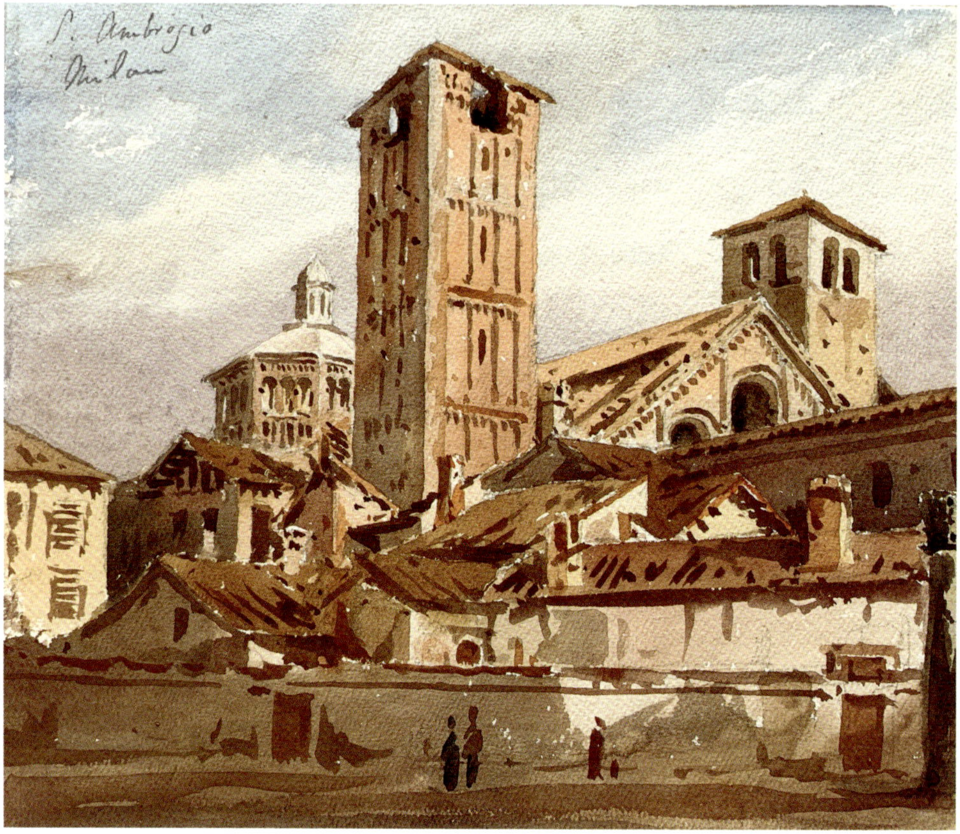

12. *Sant'Ambrogio*, Milan, 1839

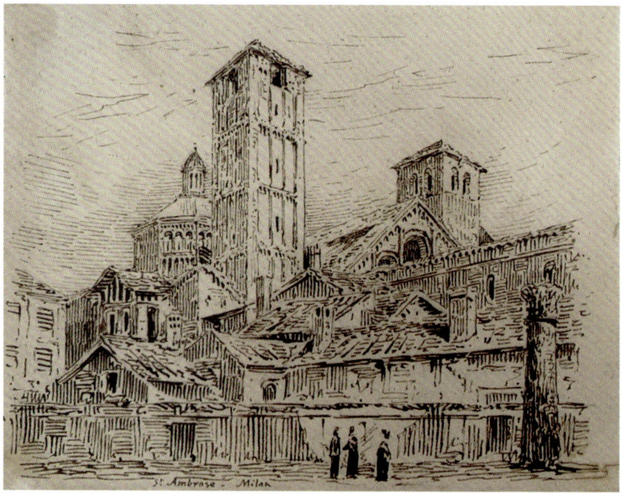

13. *Sant'Ambrogio*, Milan, 1840, pen and ink drawing for *Remarks*

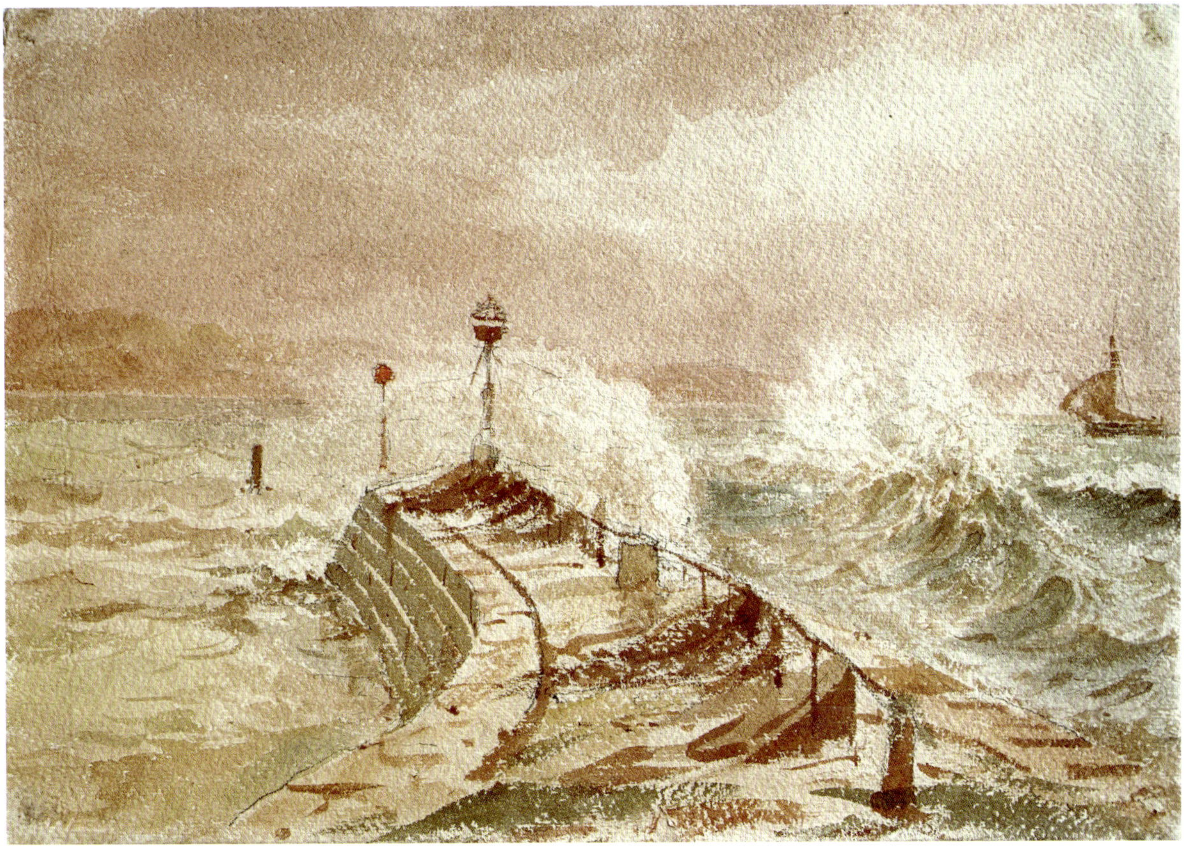

14. *Weymouth*, c. 1848

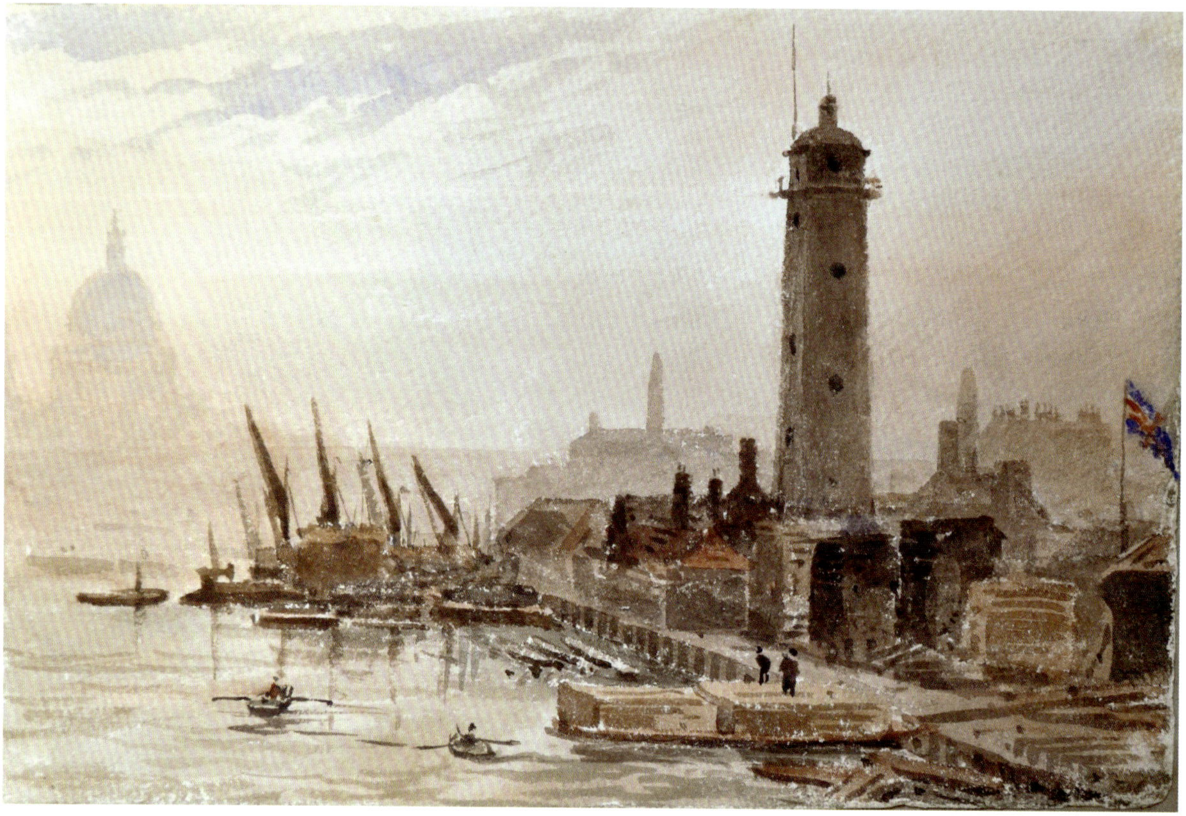

15. *From Waterloo Bridge*, c. 1830s

With this first book, Petit became the leading opponent of the Gothic Revival for church architecture. A pioneer of preserving existing old buildings, at the same time he advocated that modern architecture should be original, building on all earlier traditions and not copying one style deemed 'correct'. Somewhat heroically he held these positions until his death in 1868. From the mid-1840s, he started delivering public lectures where he exhibited his watercolours, partly to illustrate what he was saying. One report noted that over 100 of Petit's pictures were pinned to the walls.

Throughout his life Petit painted modern utilitarian structures (for example the shot tower in 15 above) to show their architectural power in contrast to the artificiality of Victorian revived Gothic. But the majority of his pictures were ancient churches, only genuine Gothic never modern ones, and natural landscapes.

Petit's church paintings aimed to capture the character of those ancient buildings, their diverse beauty and centrality in the community. Some 800 of these pictures were reproduced in his publications. His wider scenes and landscapes, on the other hand, showed the particular beauty of nature, the work of God. This understanding can occasionally be found in his books, but is voiced directly and often in his poem, *The Lesser and the Greater Light*. Its goal was to reconcile science with a belief in God. Petit was by no means alone in

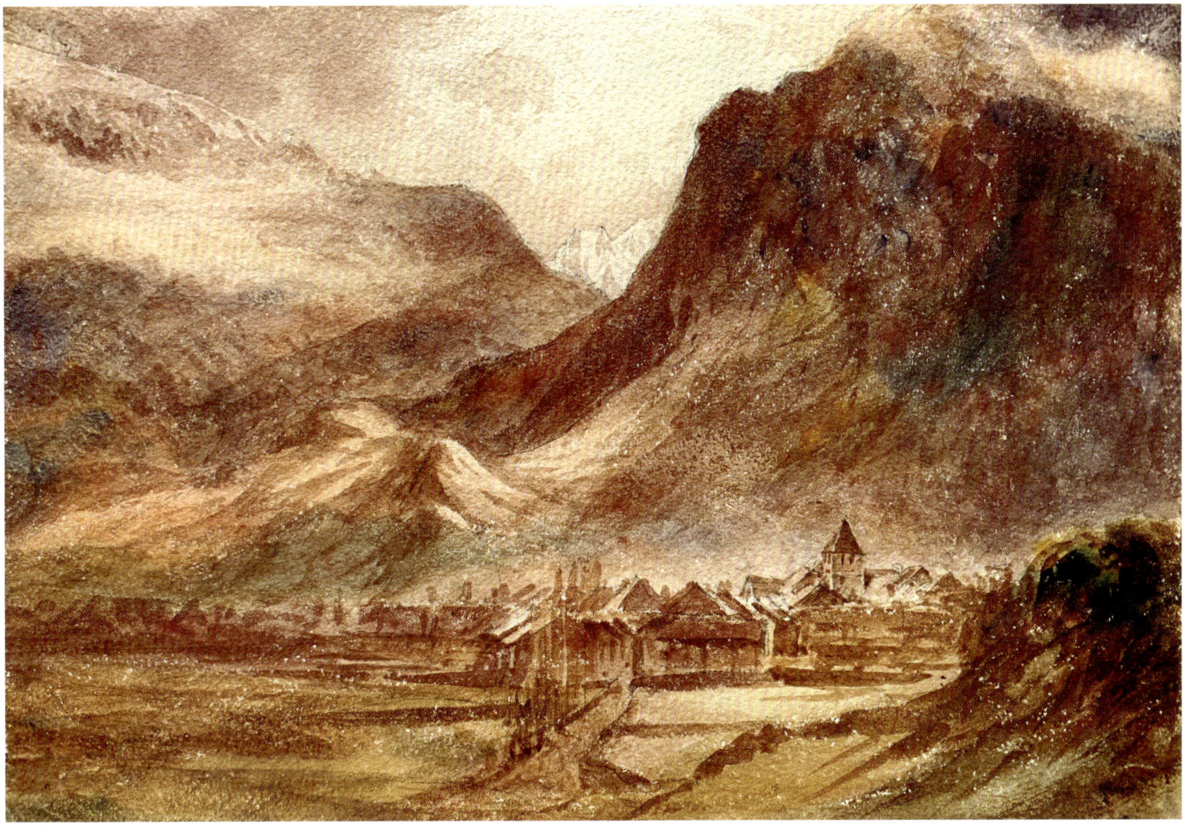

16. *Val d'Ossau, Pyrenees*, 1852

facing this question in the mid-nineteenth century. For Petit, the wonders of nature are both perceived and understood through science while, at the same time, they are a proof of God's existence:

What ! Shall we own the written witness true
And not the record of creation too?
Are they but freaks of chance or toys designed
To cheat and dazzle some enquiring mind?[6]

In taking this serious approach to landscape Petit's work reflects what Ruskin had called for. *Modern Painters* criticised all previous landscape art before J.M.W. Turner (1775–1851), which *'has never made us feel the wonder, nor the power, nor the glory of the universe; it has not prompted to devotion, nor touched with awe.'*[7] In directly addressing that challenge (16 above), Petit is Ruskinian; and some of Ruskin's *Modern Painters* helps us appreciate Petit better.

Mountain, marine or simple village scenes, often with a church in the distance, convey the spirituality of nature, but only the beauty that is there, not some idealised approximation, no artificial picturesqueness. In one of his speeches in 1856, Petit wrote: *'...it is certain that a studied picturesqueness, if not wholly valueless, is incomparably of less value than that which is inartificial.'*[8] That sentiment Petit applied equally to Gothic Revival architecture and to his art of medieval Gothic and landscape.

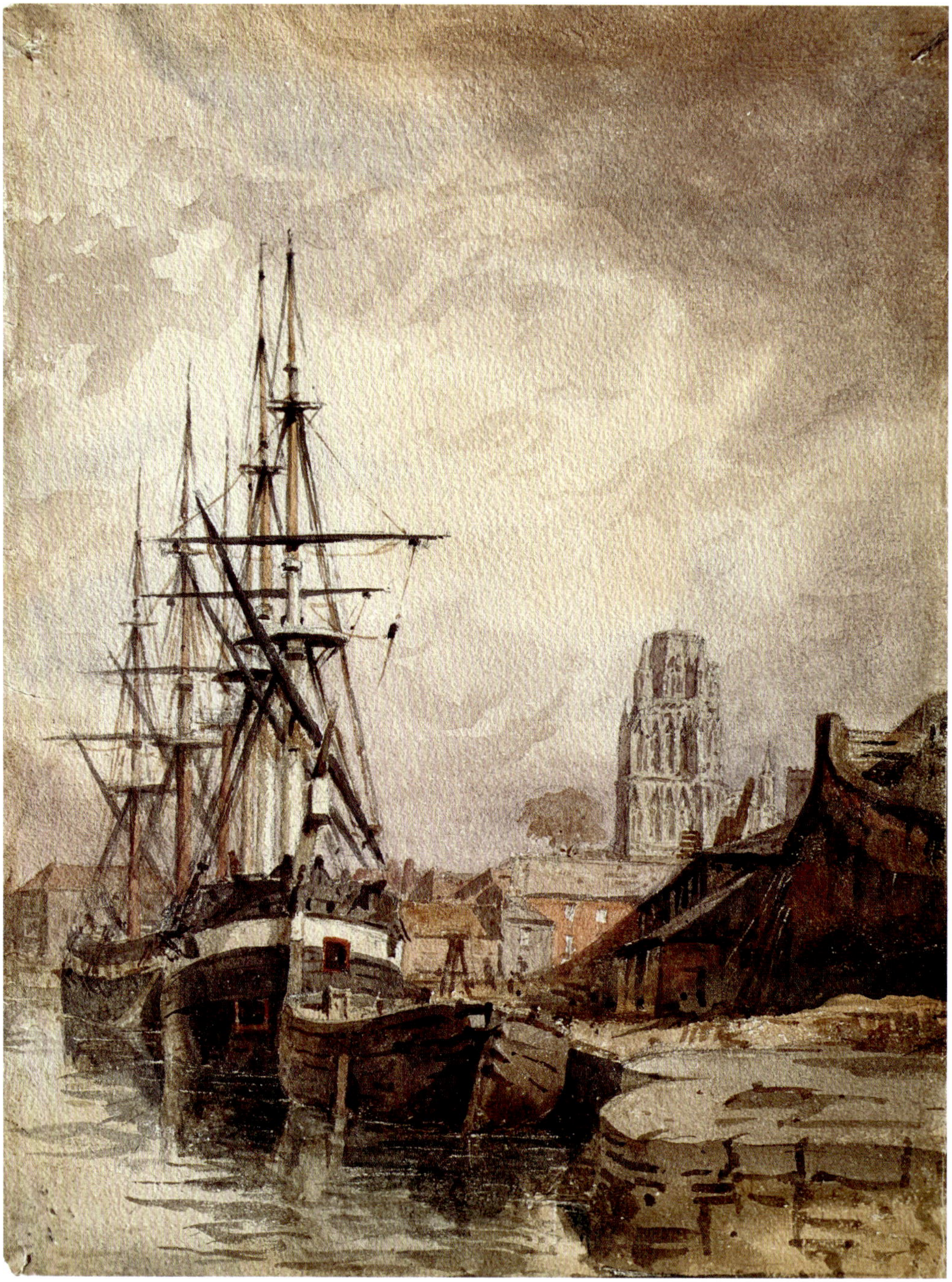

17. *St Mary's Redcliffe, Bristol*, c. 1849

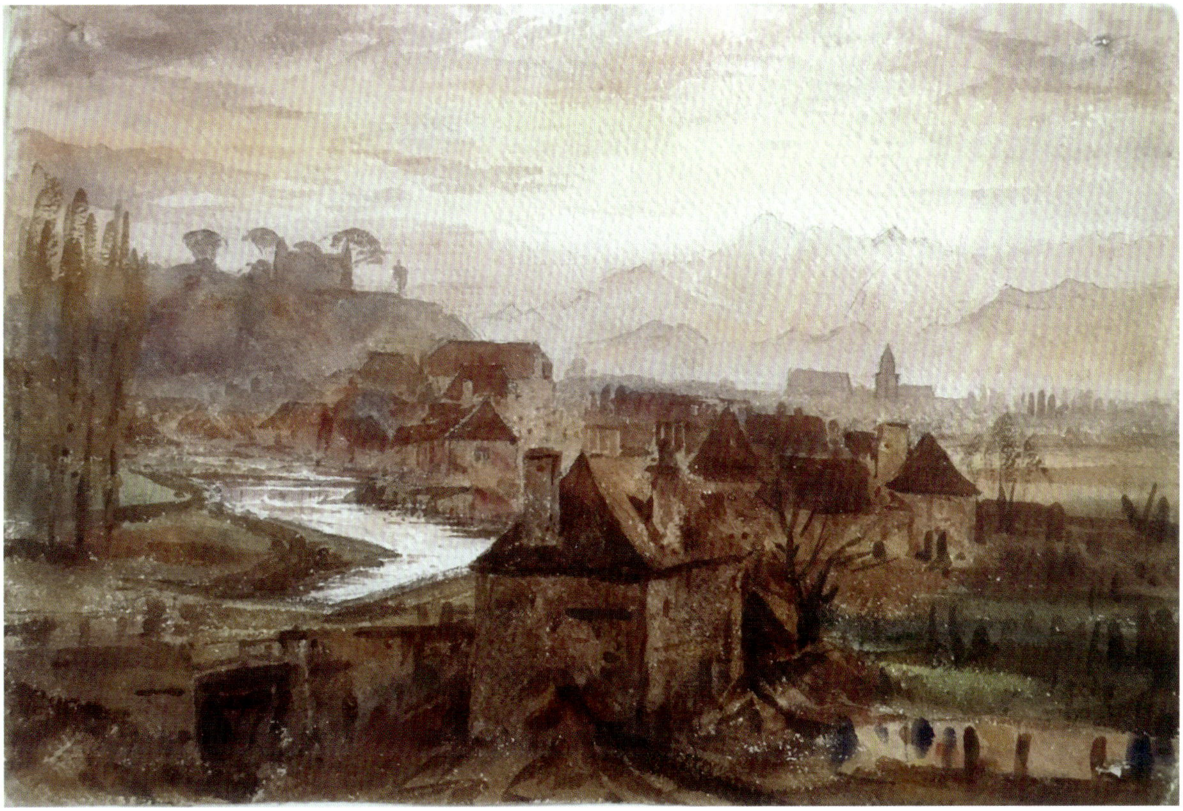

18. *Near Pau, Pyrenees,* 1852-3
Courtesy The Ian Cooke Collection, National Library of Wales

Unlike Ruskin, however, Petit was forward looking, believing that, in art as well as in architecture, artists had to improve and build on what had gone before: *'No true artist, whatever be his branch of art, will rest content without doing something towards its improvement.'*[9] Petit's art exhibits that originality: impressionistic in technique to capture immediate effect, well before that trend became more fully developed, albeit in more vivid colour, on the continent.

Petit's serious motivation emerged in the 1830s, while he was working as a curate, and only intensified over the years. Like Ruskin this intensity of purpose sets him apart from others, professional or amateur. He was steadfast and robust in defending his views on architecture, but in contrast to Ruskin, Petit was unfailingly courteous, as even his opponents acknowledged. Modest, he also took no interest in his own legacy whether artistic or architectural.

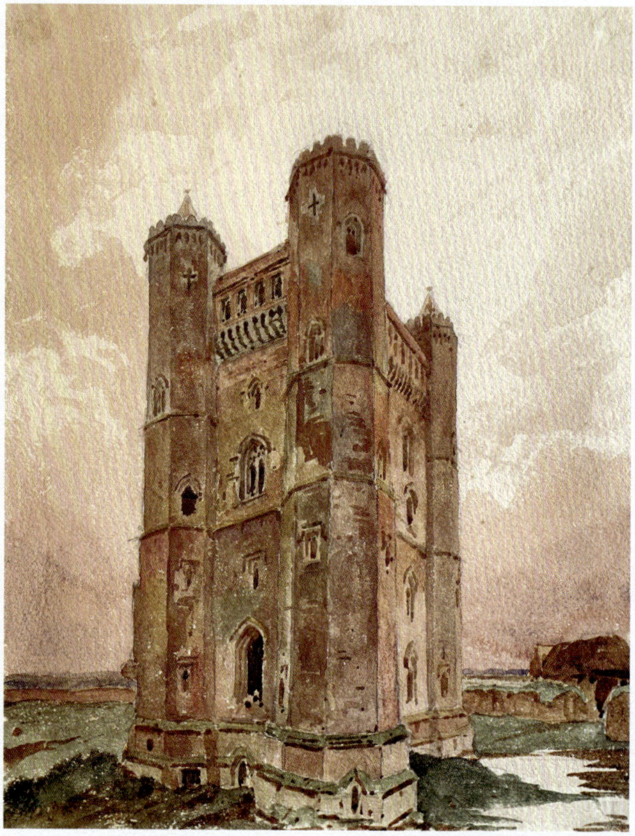

19. Left: J. L. Petit,
Tattershall Castle,
Lincolnshire, c. 1844

20. Bottom left:
Peter De Wint,
St Augustine's Gate,
Canterbury, undated
c. 1820s

21. Bottom right:
John Sell Cotman,
A Castle in Normandy,
undated c. 1820s

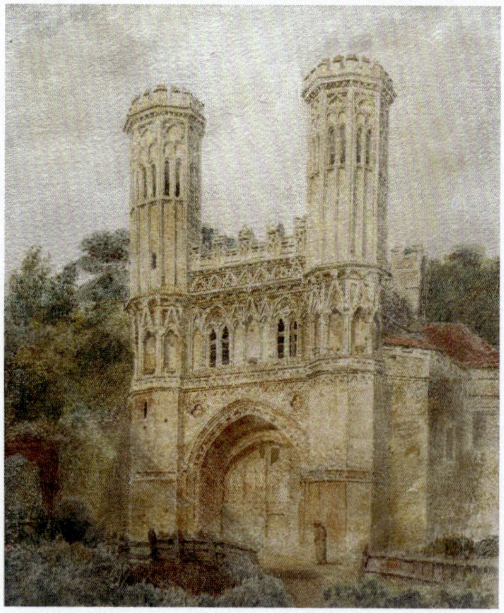

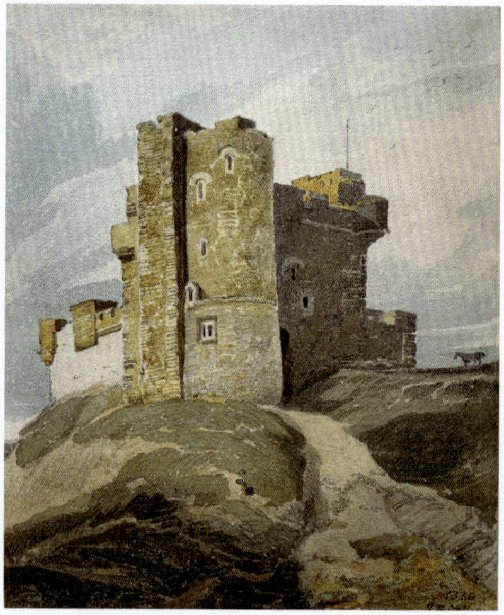

Petit and his Contemporaries [10]

Are we not to look for the best examples of a style when its vigour has not been softened away by continued attempts at finish? When there still remain some roughnesses, which, so far from displeasing, give a certain point and character that might otherwise be missed.
J. L. Petit *On Architectural Refinement*[11]

British Watercolour Traditions

The golden age for British watercolours ran from the latter quarter of the eighteenth century until J.M.W. Turner's death in 1852. Artists at that time often presented romanticised visions of real or ideal landscapes or urban scenes to meet the market for what was considered to be 'picturesque'. Petit started in this period and drew on these traditions.

Petit's early work has been compared to that of both Peter De Wint (1784–1849) and John Sell Cotman (1782–1842), two leading names associated with the more 'avant-garde impressionistic'[12] watercolour art of the first half of the century. Petit would have been aware of both artists. The first comparison shows similar compositions by each of the three. Those of Petit and De Wint are actual, picturesque, buildings; Cotman's, on the right, is his own invention, an artificial picturesque created to meet demand. The level of finish is higher in the Cotman in comparison with the De Wint, and in the De Wint in comparison to the Petit. However, the comparison serves to show how Petit's early work is grounded in this nineteenth-century watercolour tradition, and that by 1845 he is already starting to move on from that.

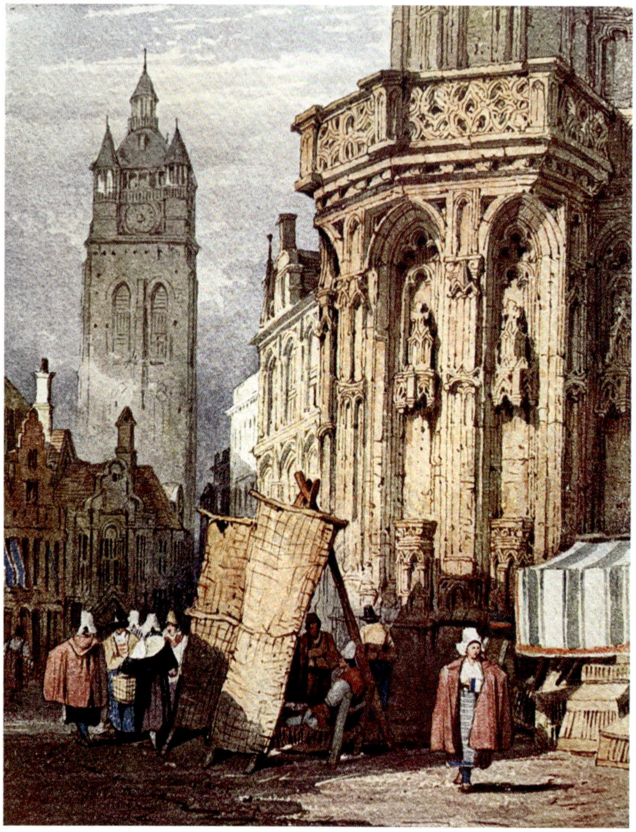

22. Samuel Prout, *View in Ghent*, c. 1823
Plate 1, *Sketches by Samuel Prout in France, Belgium, Germany, Italy and Switzerland*, ed. Holme (London 1915). One original is in the British Museum

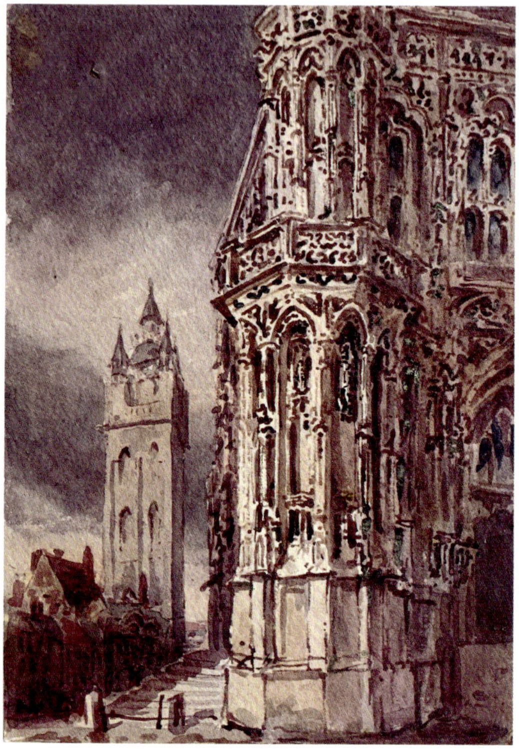

23. J. L. Petit, *Hôtel de Ville, Ghent*, c. 1832-4

Other British watercolourists prepared pictures with much more intricate detail. Delicacy was one of the virtues of the medium. Among such artists, Samuel Prout (1783–1852) became the most renowned for architecture with his European Gothic town scenes from the 1820s. On the back of these he was appointed watercolourist to the king. He and Petit were friends, publicly praised each other, and owned each other's pictures. Here we see their contrasting versions of a single building, the Hôtel de Ville in Ghent. Petit visited the Netherlands and Belgium from Harwich during his time as curate at Bradfield and Mistley, Essex, from 1828 to 1834 (see also opposite, 24). He would later write in *Remarks: 'This building is familiar to all who are acquainted (as who is not?) with Mr Prout's drawings.'*[13]

In his picture, Petit deliberately avoided the commercial picturesque, the romantic view of old Gothic and refined finish, in favour of something altogether rougher and yet more serious.

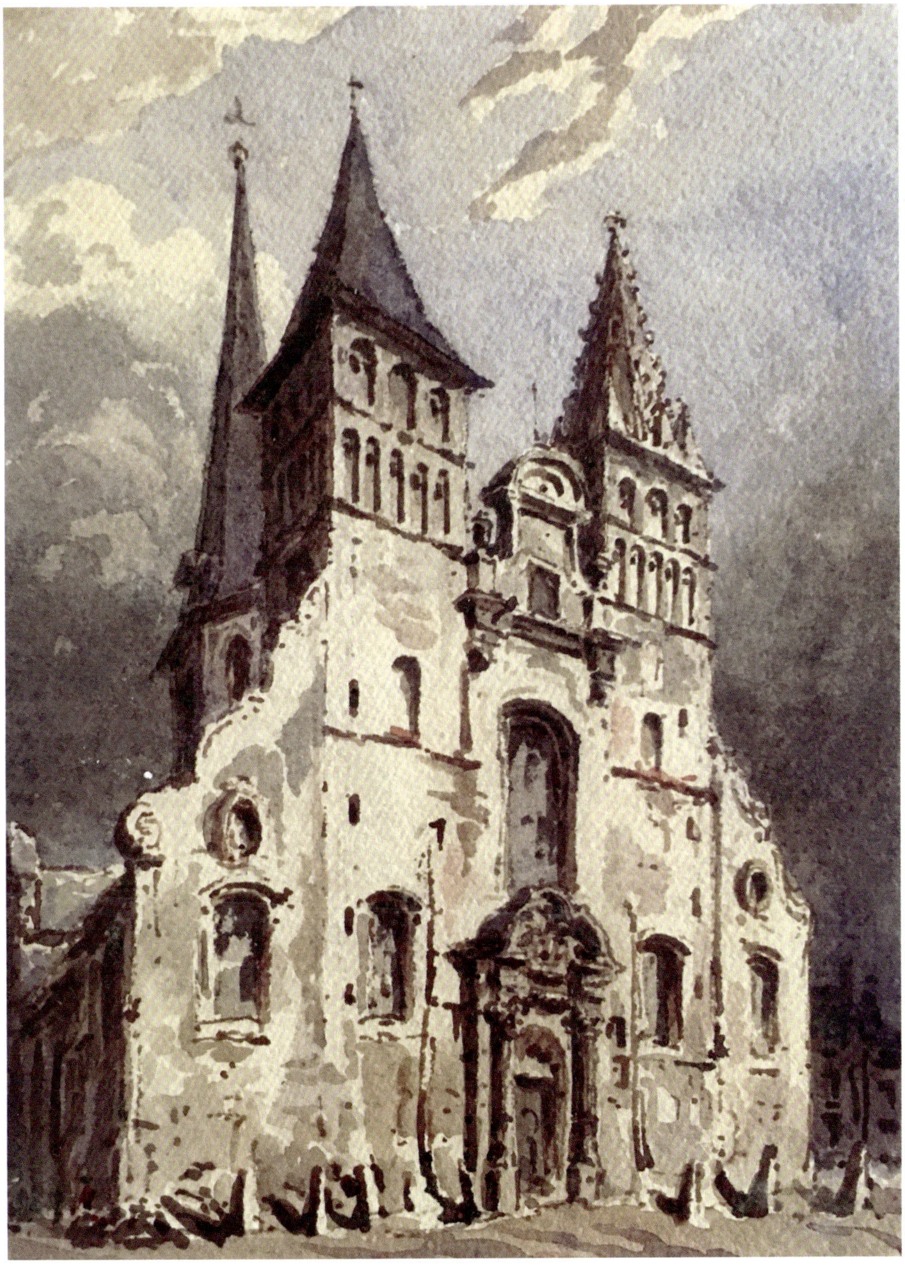

24. *St Jacques, Ghent*, c. 1832-4

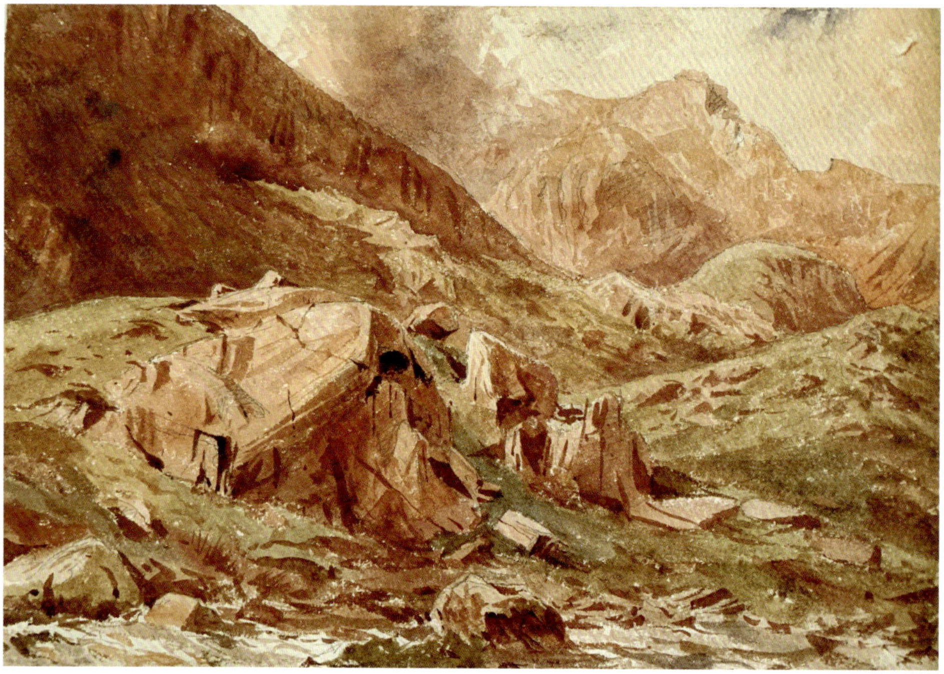

25. Above: J. L. Petit, *Near Llanaber,* North Wales, 10 September 1862

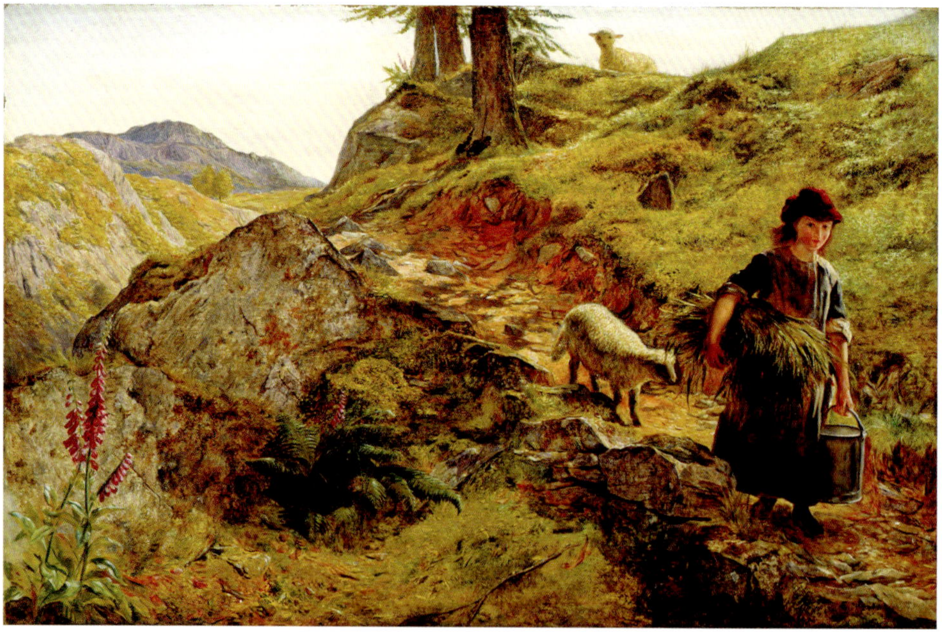

26. Above: Ebenezer Newman Downard, *A Mountain Path at Capel Curig,* 1862 (oil) Courtesy Tate

More Ruskinian than the Pre-Raphaelites

In the 1850s, following the death of Turner, British art made a radical break with what had gone before. Initially strongly influenced and supported by Ruskin, the Pre-Raphaelites are known for their historical scenes, full of allegory, and their female portraits. Their landscapes, less well-known now, were extraordinary in capturing minute detail. However, by 1855 Ruskin had become disillusioned with their ability to capture the awesome aspect of nature:

> *'...they were almost destitute of the power of feeling vastness,'* he wrote, and *'allowed their fancies to be caught by a bit of oak hedge, or the weeds at the side of a duck-pond'.*[14]

This focus on detail to the exclusion of 'noble scenery full of majestic interest' is illustrated by the next comparison, of Welsh mountain paths (25) and (26). That by Ebenezer Downard (active 1849–89) is about as different to Petit's as one could be, in its objective as well as in the approach taken. Downard has painted an idealised vision of the countryside and farming: a beautiful, gleaming landscape and a ruddy-cheeked milk maid followed by an adorable innocent lamb; even the weather is perfect. Above all everything is painted in detail. Petit's sketches capture the roughness and character of the North Wales hills as they are. His pictures are rough by comparison, certainly, but they aim directly at that vastness that the Pre-Raphaelites avoided.

Although Ruskin praised finish, he also went to some length to elevate the greater importance of the motivation of the artist: *'The fact is both finish and impetuosity, specific minuteness, or large abstraction, may be the signs of passion, or of its reverse'.*[15] Describing their own creations as *'wall decorations',*[16] in clear light and rich colour, the Pre-Raphaelites could not be further from Petit's art, which deliberately lacked the polish as well as the detail. From our standpoint, accustomed to the excitement of contemporary art, nineteenth-century finished exhibition landscapes can now appear somewhat staid and artificial. With our modern eye, we can appreciate Petit's rough immediacy.

And thus it is that, for the most part, imperfect sketches, engravings, outlines, rude sculptures, and other forms of abstraction, possess a charm which the finished picture frequently wants. For not only does the finished picture excite the imagination less, but, like nature itself, it taxes it more.
John Ruskin, *Modern Painters* vol I[17]

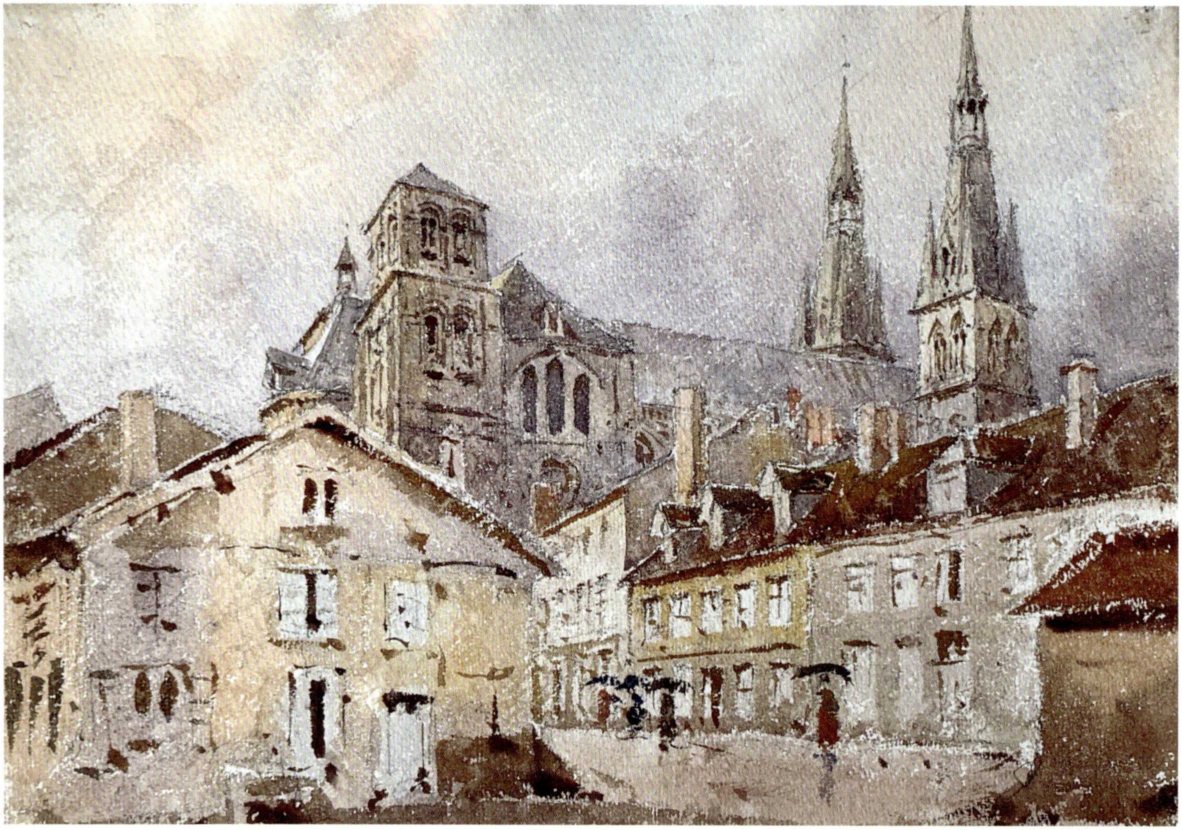

27. J. L. Petit, *Notre-Dame, Châlons-sur-Marne,* 9 October 1855
28. Opposite page: Camille Pissarro, *Pontoise, The Road to Gisors in Winter,* 1873 (oil)
Courtesy Wikimedia Commons; original: Museum of Fine Arts Boston, 48.587

Pre-Impressionist in Subject and Technique

While completely different from Pre-Raphaelite paintings, many Petit pictures compare quite closely to the work of French artists of twenty years later. This should not be as surprising as it sounds. Turner and the other outdoor sketchers among the watercolourists, notably De Wint and David Cox (1783–1859), had already travelled some way towards Impressionism by 1850. The surprise might be more why no other British artist continued along that path except Petit, working outside the recognised academies.

Exploring the visual impact of real-life everyday scenes, without allegory or artifice, and visible brush strokes that create an illusion of infinite depth are just the first stages of Impressionism. Initially, the Impressionists would be accused of producing unfinished, crude work, and they increasingly compensated with rich colour, playing with the effect of light. The muted colours of an early Pissarro street scene allow several possible Petit comparisons (for example 27), which would not be the case with the French artist's later more colourful urban scenes. Petit's focus here is on the church and its relationship with the town, while Pissarro's is on the everyday street itself.

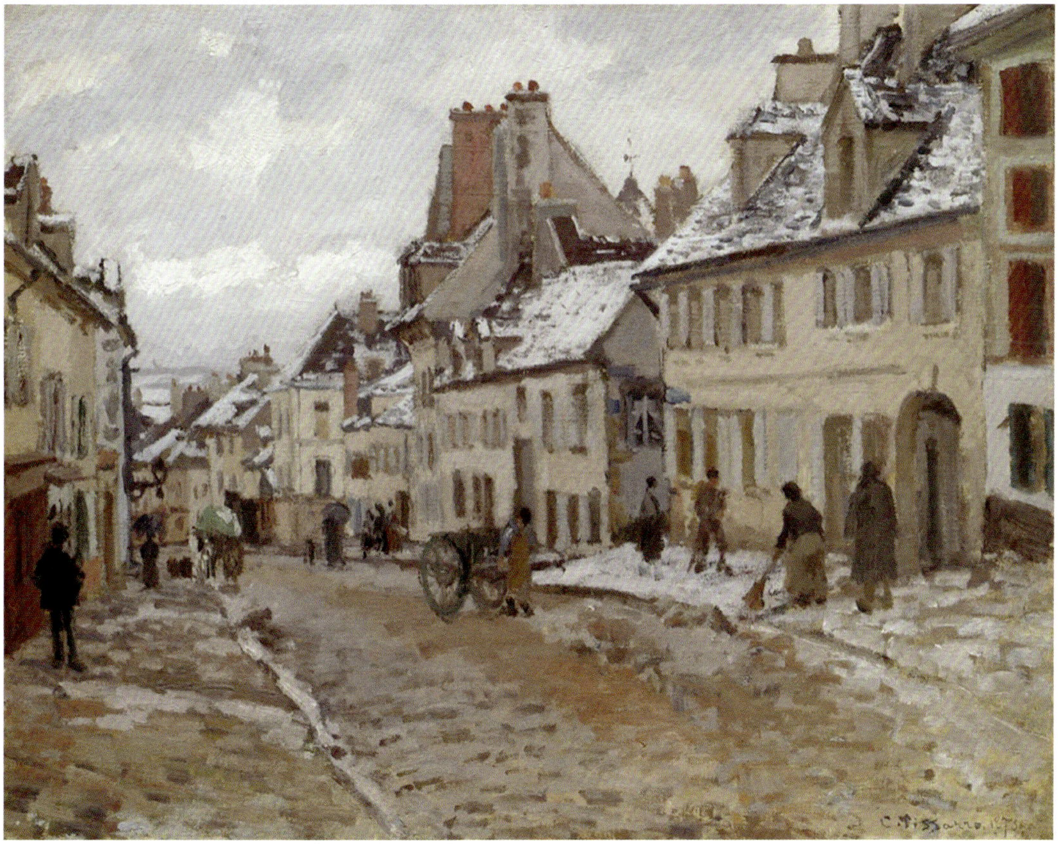

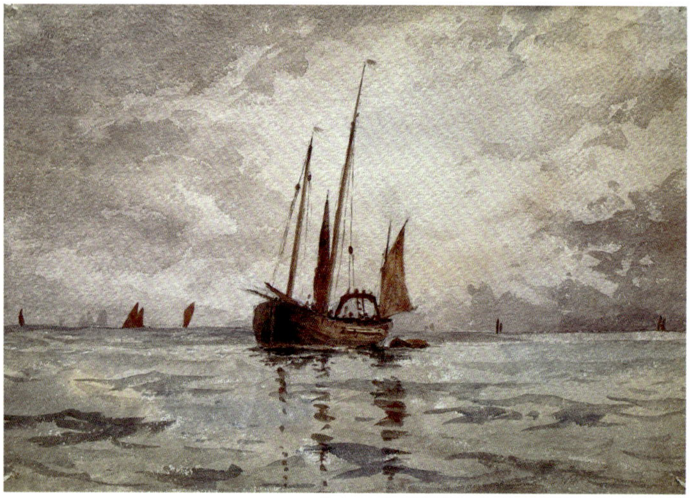

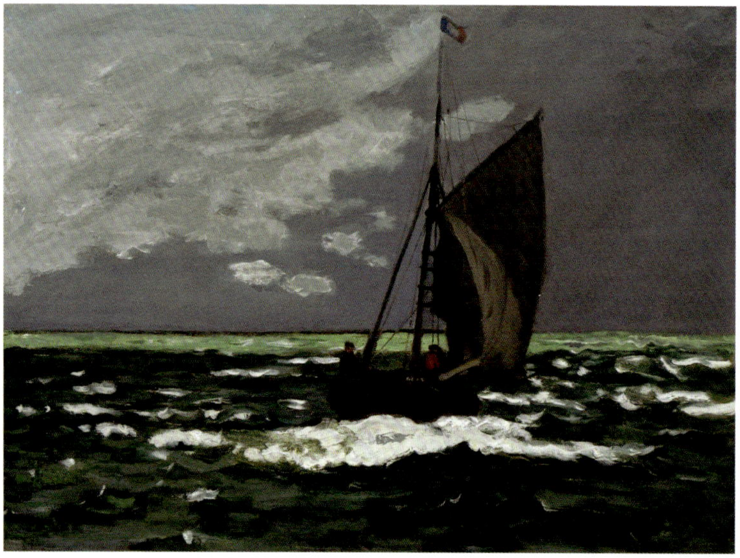

29. Top left: J. L. Petit,
Fishing Boat off Torquay, c. 1848

30. Left: Claude Monet,
Seascape, Storm, 1866 (oil)
Courtesy The Clark Art Institute, 1955.561

Comparing a Petit seascape with an early Monet, the compositions are practically identical (29, 30), just their medium, scale and colour differ. In similar seascapes in later years Monet went on to use brighter colour and blurred the clarity of the boat's form to create movement.

Petit rarely indulged in colour and never as richly as a full oil treatment allows. He also rarely focused on the effect of light for its own sake. One exception is this snow scene outside Lichfield (31, opposite). Pissarro (32, opposite) and Monet often painted such scenes to capture the unusual light effect of fresh snow; British painters did not. In everyday subject matter, in technique and in the underlying objective to capture the effect or impression of a scene, there is remarkable similarity. However, the impressions Petit conveyed often tended to be more spiritual, and serious, at least overtly. Monet occasionally painted churches, but never quite as austerely as Petit and with greater emphasis on the sky (see frontispiece comparison).

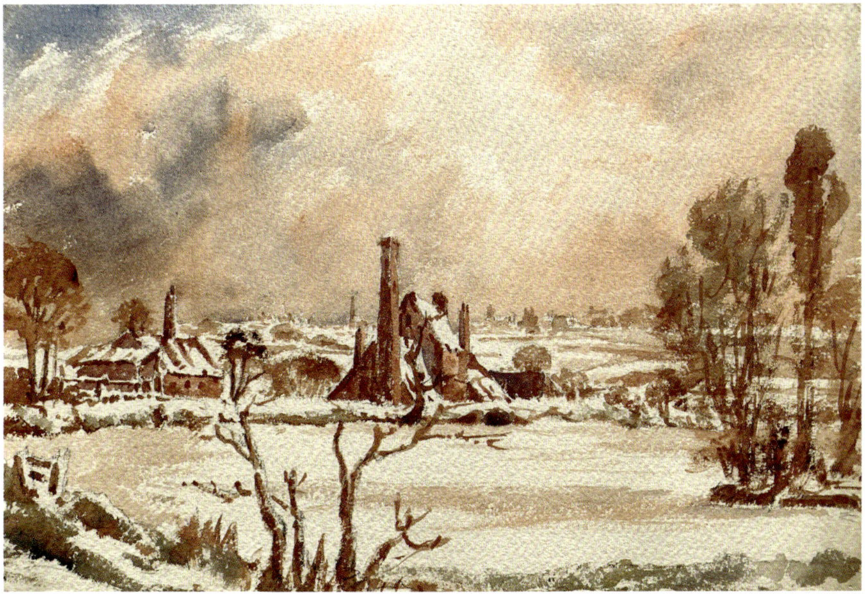

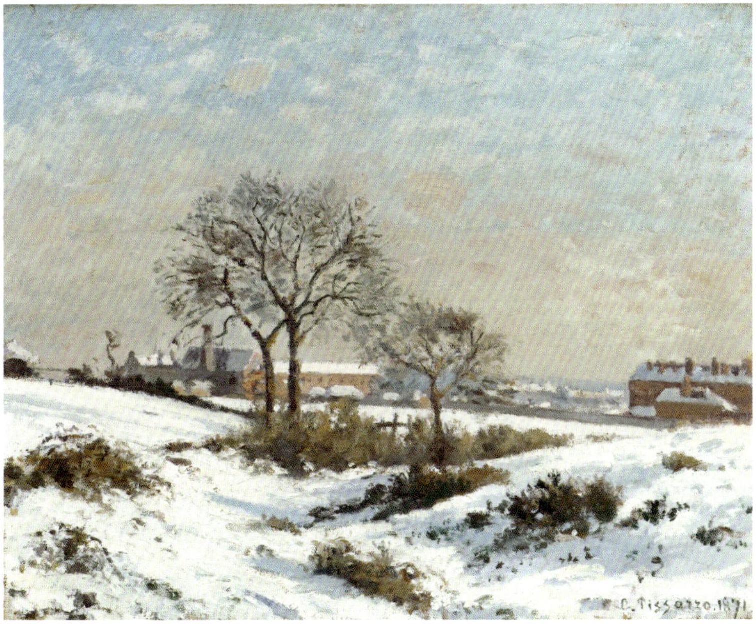

31. Top: J. L. Petit, *Huddlesford Mill,* near Lichfield, 13 February 1855

32. Left: Camille Pissarro, *Snowy Landscape, South Norwood,* 1871 (oil) Courtesy Los Angeles County Museum of Art, M.2005.70.116

From 1854 Petit travelled most years to France. Sometimes he was there for several months, both revisiting favourite locations and adding more to his knowledge. He visited and painted in all the locations associated with the emerging generation of artists including Normandy, the Forest of Fontainebleau (see p. 94), Arles and Paris. This helps in finding similarities. It is not meant to imply that their paths actually crossed; his correspondents and acquaintances are still unknown.

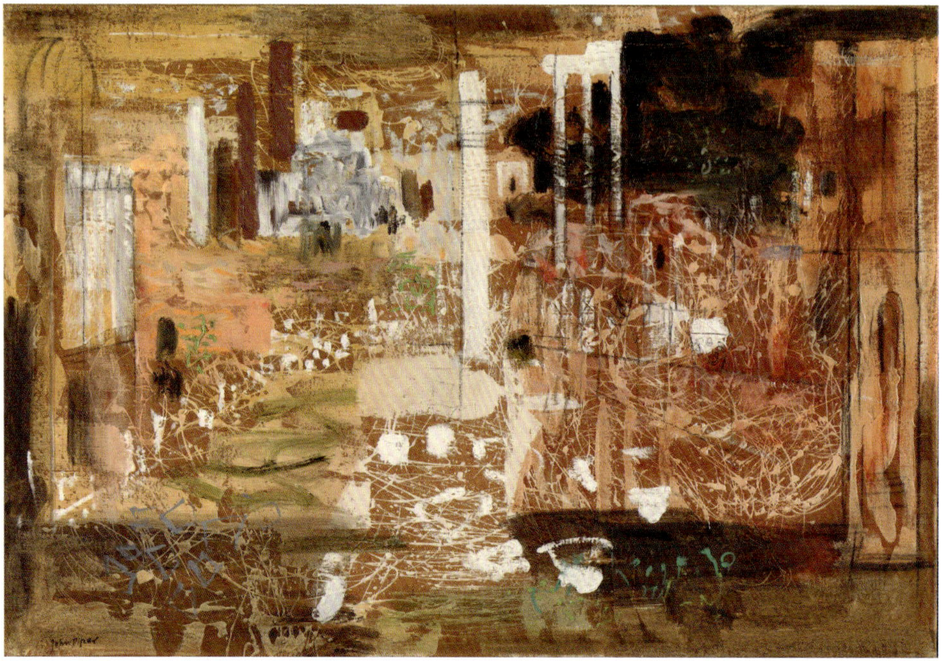

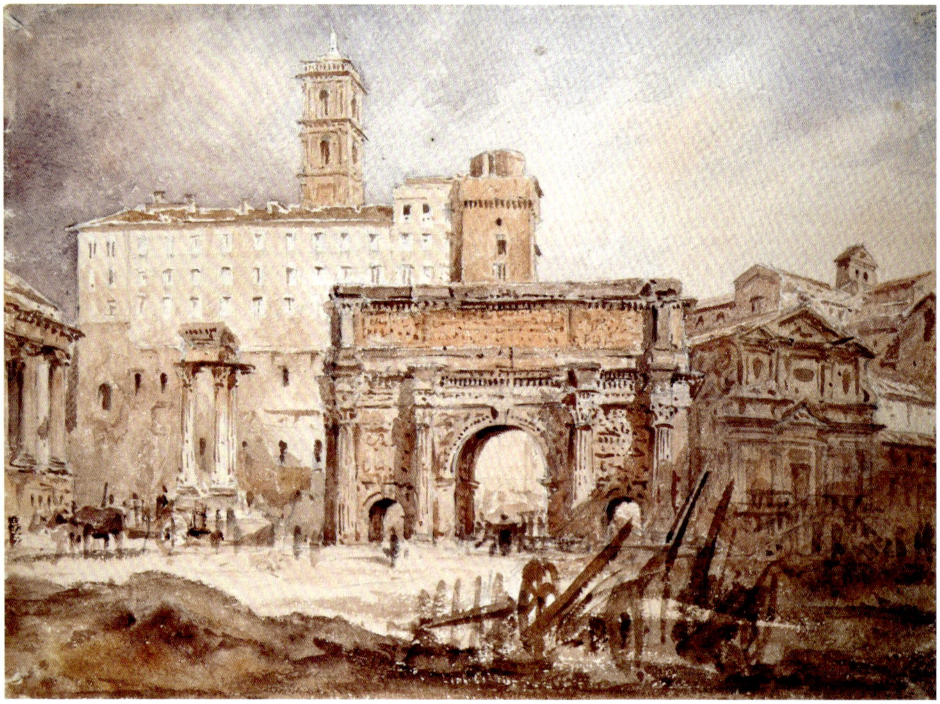

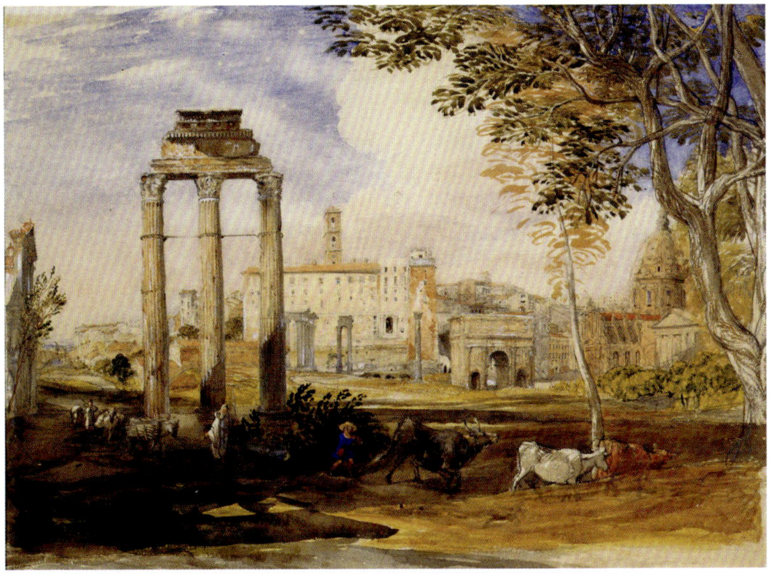

33. Above: Samuel Palmer, *The Roman Forum,* 1840s or 1850s
Image by Birmingham Museums Trust, licensed under CC0
34. Opposite page top: John Piper, *The Roman Forum,* 1961 (oil on canvas) Courtesy Tate and The Piper Estate
35. Opposite page bottom: J. L. Petit, *Roman Forum,* 17 May 1854

Modern before his Time

On occasion Petit's landscapes seem to anticipate techniques used even further ahead of his time. In the final comparison, the view of the Roman Forum by John Piper [1903-92] (34) is a century later than the Petit or the Palmer, both mid-Victorian. However, artistically, the Petit (35) is mid-way, retaining form and accuracy, but already a long way beyond conventional Grand Tour watercolours such as the Palmer (above).

In architecture Petit constantly argued that the Gothic Revival was *'doomed to gradually fade away on its development to meet the views and exigencies of the present'.*[18] This proved to be the case although only after Petit's death. To the shock of contemporary architects, Petit praised Victorian *'engineering works, which display a power, and, I will add, a perception of architectural propriety, not surpassed in the greatest works of the Romans'.*[19] He advocated building on all previous traditions, from across Europe, and not starting from scratch. Thus it should not be surprising that in his art, Petit practised what he preached. Pre-Raphaelitism and the subsequent Aesthetic Movement had very limited impact on the continent (the USA is another story) and also gradually faded away; while Impressionism, which Petit's landscapes and his rock and tree studies anticipated, led on to most later art.

Petit's modern style can be immediately accessible today, when much other Victorian art often appears posed and overly composed. However, the question of a serious moral purpose in art is more controversial. The spiritual aspect of Petit's natural landscapes and his reverence for buildings devoted to spiritual life are not such common contemporary art themes (Piper is a rare exception). But perhaps that reflects our limitations rather than Petit's.

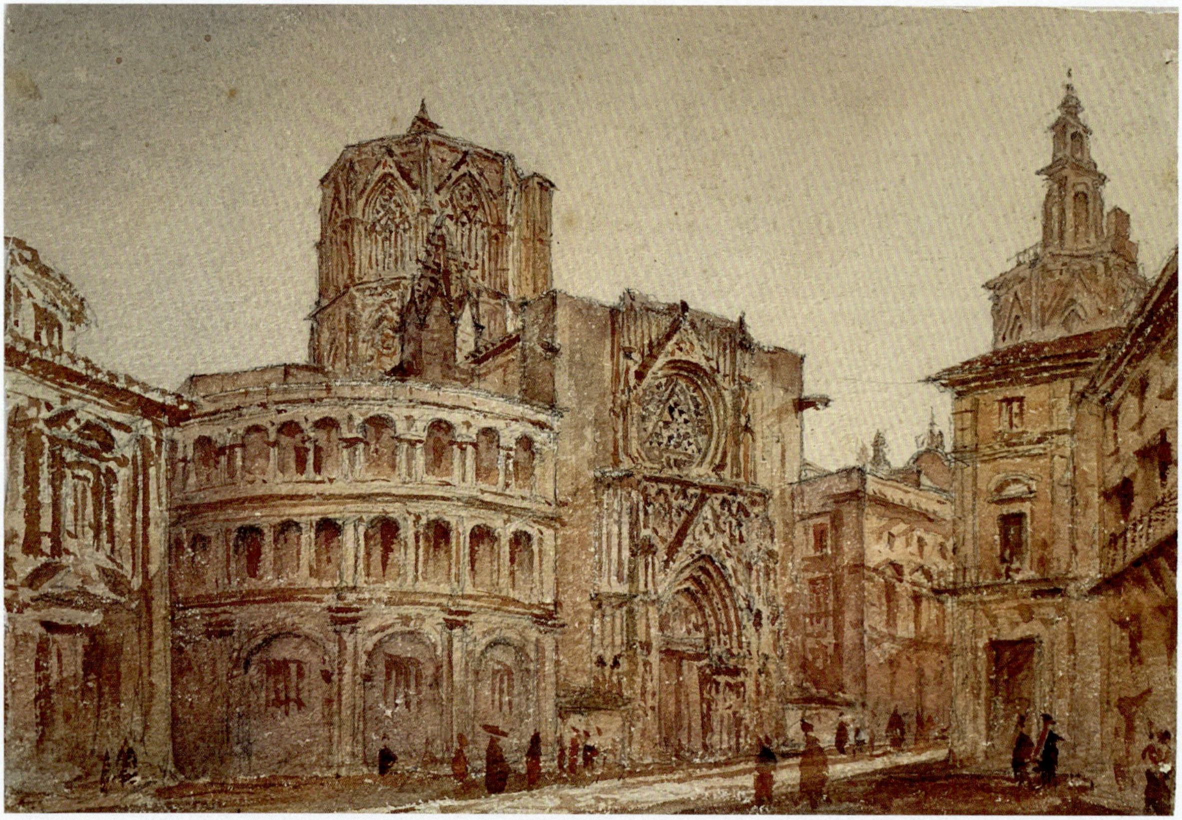

36. *Valencia Cathedral,* 15 December 1858 (damaged)
From a family descendant and believed to be picture 183
from the exhibition of 1869

Then and Now, Rediscovering Petit

I make no apology for the roughness of my sketches…my wish is rather to excite than to indulge [the reader's] curiosity.
J. L. Petit, *Remarks preface*

After Petit's death in 1869, the annual Architectural Exhibition gave up one of its two halls to a last exhibition of Petit's art, showing over 300 works, presumably selected by his sisters. Then the bulk of his art, over 10,000 pieces in total, was stored. One thousand works were gifted in his will to other family members, to be selected by them.

The ones taken were, unsurprisingly, often those of the well-known destinations in Europe, Rome, Venice and so on, those from his 1865 trip to the Middle East and also those of London. *Valencia Cathedral* (opposite) is a typical example of those chosen and removed from the main hoard by family. Sadly, few of these have been traced and the majority of those have been damaged by light. Such grand urban scenes show a further aspect of Petit's art which is largely lost.[20]

The hoard that went into storage probably consisted of 11-14,000 J. L. Petit pictures, 5-6,000 in albums, mostly from the early years, and the rest in folios of around 100 each, from which the 1,000 for other family members had been taken. However, the six main dealers and others known to have bought the lots - dumped mainly at Sotheby's Billingshurst, sometimes 300 pictures to a lot - only account for 8,000 J. L. Petit pictures at most.

The condition of some of the lots would indicate that some whole folios and albums may well have been entirely lost to damp (see 40); and this is supported by almost completely 'missing' folios - for example, the 'F', 'G', 'H', 'J', 'K' and 'N' folios in the alphabetical series from the late 1840s to 1855.

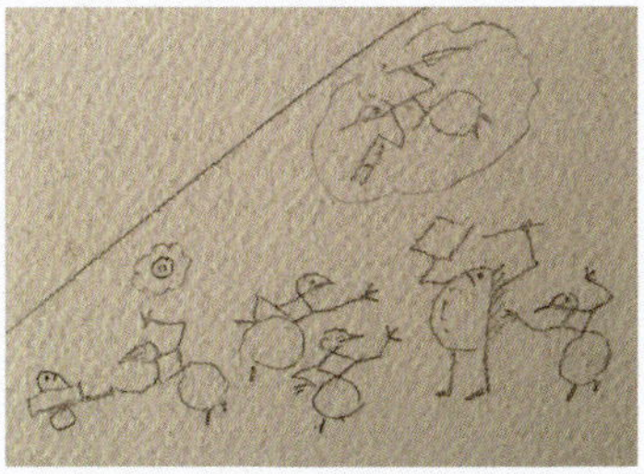

The Doodles

D2. 7 May 1863, at Bricquebec, Petit being bothered by children and wishing his sister was there to chase them away

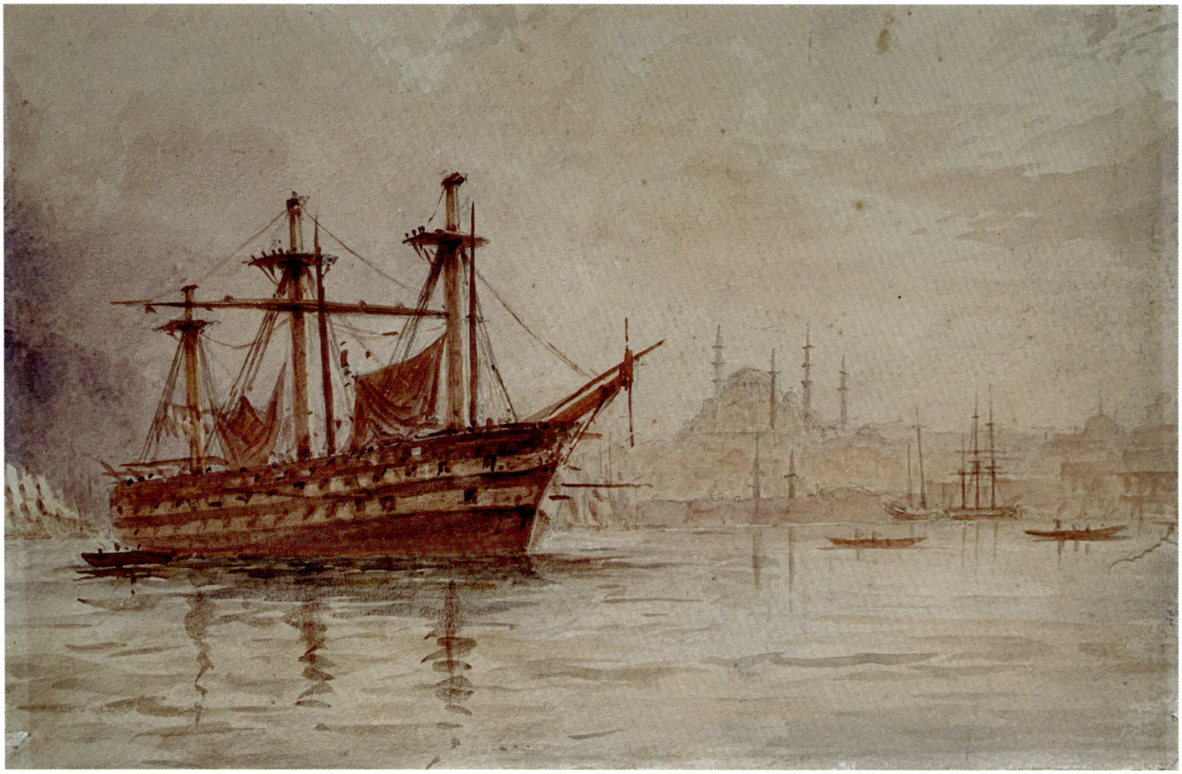

37. *Golden Horn,* 13 November 1857 (damaged)
From a family descendant and believed to be picture 320
from the exhibition of 1869

The dealers, including one in the USA, broke up the albums and lots and widely dispersed the pictures. The opportunity to view Petit's work as a whole was missed and this is the first attempt to pick up the pieces.

To carelessness, poor storage and dumping must be added one further problem. The auctions mixed up Petit's pictures with between 1,000 and 2,000 of his sisters' pictures, which had been stored together and were all sold as Petit's.[21] Altogether a disastrous way to reintroduce an artist who was by then practically unknown.

Contemporaries had admired Petit's work. For example, Sir George Gilbert Scott recalled, *'He was of a noble, generous nature, both as a scholar, as a gentleman, and as a most original artist.'*[22] Philip Delamotte, a professor of art and pioneer of photography, included him alongside nine other great earlier watercolourists as one of the greatest for *plein-air* sketching, in his book *The Art of Sketching from Nature*, published in 1878. Delamotte noted in conclusion: *'...genius is the word by which the world characterises the man who can work most, and who, for its own sake, loves his work most'*, and followed this ending by the illustration shown here (see below).

Even though Petit himself never sought fame, there is now the opportunity for this unconventional artist to be appreciated again.

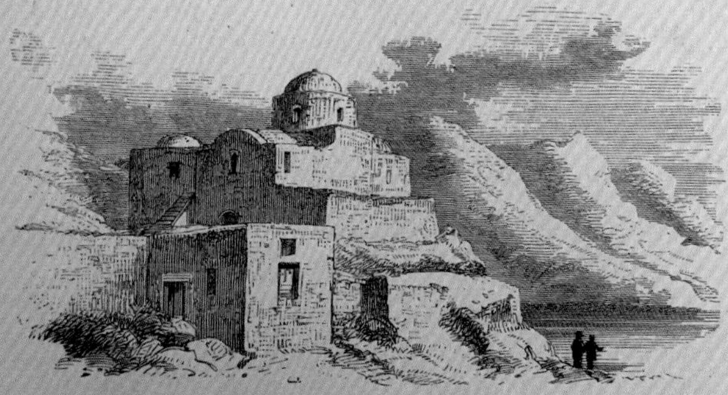

From a Sketch by Rev. J. L. PETIT. Fig. 14.

38. *From a Sketch by Rev. J. L. Petit.* Philip Delamotte's *The Art of Sketching from Nature* (1878)

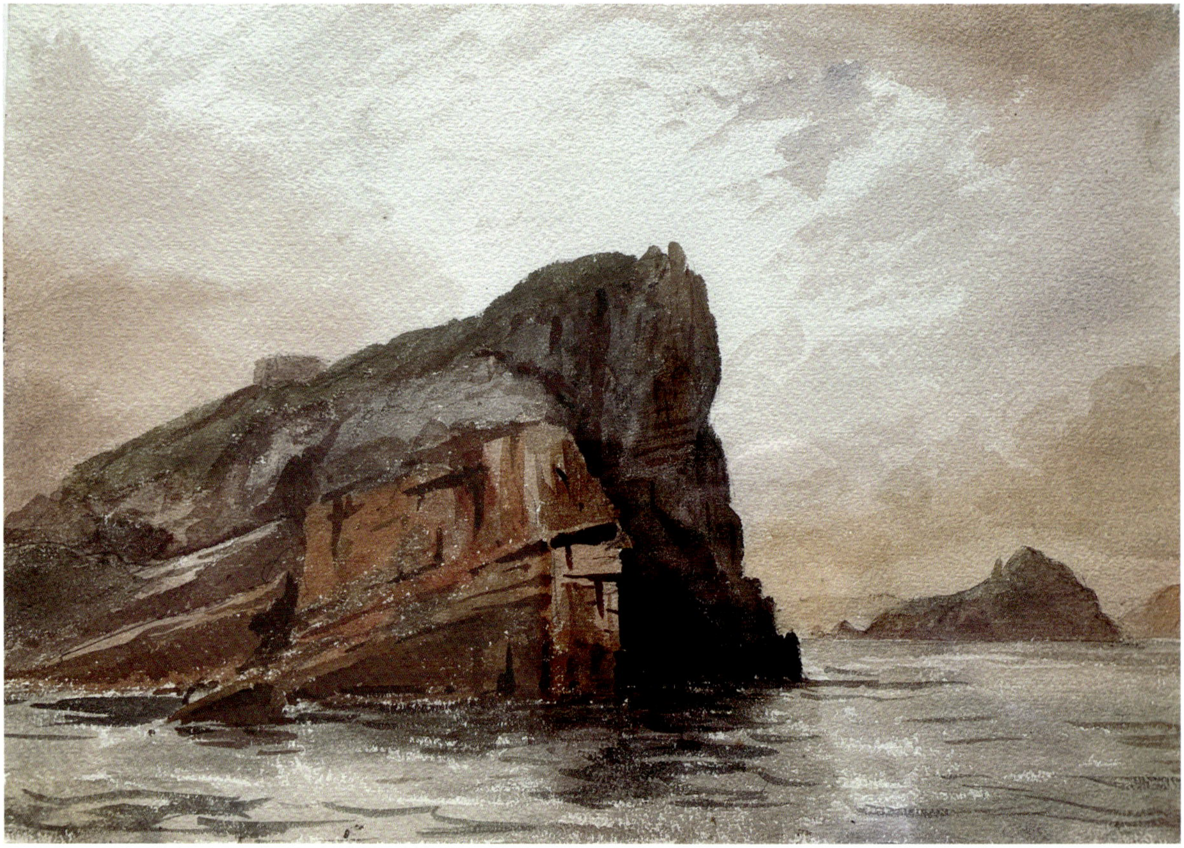

39. *Thatcher's Rock,* off Torquay, c. 1848
40. Opposite page: *Gloucester Cathedral,* c. 1835 (damaged)

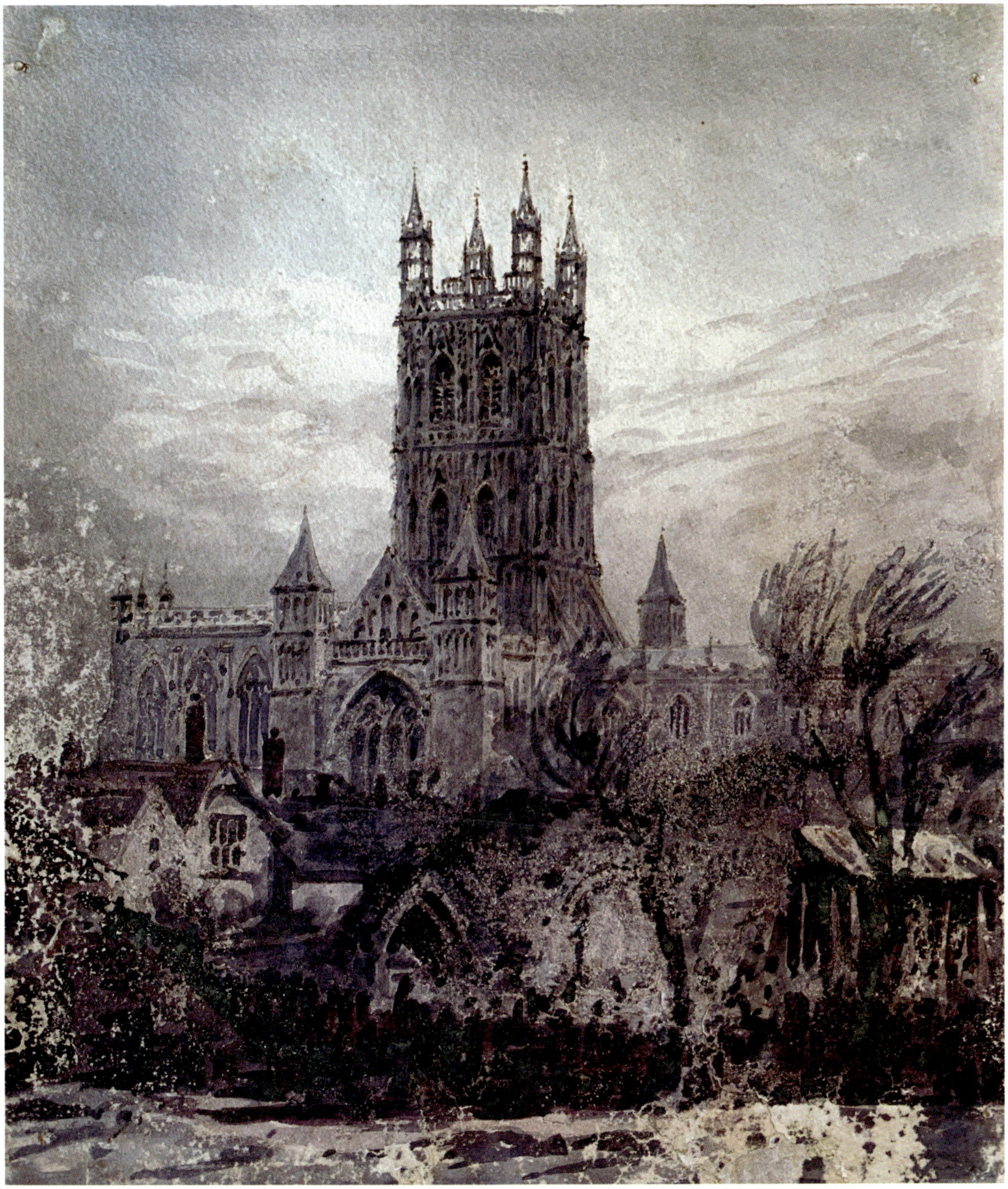

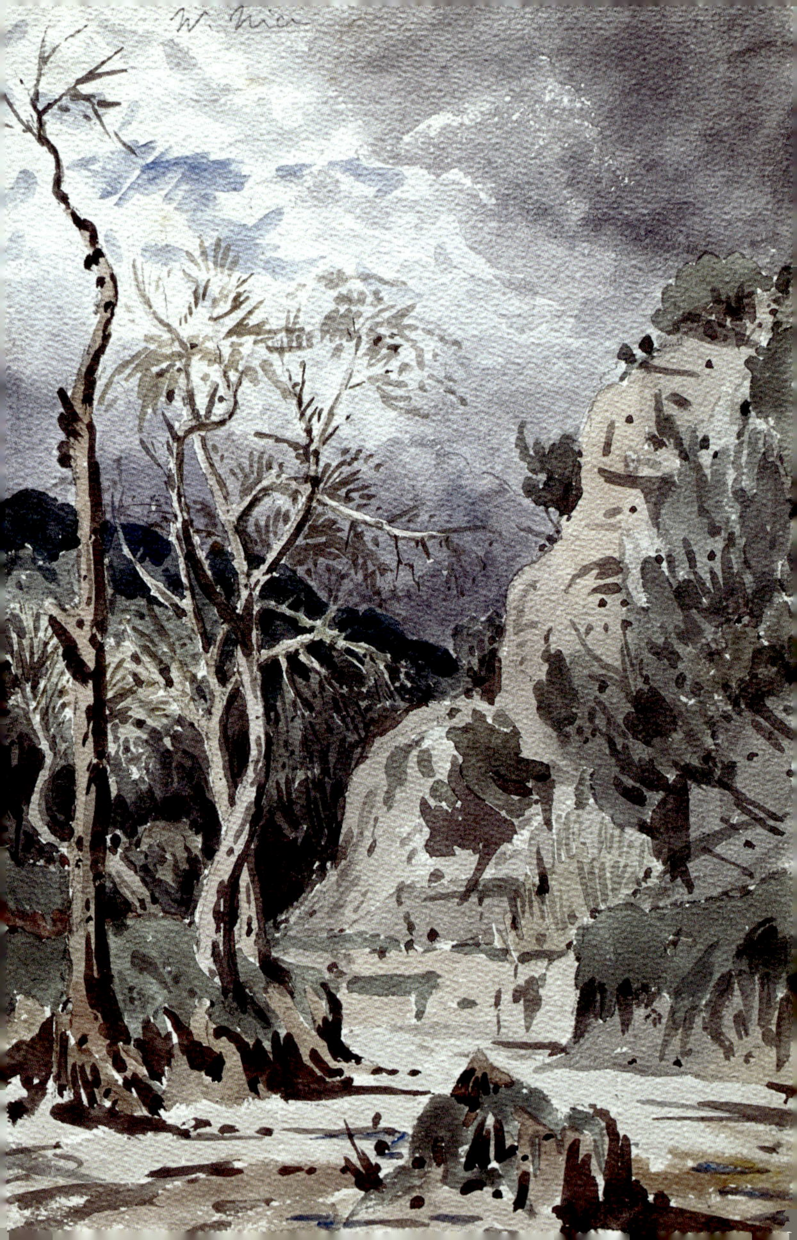

Early Art:
Until the Late 1840s

41. Opposite page: *Near Nice,* 1839

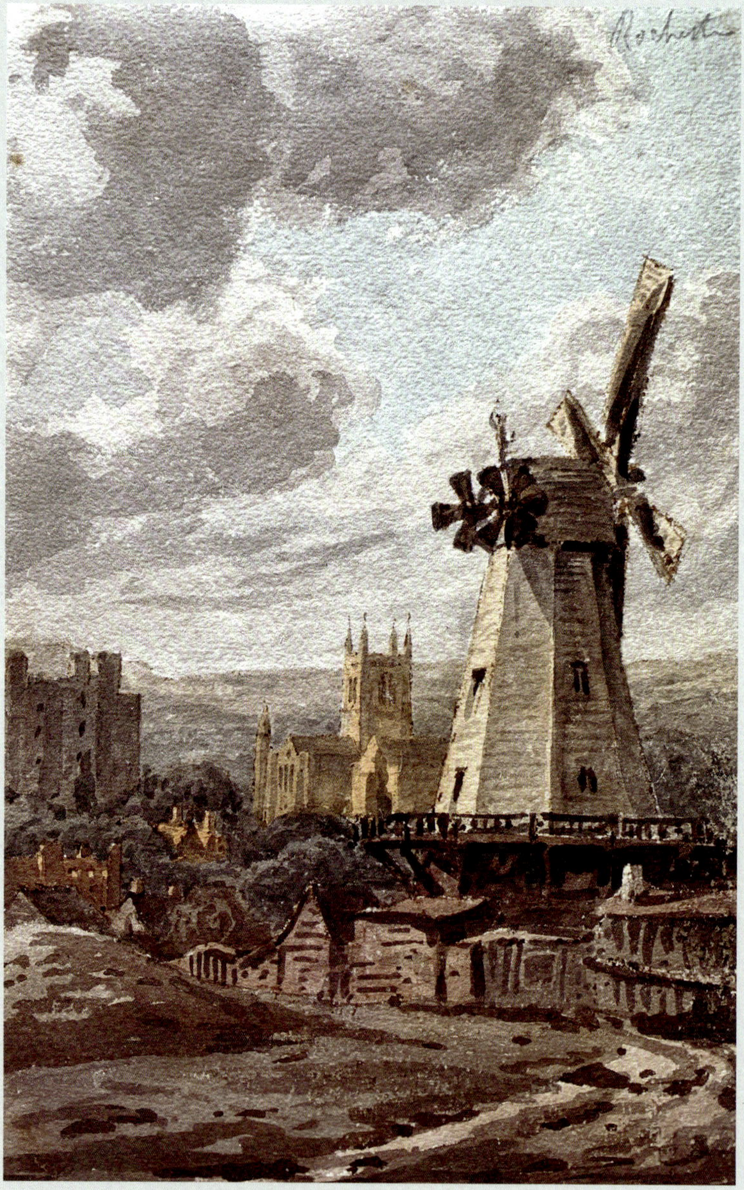

Early Landscapes

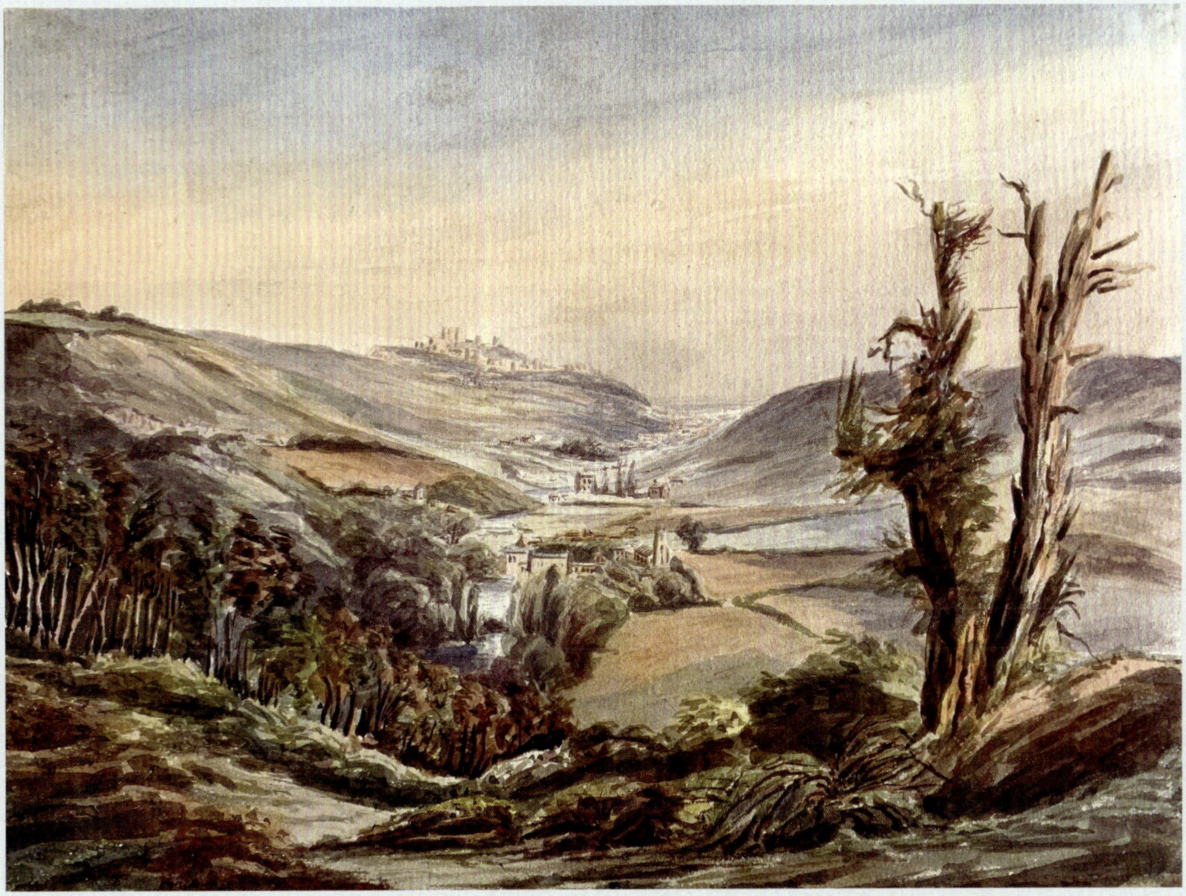

42. Above: *Road to Dover,* 1828
43. Opposite page: *Rochester,* 1830s

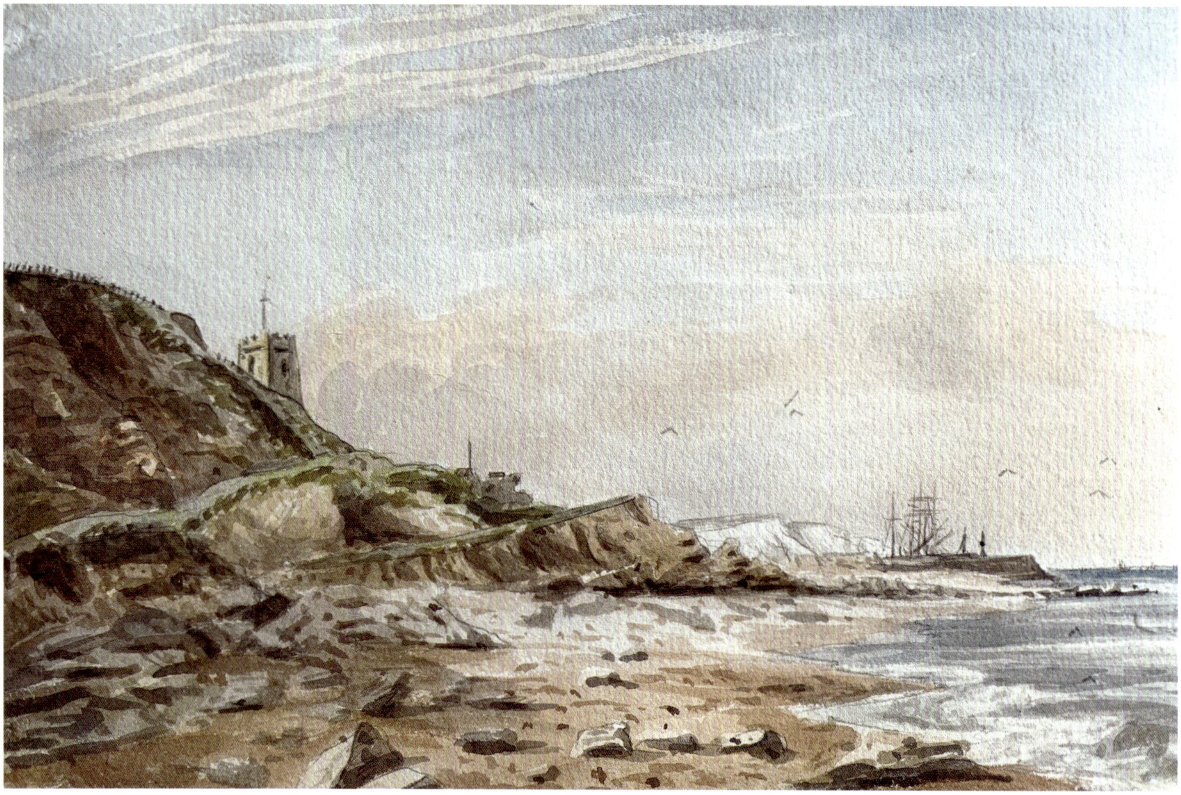

44. *Folkestone*, c. 1828

...all Mr Petit's early sketchbooks prove that he thoroughly understood all the minutest detail both in architecture and shipping, for many of these books contain most beautiful and highly finished details.
P. H. Delamotte *The Art of Sketching from Nature*

Petit's earliest known paintings date from the 1820s. These were more traditional landscapes, and he continued in this vein to a greater or lesser extent during the 1830s. They often show a finer level of detail, demonstrating that the later rougher style was deliberate (43-45). It is not known if Petit took art lessons other than at school. However, his maternal grandfather was the portrait painter John Astley (1724-87) and his mother Harriet painted and presumably taught her children, John Louis and nine siblings.

Pictures from this time all come from several albums that were broken up by the dealers Abbott and Holder in the 1980s. The most frequent subjects are landscapes from Staffordshire and Derbyshire. Petit made several sketching trips to the Peak District. Already at this early stage his pictures show a realistic bleak aspect of that

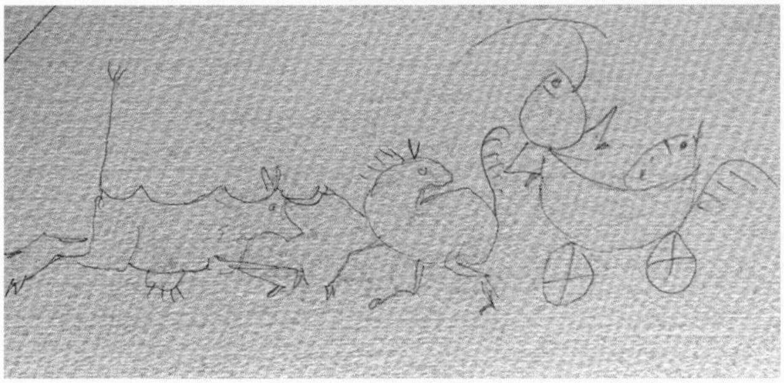

The Doodles

D3. 14 November 1863, at Cuverville
An encounter on the road

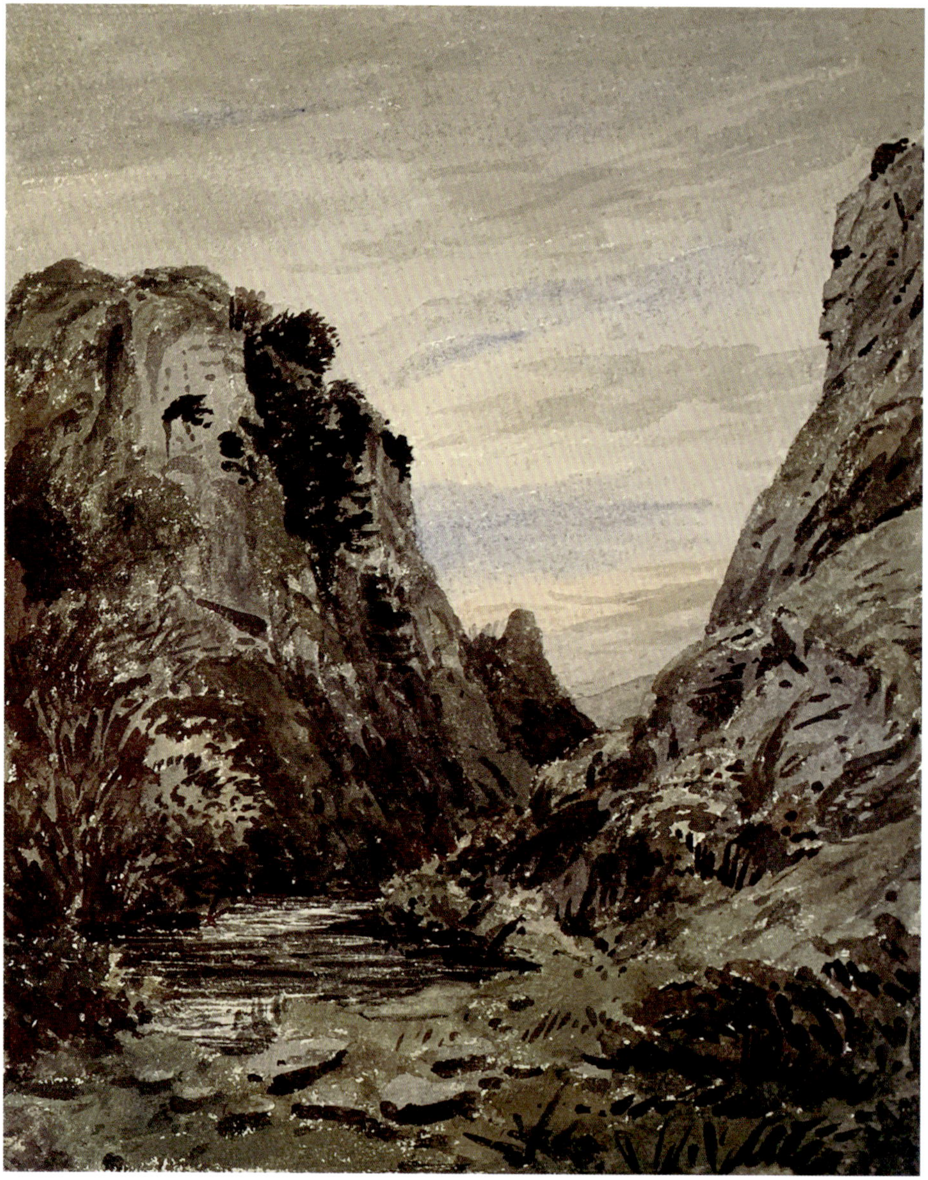

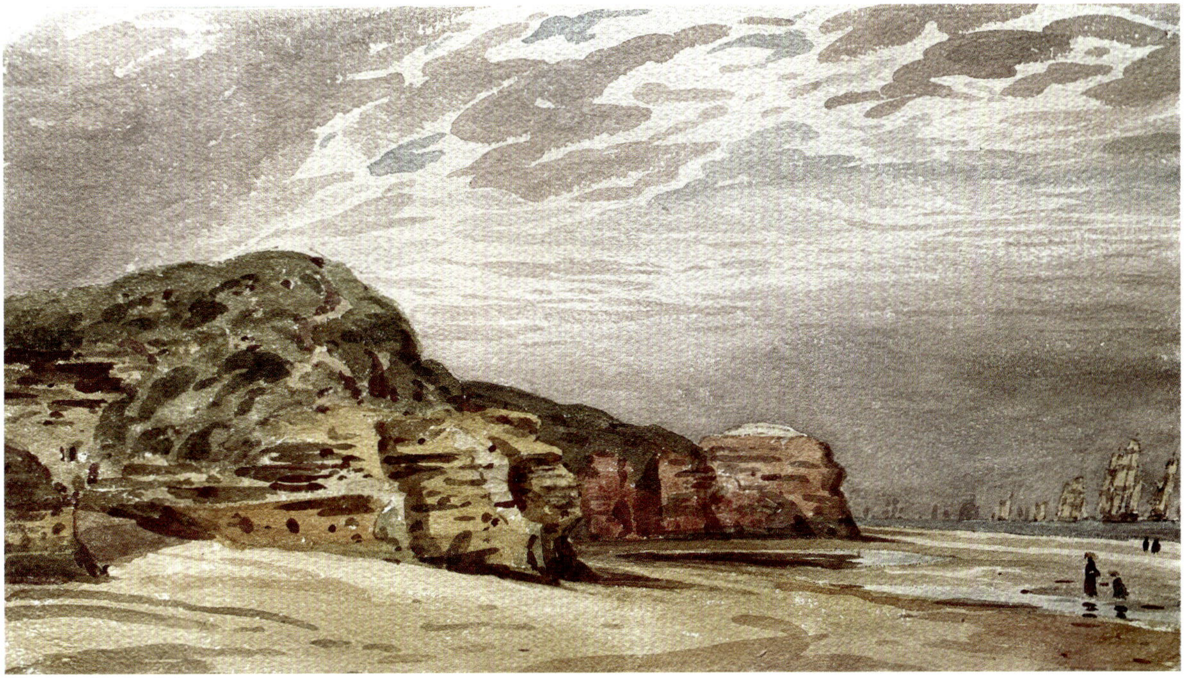

45. *New Brighton*, near Liverpool, c. 1830s
46. Opposite page: *Dovedale, Derbyshire*, c. 1836

region (46, opposite) unlike those of his contemporaries such as the Gresley dynasty of artists. There are also many pictures from Essex, Suffolk and North Kent. Rochester was an easy boat journey from Harwich where he was based. Other counties are represented with a smattering of examples.

One album was dedicated entirely to the South Kent coast. On the back of at least one picture Abbott and Holder wrote the date 1828, presumably taken from the album cover. In June 1828 Petit married Louisa Reid at Wye in Kent, and later in September started work as the curate at Bradfield in Essex. This album, full of unusually bright sunny pictures (42 and 44), might well be from a honeymoon trip that summer.

Sunny pictures would return in 1838-42 and on the trip to the Middle East in 1865 (both groups are shown later) and only occasionally otherwise. In 1840, during the first of these periods, Petit took an apartment in Hastings while completing his first book and painted along the south coast to the west.

Even at this early stage Petit's pictures generally appear to be accurate, without artistic licence, but not without exception. The fashion at the time was for an artist to embellish or adjust nature to suit his picturesque vision. No examples of such a practice are found in later groups. Even among this early group only two have been noted out of a few hundred pictures.

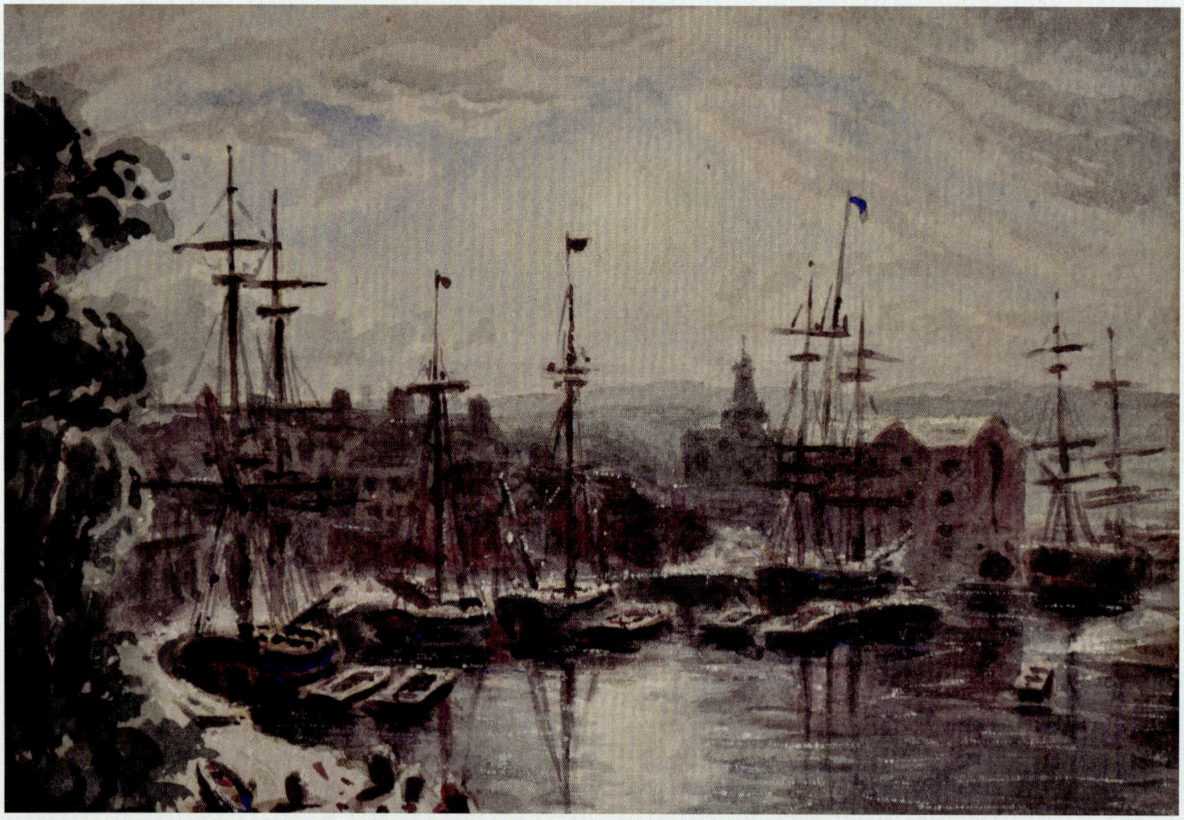

47. *Mistley*, Essex, 1832-4

A Dark Time

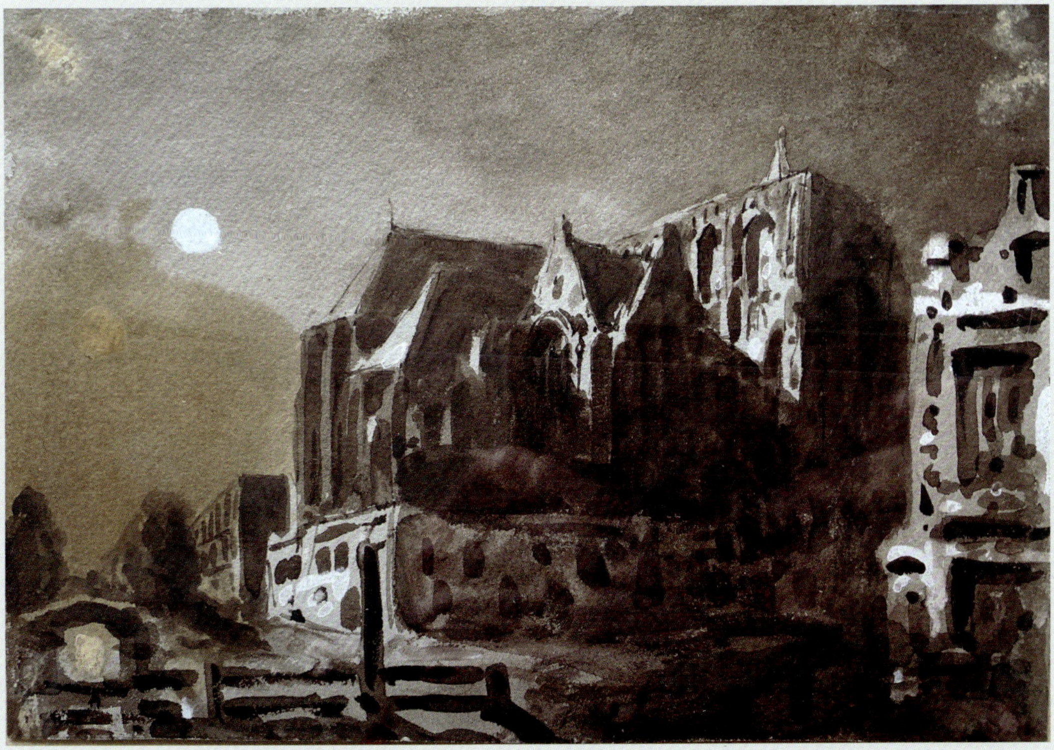

48. *'Oude Kirke'*, Delft, c. 1832-4

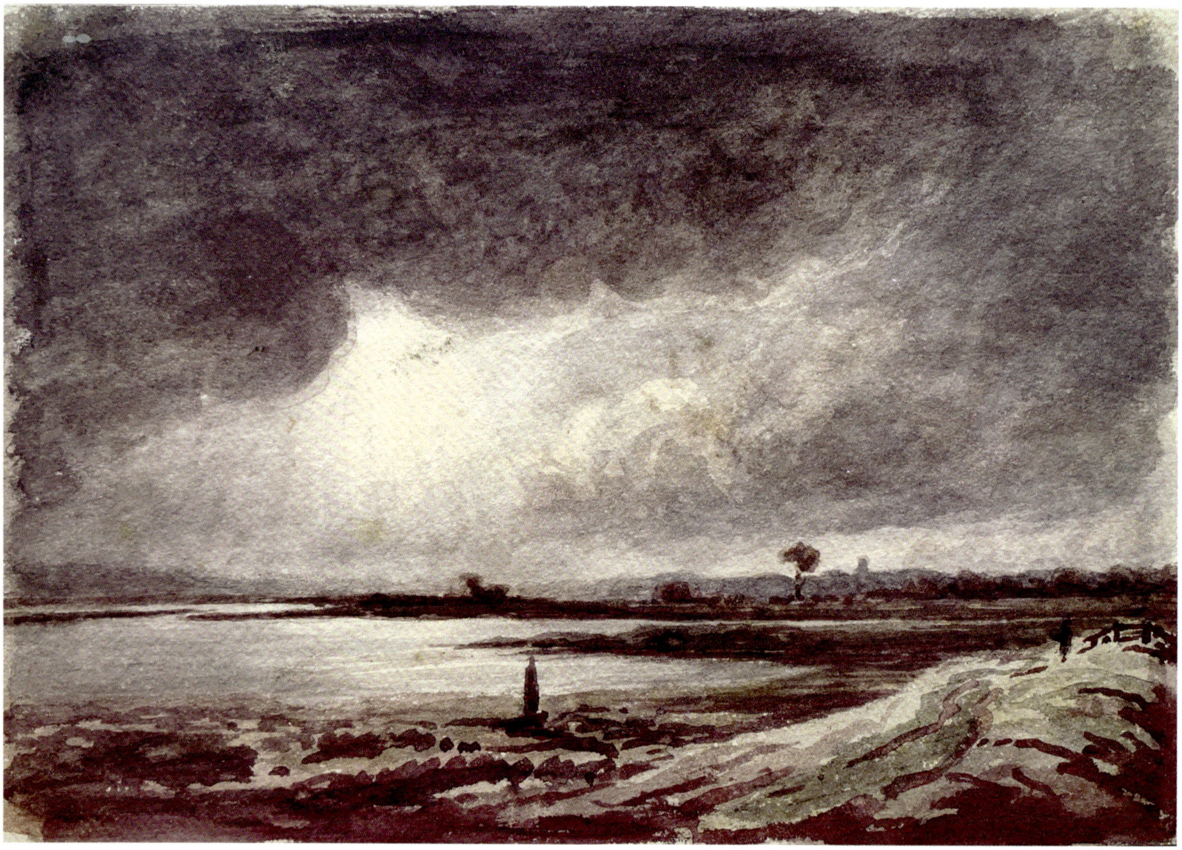

49. *Near Mistley*, Essex, c. 1832

But through the gloom in thrilling tones are heard
Man's conscious heart and God's unerring word... [23]

Petit's happy mood of 1828 did not last. From the early 1830s, he often painted in dark, monochrome tones, sometimes relieved with a gleam of light (see opposite).

A few of these dark pictures can be dated to after 1835; the last pictures in this style are from 1841. Among the earliest we find pictures of Essex and the River Stour, and also pictures from the Netherlands which he visited by ferry from Harwich, on his first known painting trips abroad (48). Petit's curacy from 1828 to 1834, was at the twin parish of Bradfield and Mistley, on the south bank of the Stour estuary, 10 miles east of Harwich. The first marine studies date from this time (47): a subject he would continue throughout his life. One also starts to find a significant proportion of churches. Not as high a proportion as in later life, but enough to date Petit's preoccupation with church architecture from this period.

Most notable are pictures of the Black Country mines and factories (50). While other artists had painted romantic views of Dudley Castle, or completed sketches showing distant factories (Turner did both), Petit was one of the first to make art from real-life industrial scenes These were not deemed picturesque and so not a suitable subject for his contemporaries. Later, Petit would praise the architectural power of such furnaces: *'Some of these taken as buildings independently of their accompaniments of fire and smoke, are absolutely grand...'*[24]

It was not until the turn of the century that Edwin Butler Bayliss, for the same region, and L. S. Lowry, for the northwest, would popularise such art.

We do not know the cause of the obvious gloom in Petit's mood. Whatever the reason, the effect on his paintings marks his first distinctive style, and his first departure from the mainstream.

The Doodles

D4. 12 September 1866, north Wales. Emma holding the umbrella while Petit drew in the rain, but still got wet.

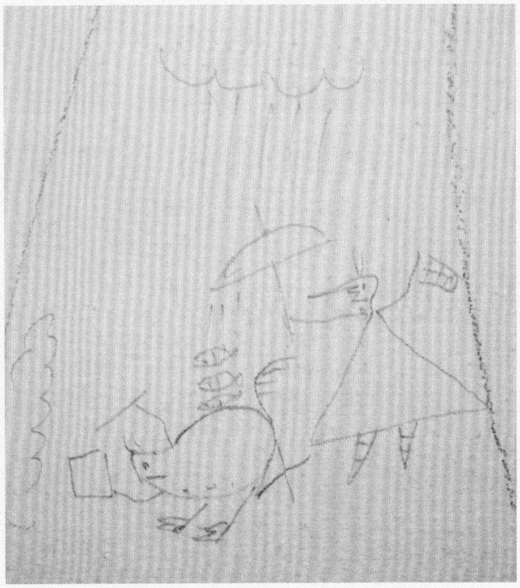

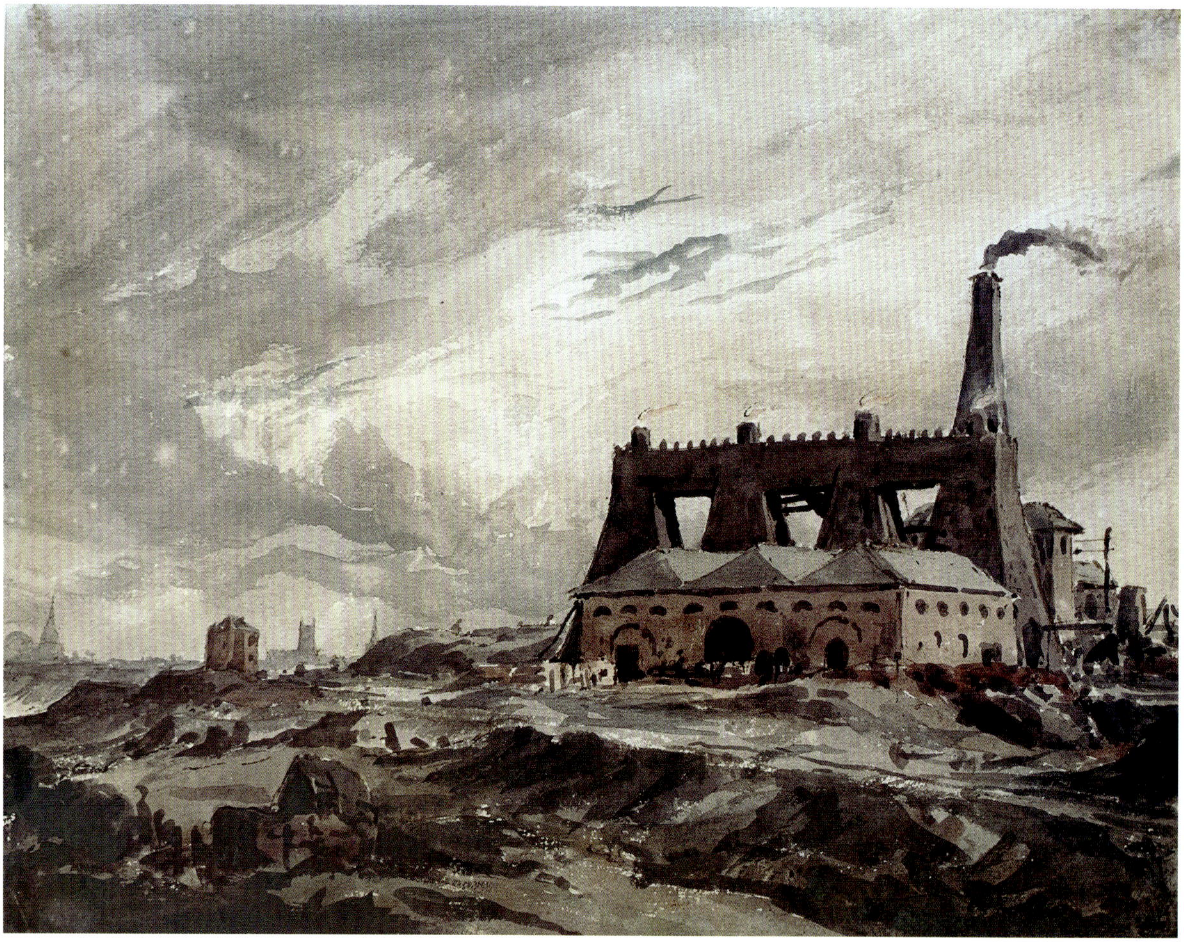

50. *Near Wolverhampton*, *c.* 1835
51. Opposite page: *Ulverscroft Priory, Leicestershire*, c. 1830s

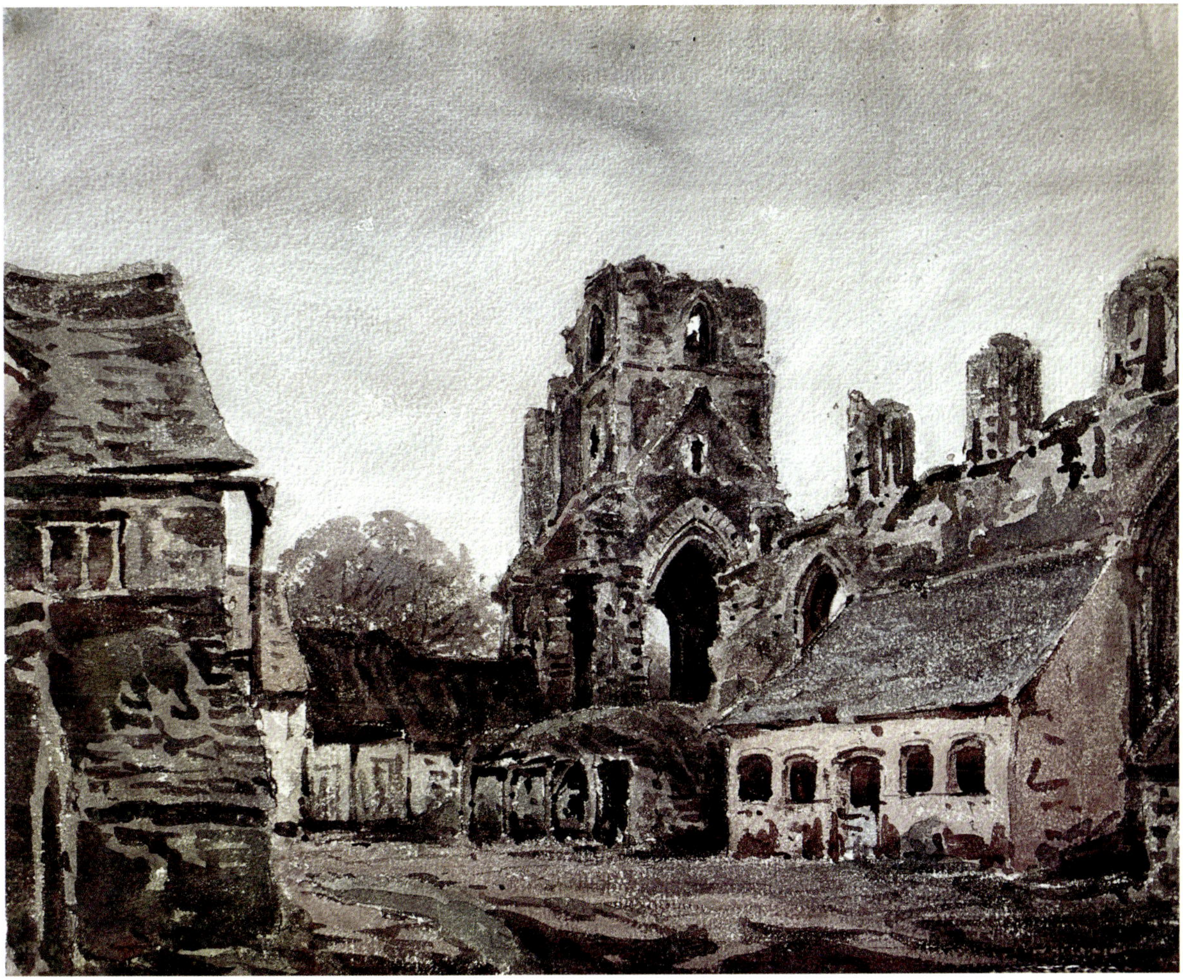

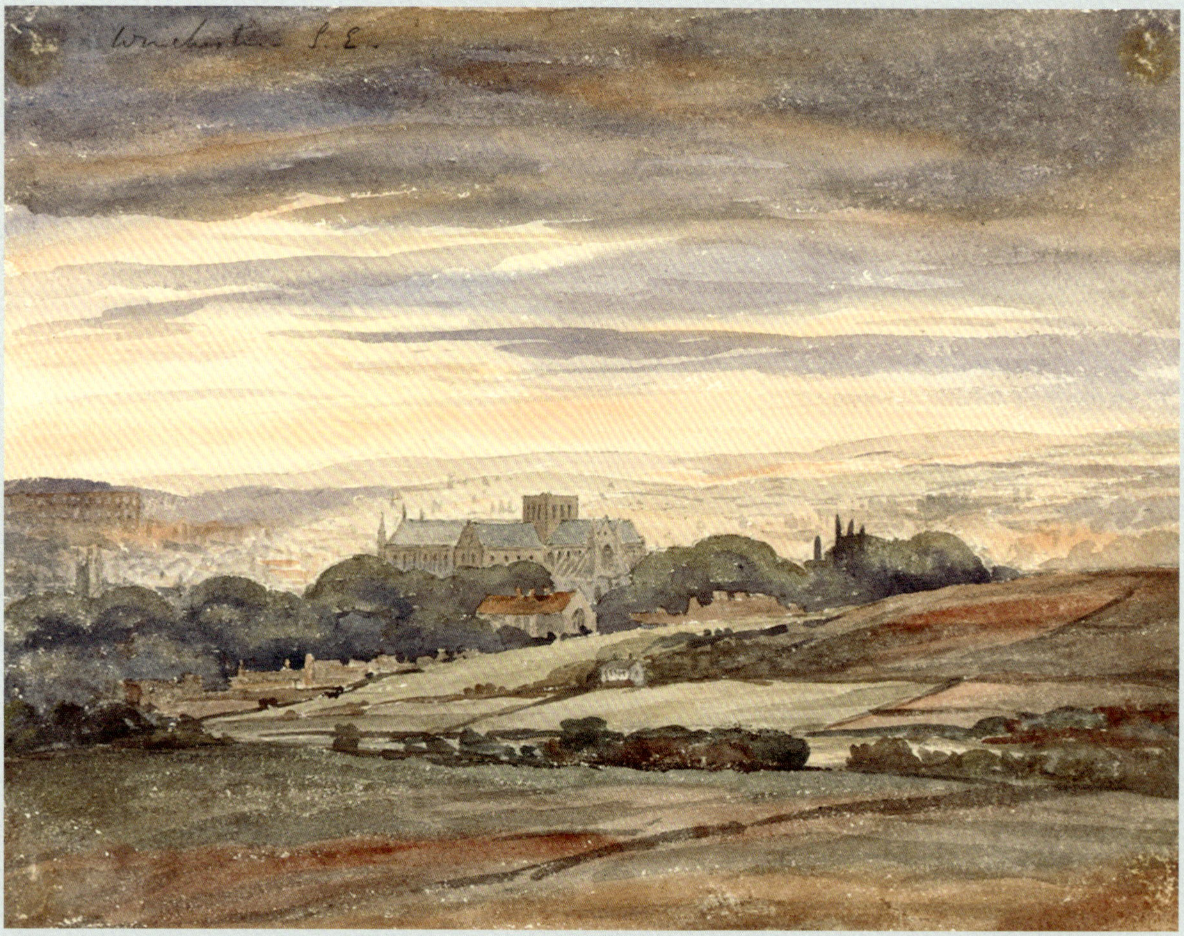

52. *Winchester,* c. 1840
53. Opposite page: *St Catherine's,* Isle of Wight, c. 1840 reproduced in *Remarks*
Both pictures courtesy Special Collections, Hartley Library, Southampton University (MS283)

A Colourful Interlude

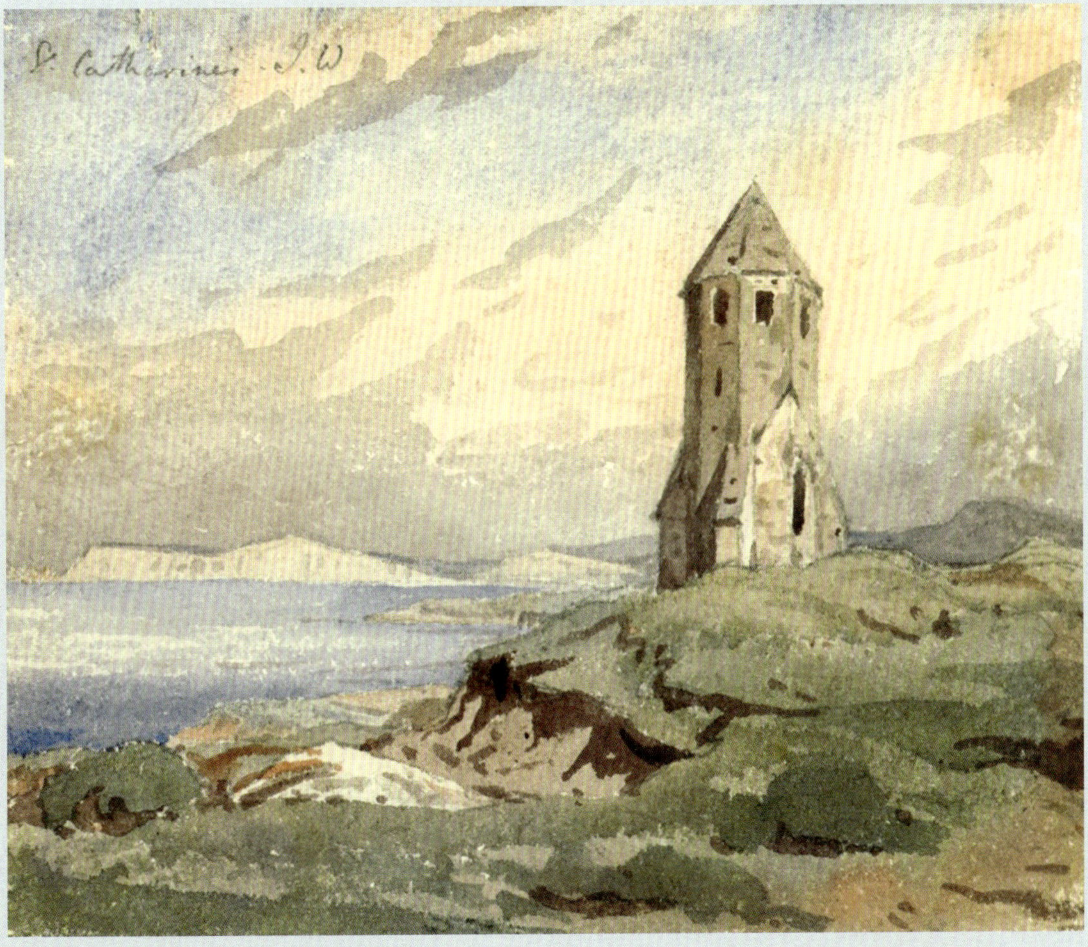

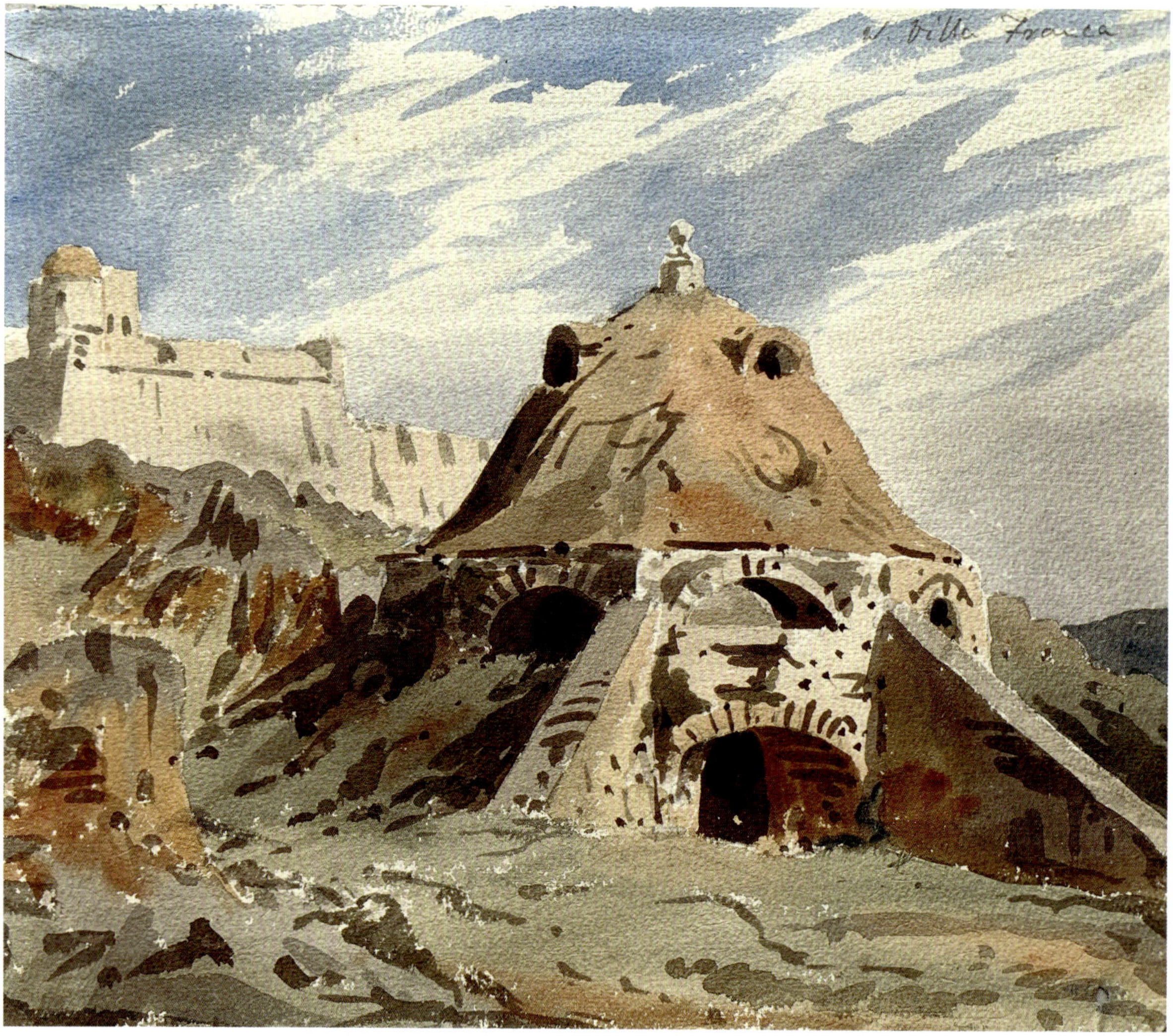

54. *Lime Kiln Near Villa Franca* (Villefranche), 1839

If an artist, in making a sketch from nature, thinks only of copying as closely as he can every line, tint and shadow, his work will on the whole be feeble and unsatisfactory. If he is intent on capturing the style of a favourite master, the result will betray mannerism...
But if he studies the scene and considers the points by which it fixes itself on his memory and uses the different combinations and contrasts which make its identity, his drawing will have character.
J. L. Petit, *Remarks on Architectural Character* (1846)

Petit spent much of the next seven years, from 1834 until 1841, working on his first book: *Remarks on Church Architecture*, in particular finding, visiting and painting the examples that he would use to illustrate it from all over Britain and Europe.

Yet suddenly, towards the end of this period, his art and presumably his mood brightened. During a three-month stay around Ashbourne from March to May 1838, there are a large number of landscapes where he seems to be experimenting with different colours and with capturing 'effect' quickly and roughly (see 55 next page). Gradually this settles to a few palettes that he takes to the south coast in either 1839 or 1840 (52, 53 previous pages) and on trips to Italy and France in 1839. The obvious exuberance reached a peak in the south of France and north Italy (54, 56) and in Normandy (57, 58).

There are many watercolours from this period of churches, or other old buildings, which did not make it into the book. Landscapes, however, are scarcer from this period and those tend usually to be quick impressionistic sketches. A few groups exist from this time, from near Nice (see 41, above) and the Isle of Wight, and the Alps, when Petit allowed himself to be distracted from his objective by *'the sublimest works of our Creator'*.[25]

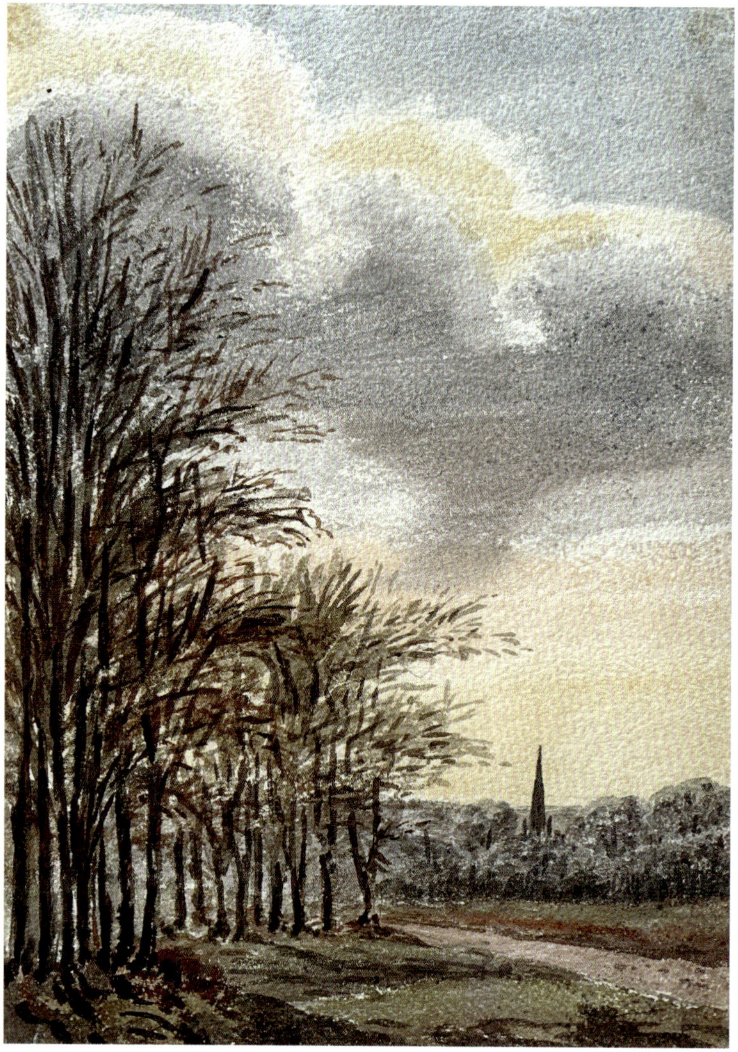

55. *Ashbourne,* Derbyshire, May 1838

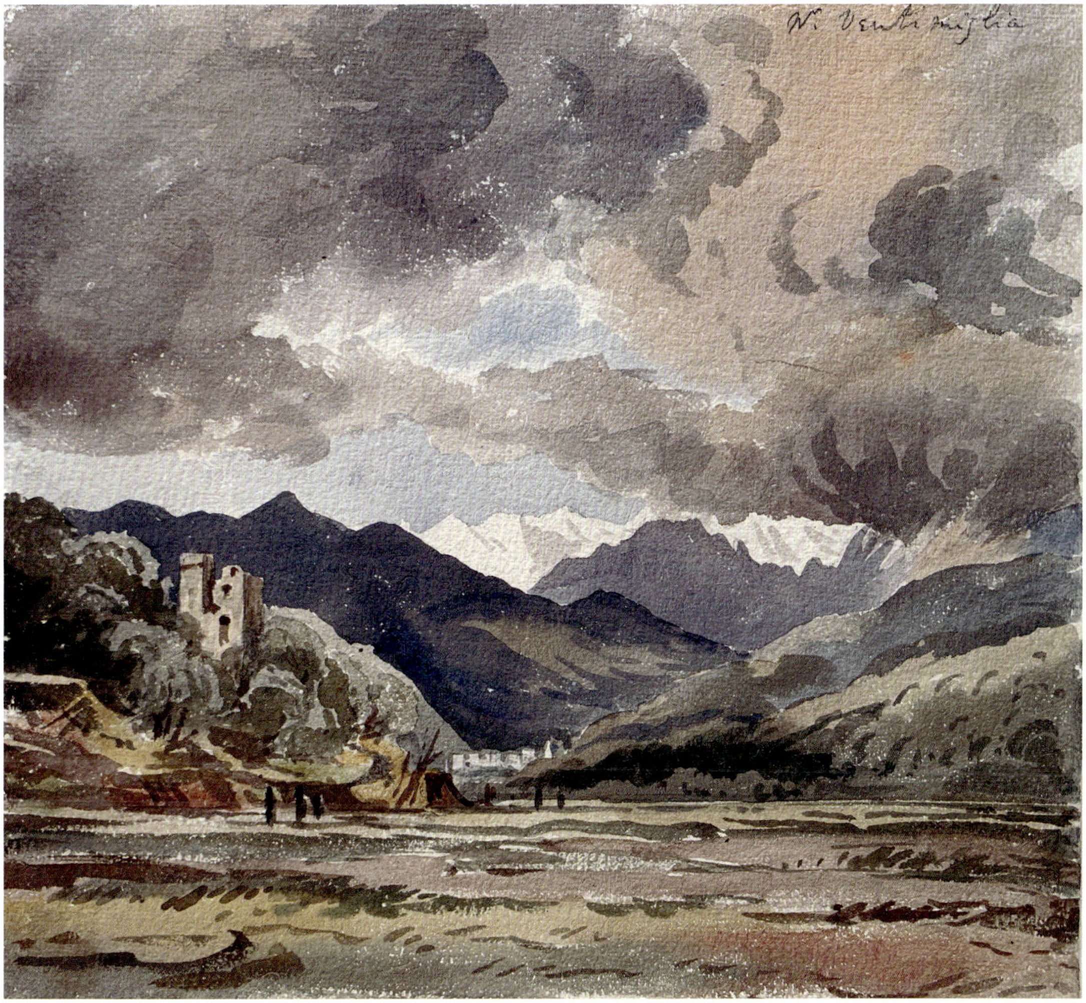

56. *Ventimiglia*, 1839

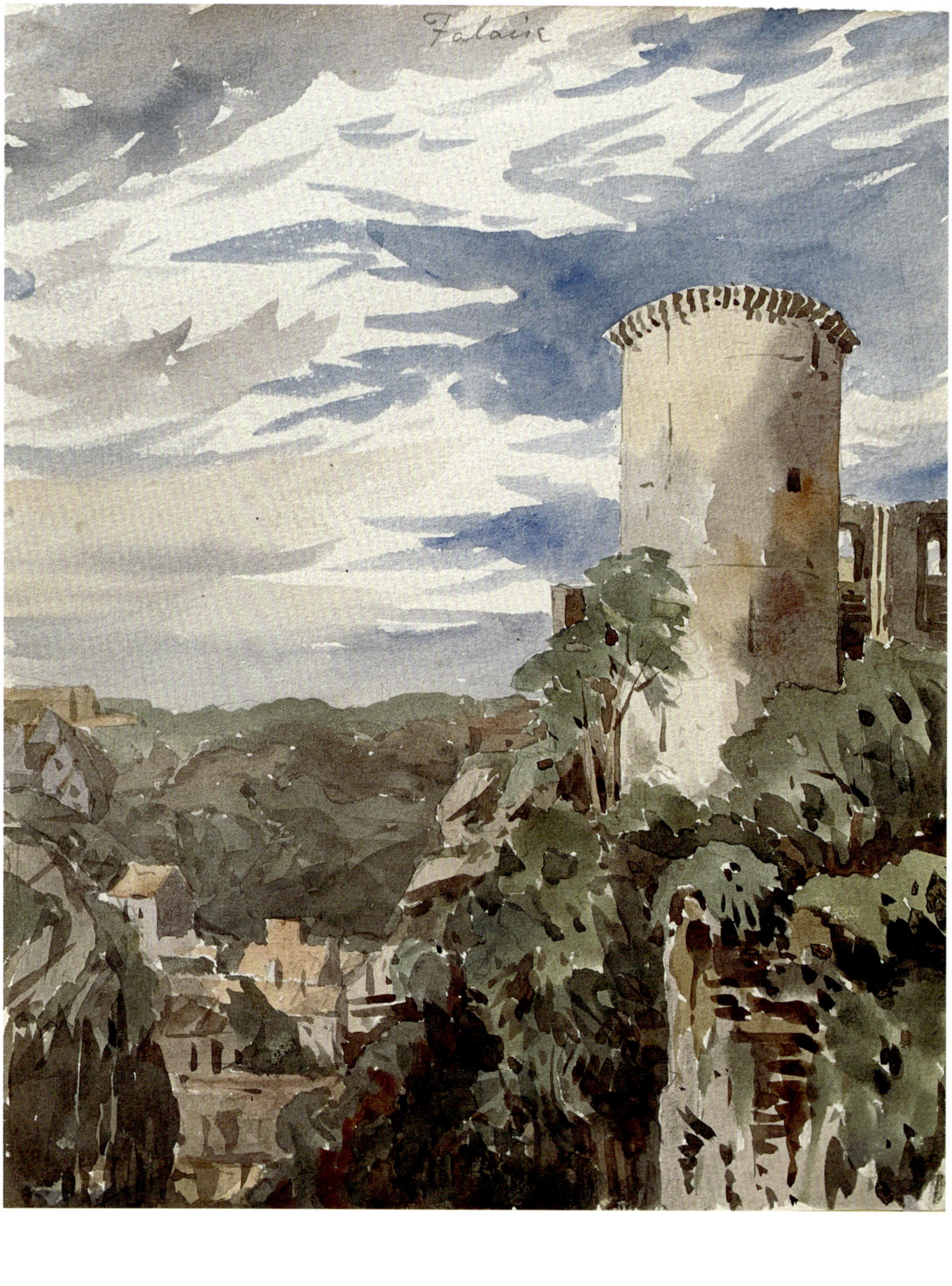
Falaise

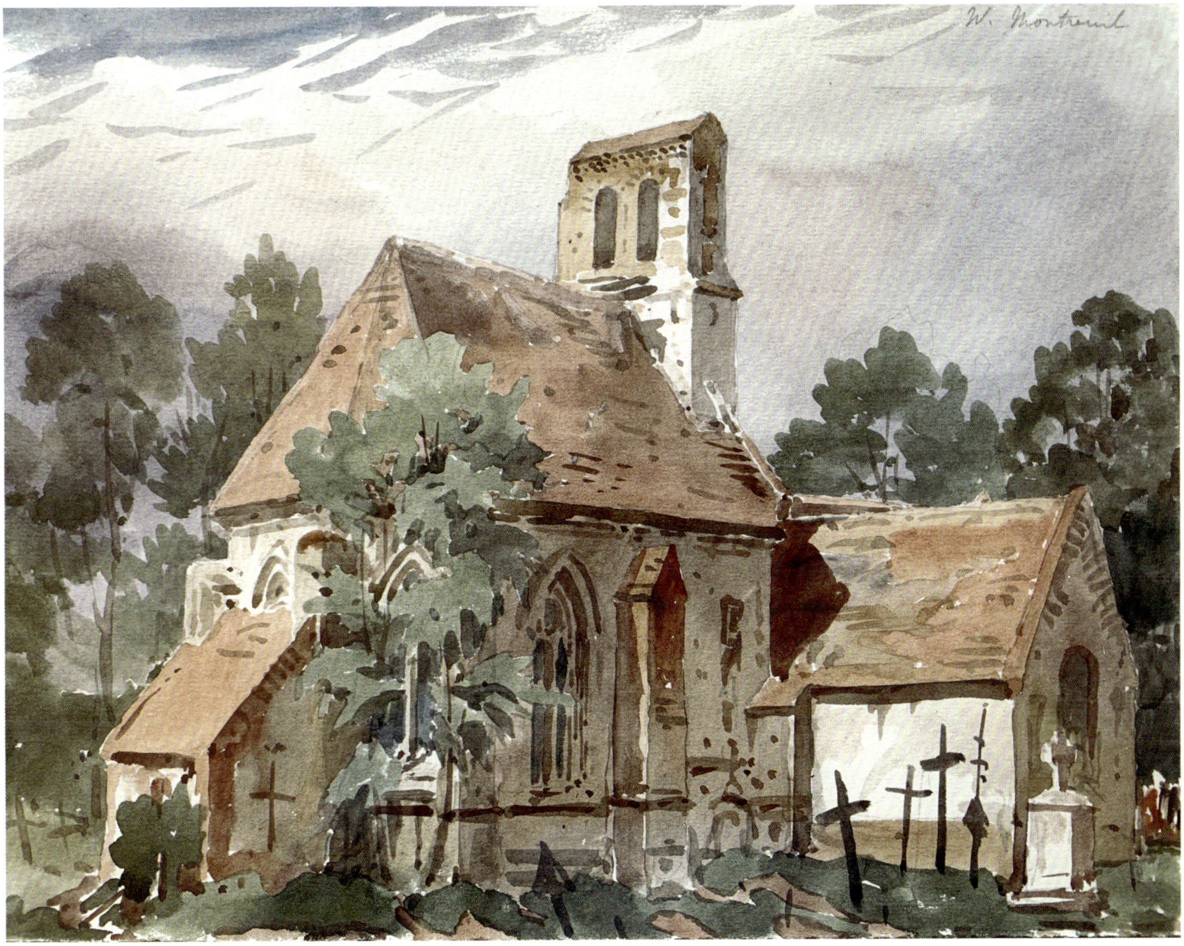

57. *Near Montreuil,* 1839 reproduced in *Remarks*
58. Opposite page: *Falaise Castle, Normandy,* 1839

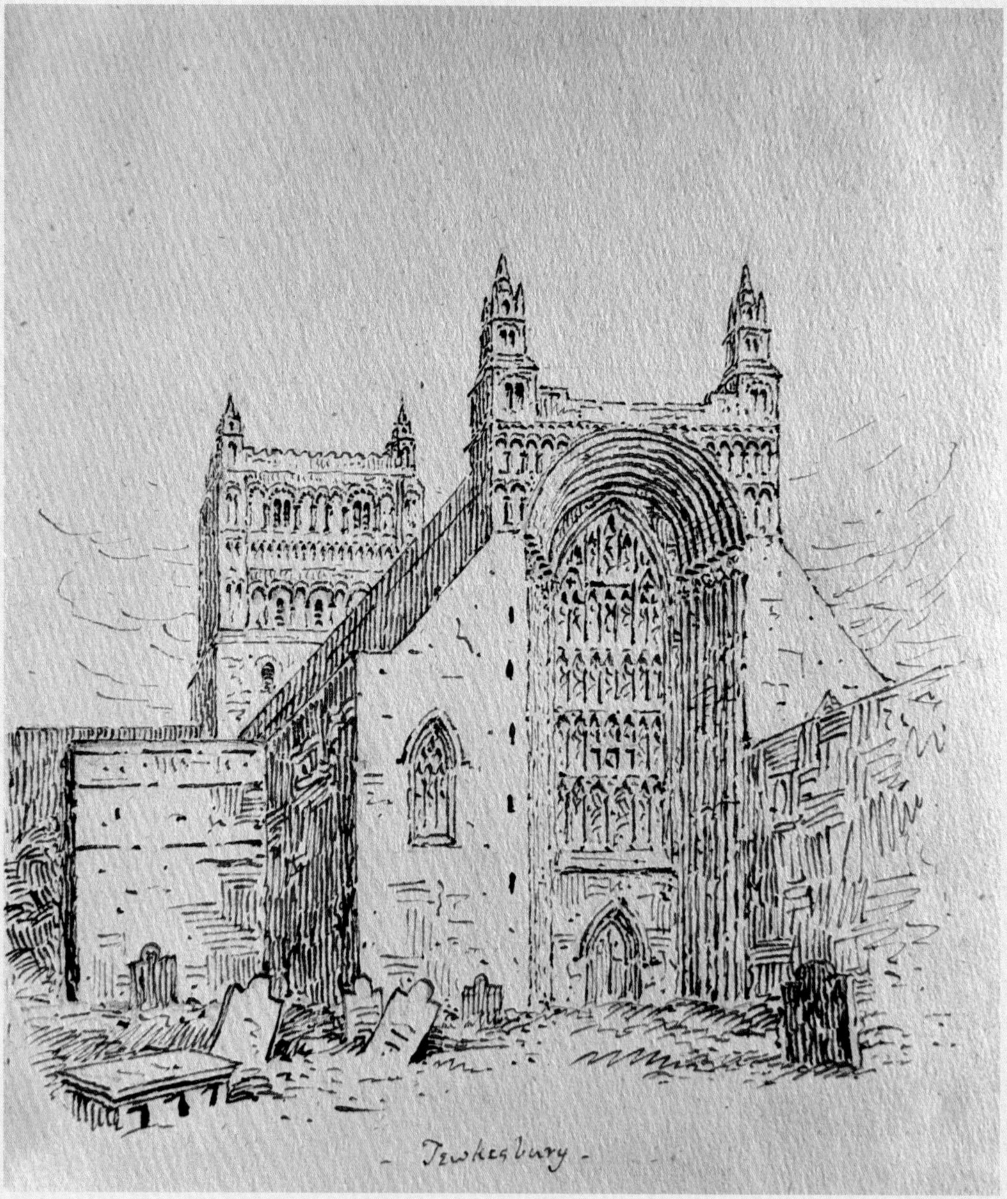
- Tewkesbury -

Pen and Ink Drawings

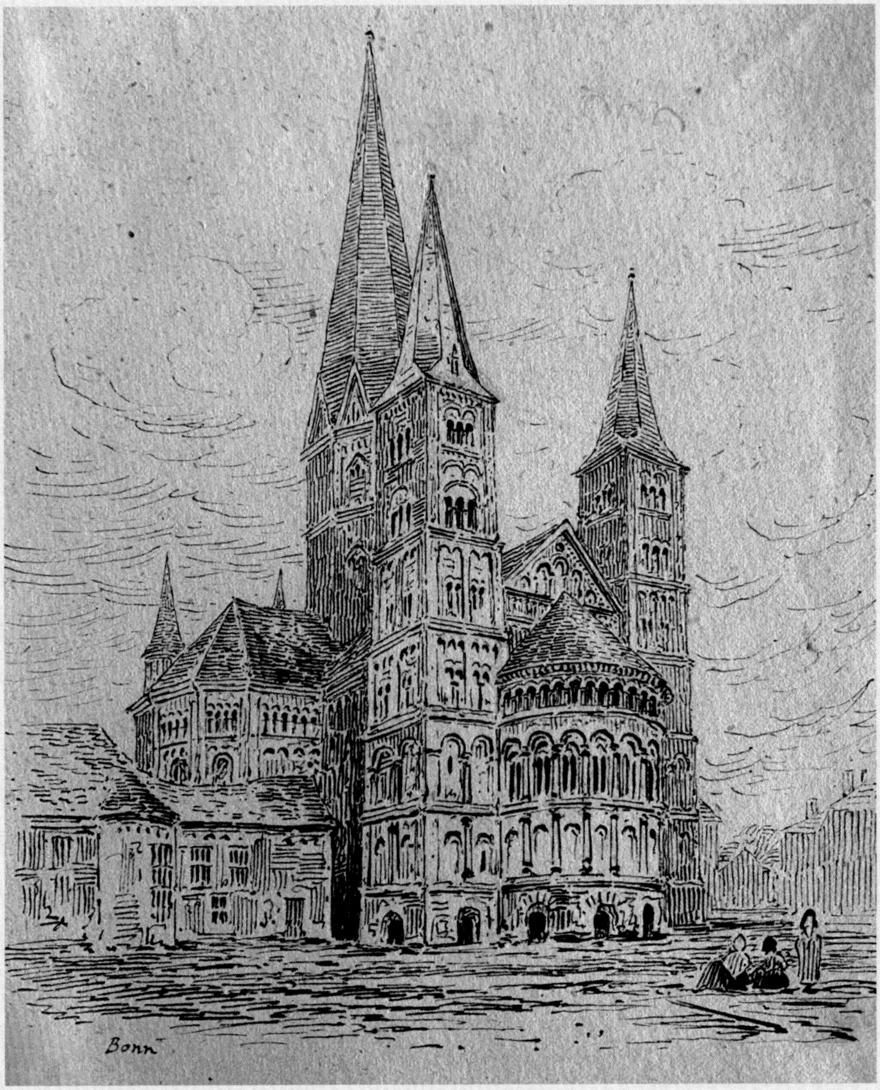

59. Above: *Bonn*, pen and ink drawing, 1840
60. Opposite page: *Tewkesbury*, pen and ink drawing, 1840

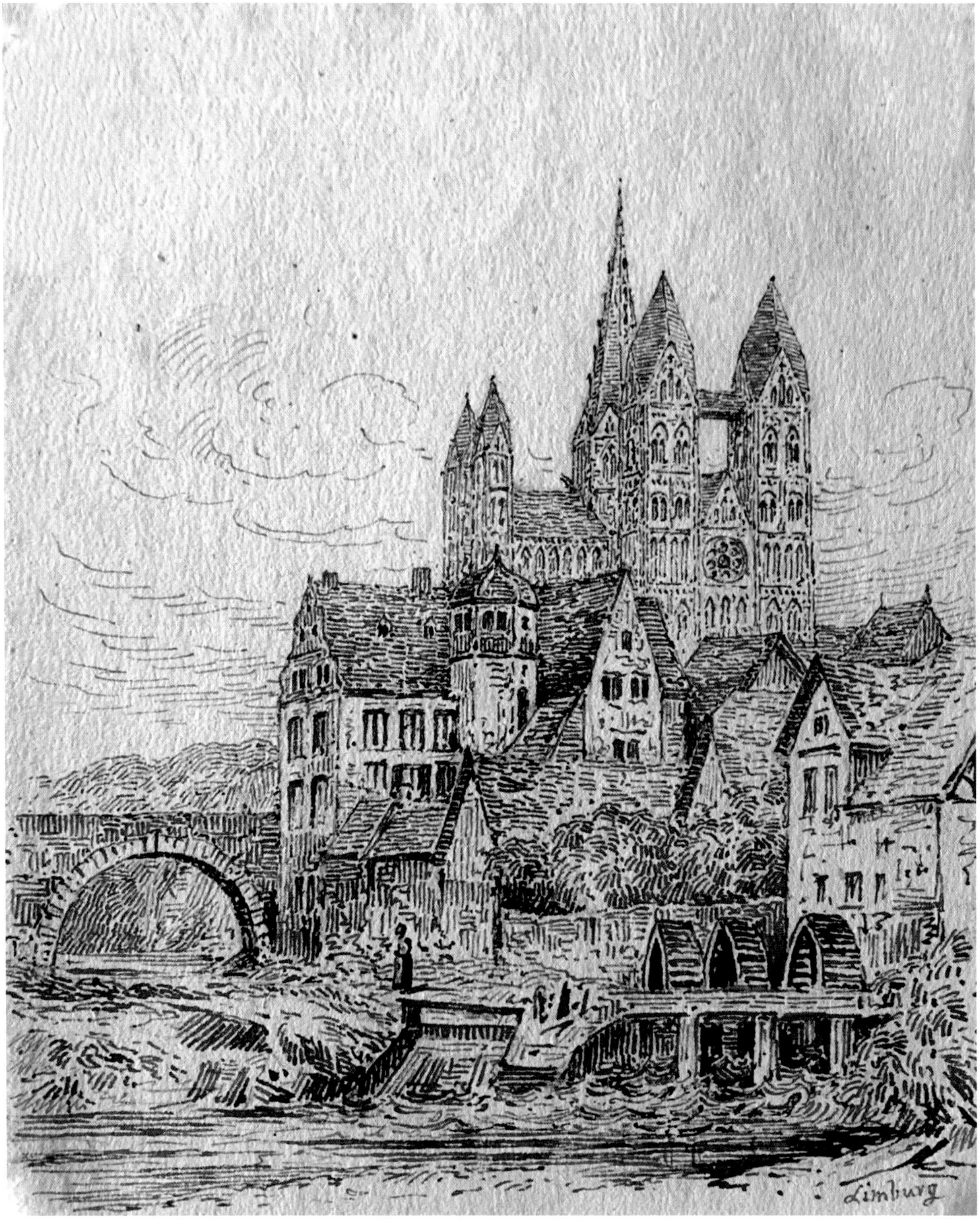

61. *Limburg on the Lahn,* 1840

I have done my best to set before the reader a sufficient variety, both in form and composition, to prove to him how wide a range can be taken by architects…to be confined neither to one country, nor one age, nor one scale of importance; to comprise not only finished and elaborate specimens, but the roughest and plainest chapels or village churches, many of which, on account of their unpretending beauty, attained solely by proportion, are invaluable.
J.L. Petit *Remarks*[26]

Petit himself prepared the pen and ink drawings for the illustrations in his publications. The first and largest group was the 290 for *Remarks on Church Architecture*. These had been lost until 2020, when they emerged unattributed in a small regional auction in Dorchester. Except for three by others, all these drawings were completed by Petit between returning from France in late 1839 and the book's appearance in March 1841. An astonishing labour best appreciated when the drawings are viewed together as one work of art - Petit's homage to medieval Christian architecture, which he loved but did not want imitated.

The *Remarks* drawings show an attention to detail and relative delicacy compared with his watercolours. In the same way that his rare colourful pictures demonstrate that Petit chose his usual austere palette deliberately, rare intricate works argue that his rough style was equally considered.

Drawings have been said to reflect *'the very spirit and quintessence of art'*.[27] In these drawings Petit's feeling for architecture is expressed differently than in his watercolours.

The *Remarks* drawings were highly praised – even by those who opposed the book's message. Indeed, the attractiveness of the drawings was used as an argument against Petit: readers should not be misled by the pretty drawings. This might be the reason why Petit retreated from his vibrantly colourful style around 1843, and mostly avoided it with the exception of the trip to the Middle East in his last decade (see p. 106).

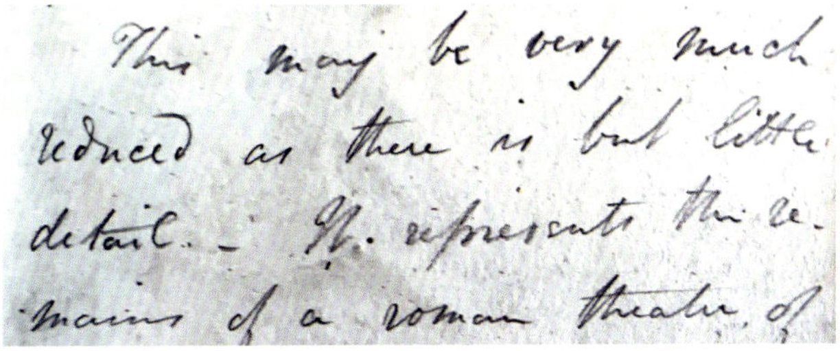
This may be very much
reduced as there is but little
detail. – It represents the re-
mains of a roman theatre of

Above: Petit wrote detailed instructions to the printer on the reverse or sometimes on the face of the drawings.

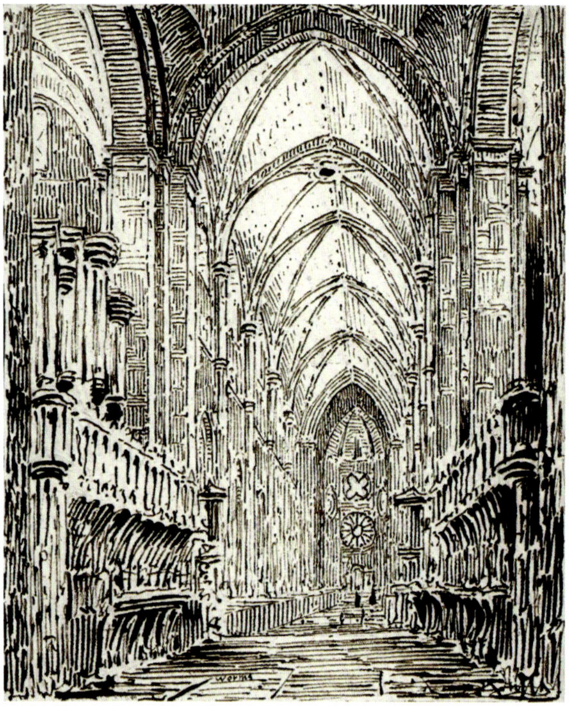
Worms

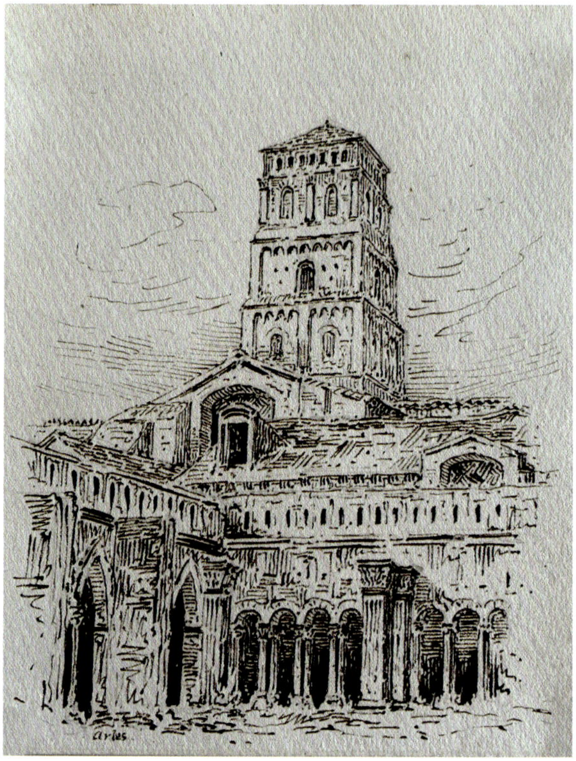
Arles

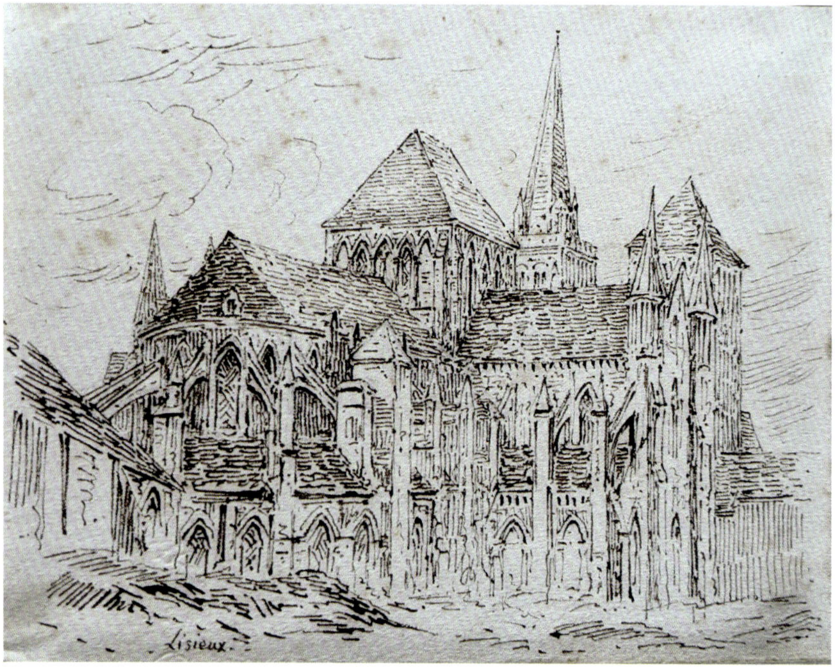
Lisieux.

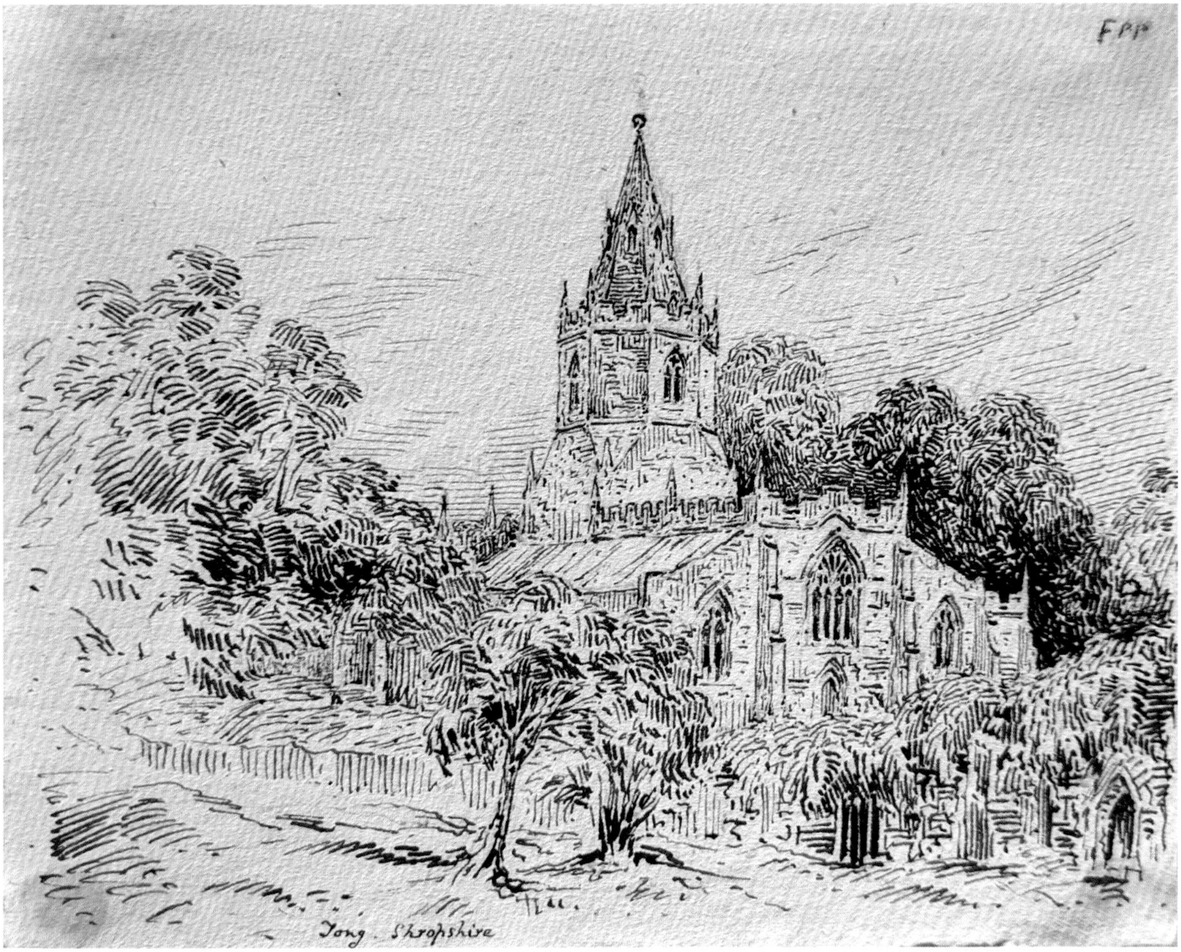

62. Above: *Tong*, Salop, pen and ink drawing, 1840
63. Oppostite page, top left: *Worms Cathedral*
64. Oppostite page, top right: *Arles*
65. Opposite page, bottom: *Lisieux,* all pen and ink drawings, 1840

Subsequently, between 1845 and 1868, Petit did approximately 300 other drawings for his articles in the *Archaeological Journal*. He gifted them all to the Archaeological Institute. Their current whereabouts are unknown. For his last major book, *Architectural Studies in France* (1854), Petit completed 90 drawings which were produced using the new anastatic copy technique. These were much rougher. The originals of those are also not traced.

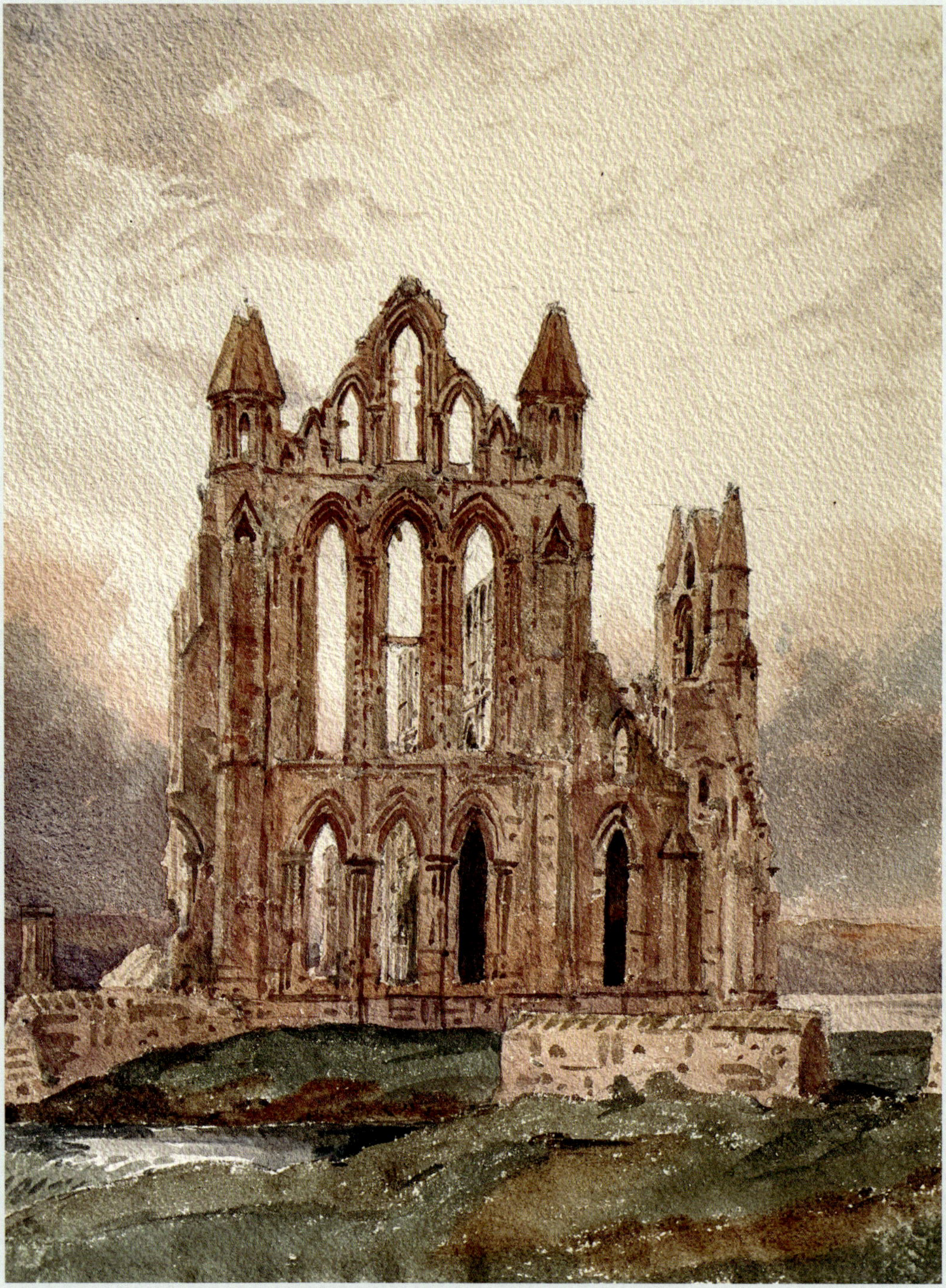

66. *Whitby Abbey, Yorkshire*, c. 1844-5

Mid-1840s
Albums and the Gothic Ruins

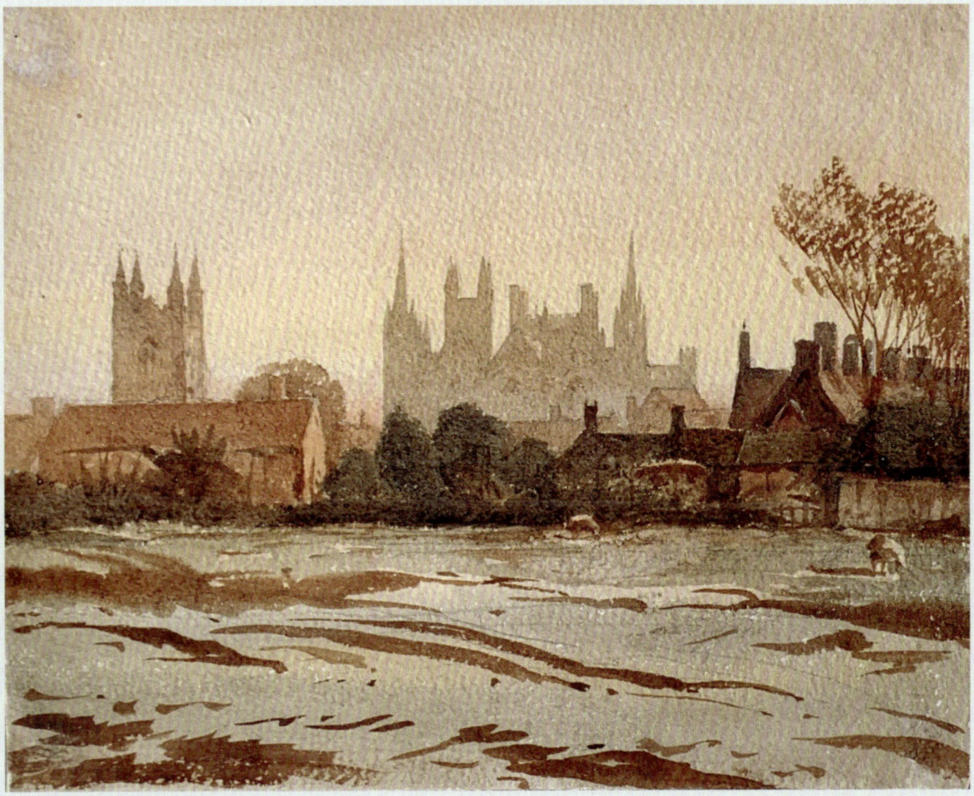

67. *Peterborough Cathedral*, 1843

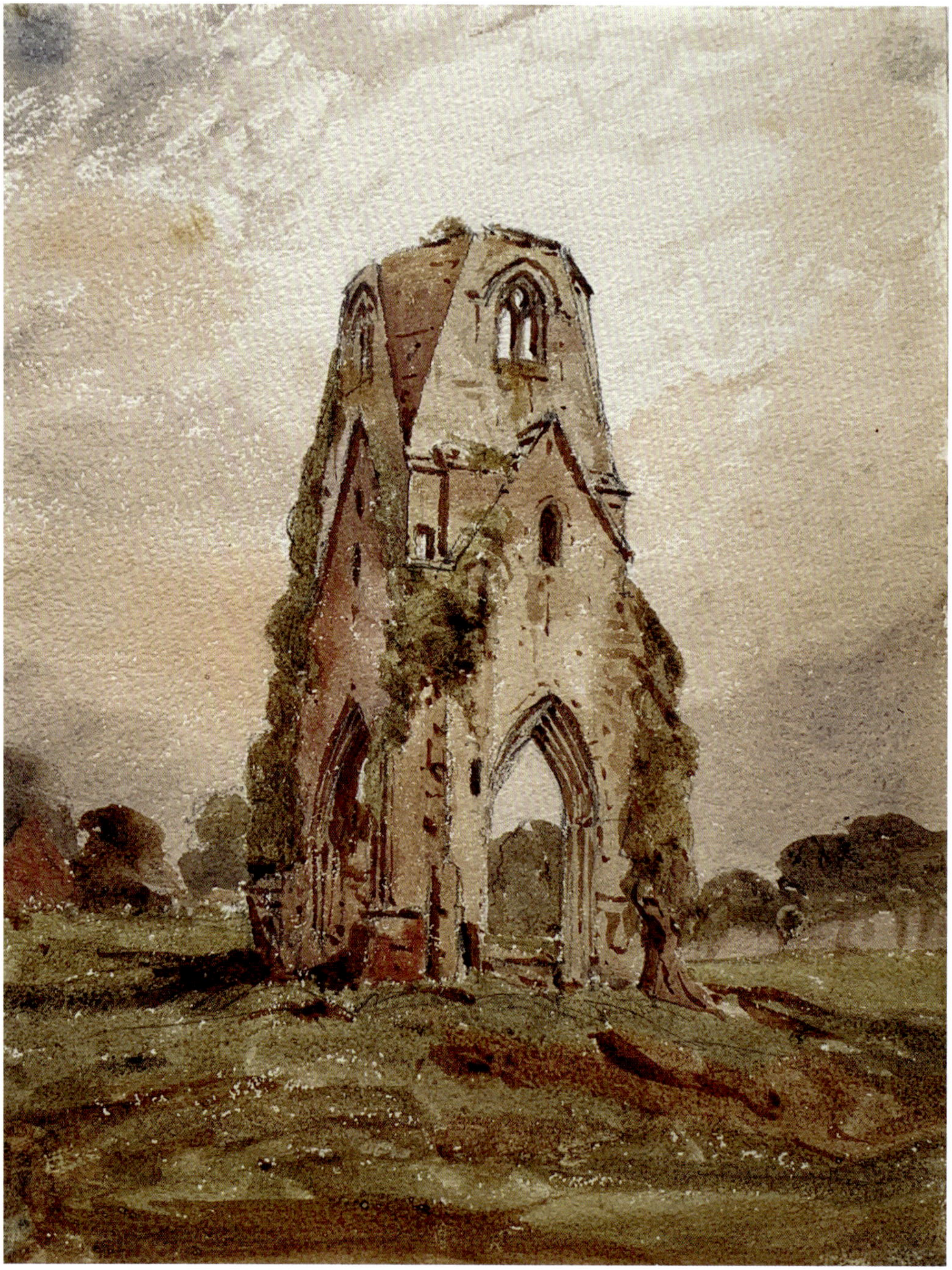

68. *Maxstoke Priory* (nr Coventry), c. 1845

The Gothic style is not a bad style, nor are the architects of the present day bad architects, yet the two do not agree together, and the result is unfavourable to both.
J. L. Petit *Architectural Studies in France*[28]

Following the exuberant style of 1838-42, Petit mostly avoided bright colour that could distract from his purpose. In the 1840s we start to see a clearer split between the architectural sketches, where he took portraits of the buildings he wanted to note, and the landscapes – both pure landscapes, and those where he captured 'the effect' of a church in its wider setting.

Petit also started to paint larger pictures – 37 x 27 cm – which would become the standard for the rest of his life. Possibly they became larger and standard sized as a result of the need to exhibit. The red-brown washes that underlie most of his sketches also became predominant from now on.

The series of ruins from 1845 (66 and 68) are most notable as markedly differing from the Romantic treatment of a Gothic ruin, where the artist often added his own fancies to make it more picturesque. This was still the age when a wealthy landowner might build a quaint ruin for his garden. Petit's pictures were accurate, and were presented to show the violence and savagery of the societies that produced Gothic.

'Its savageness and its air of mystery which constitute its greatest charm are wholly out of place in this age of refinement and realities.'[29]

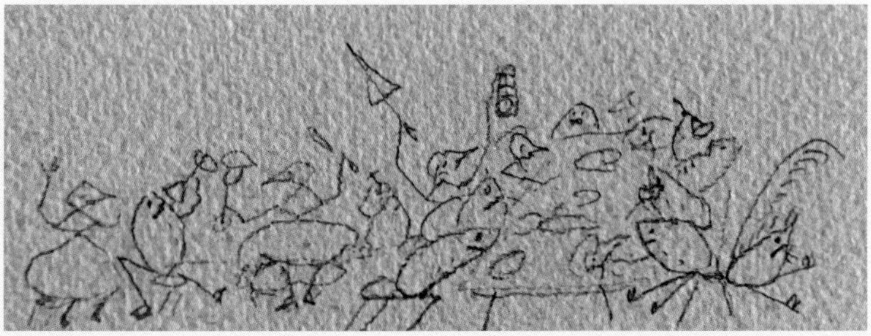

The Doodles

D5. 27 July 1861, at Crowland.
A celebration or a rowdy pub dinner. The umbrella indicates which is his sister Emma, and Petit is the character with the long tail at right

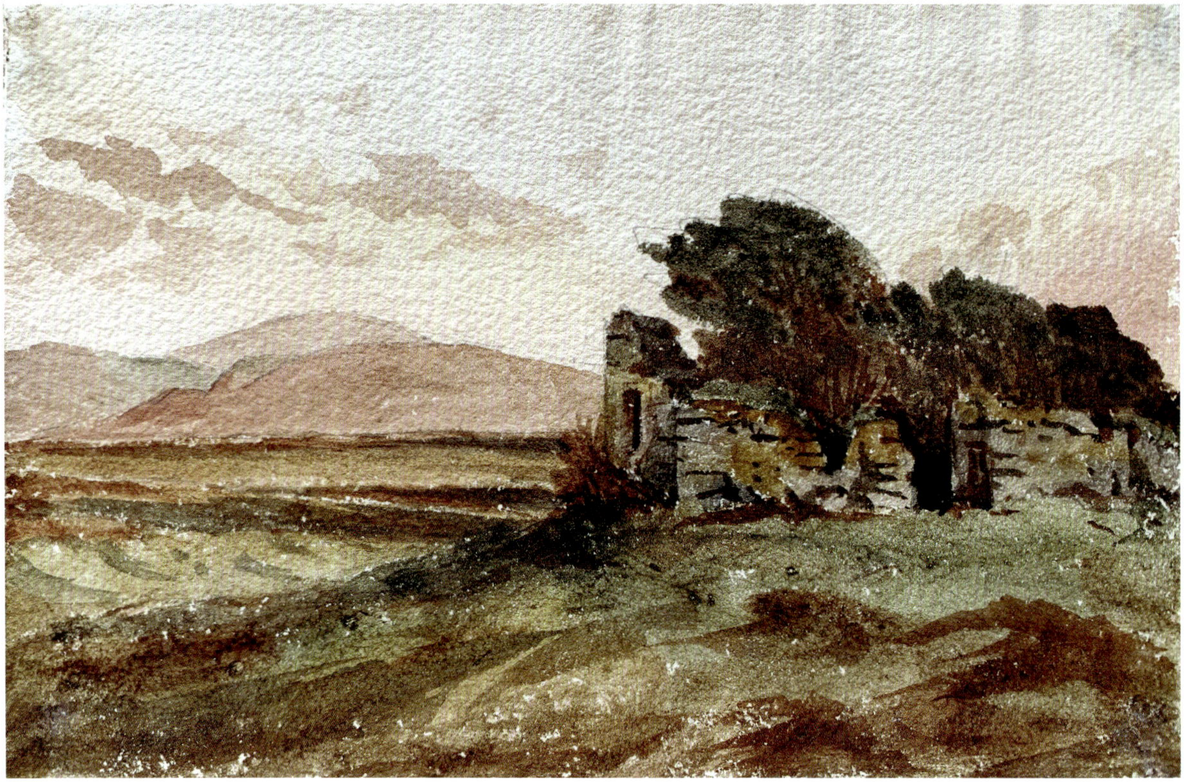

69. Tholtan, Isle of Man, c. 1843

On at least two occasions between 1843 and 1845, Petit journeyed to the Isle of Man to help a friend, The Rev. John Thomas Clarke, with his transformation of a depressed rural region, St Mark's. Petit contributed to its architecture and completed over 30 landscapes (69). This series fills a gap in Island art before its own school established itself later in the century.[30]

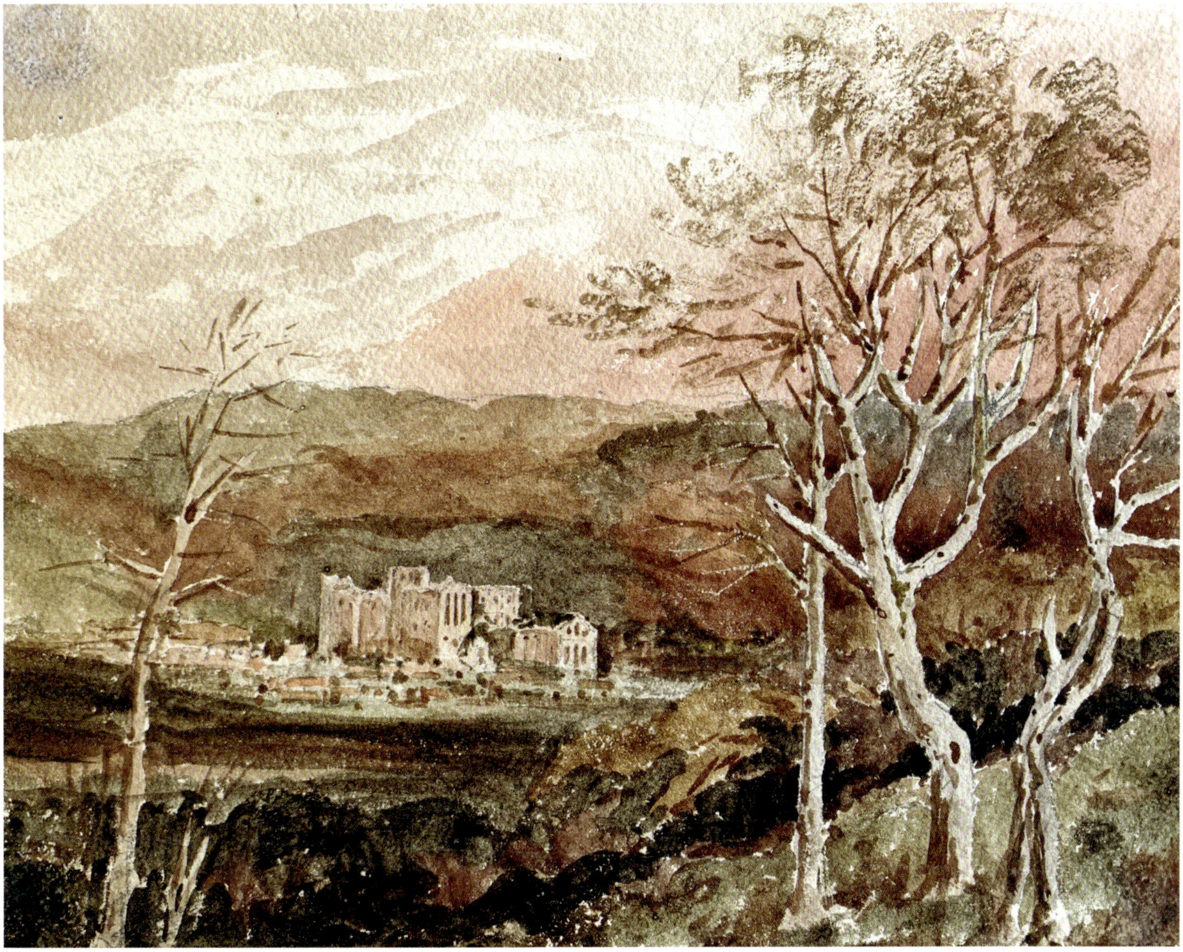

70. *Rievaulx,* Yorkshire, c. 1844–5

In 1844–5 Petit painted extensively in Yorkshire (70).[31] Landscapes from these two years are practically exclusively from that county. Later in the decade the West Country, from Gloucestershire to Dorset, seems to have been the focus including pictures along the coast from Torquay to Portland (see 14 and 39 earlier). Church pictures, however, during the 1840s come from all over Britain, during which time Petit produced four small books of speeches, and several articles. No continental trips, on the other hand, have been confirmed from 1839 until 1851.

Later Art: Late 1840s to 1868

1. Architectural Studies

2. Later Landscapes

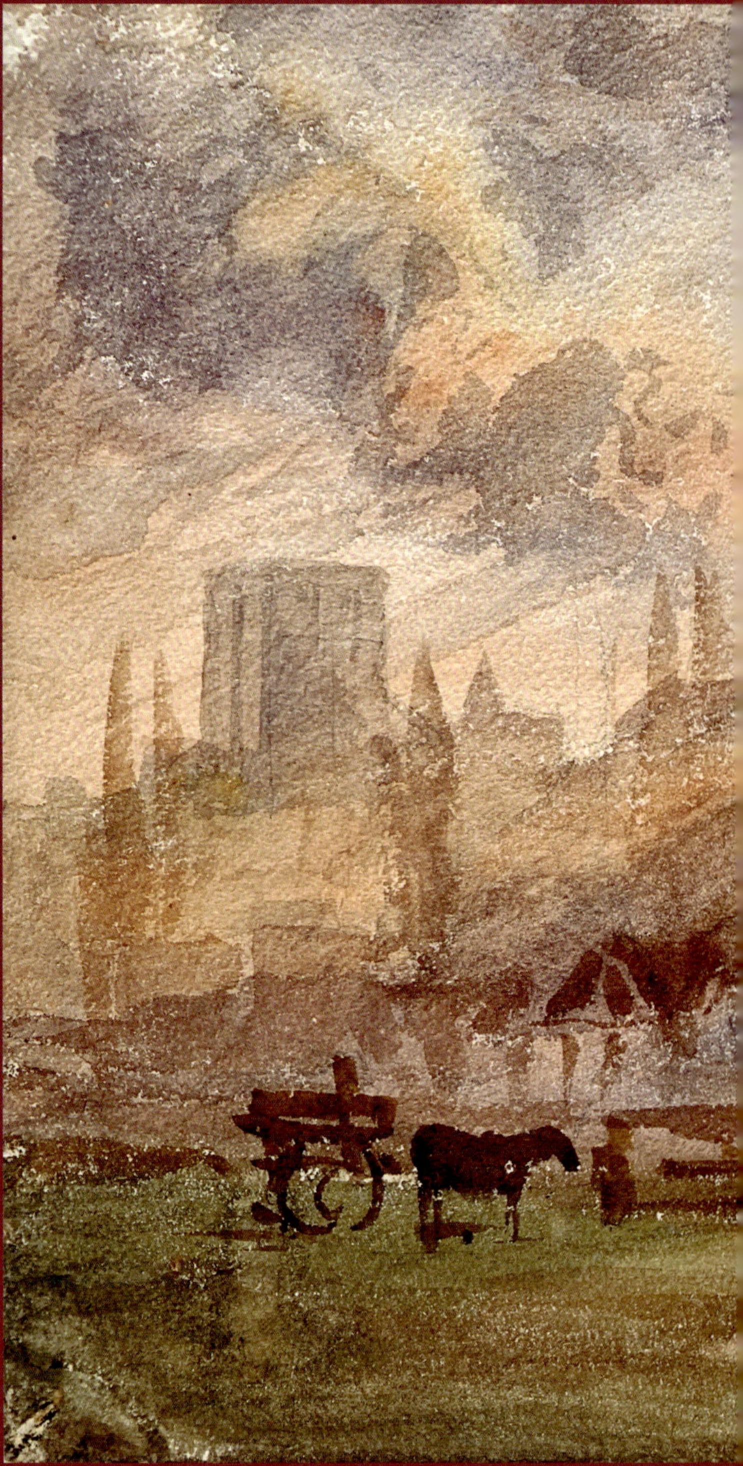

71. *Loches*, 3 April 1854

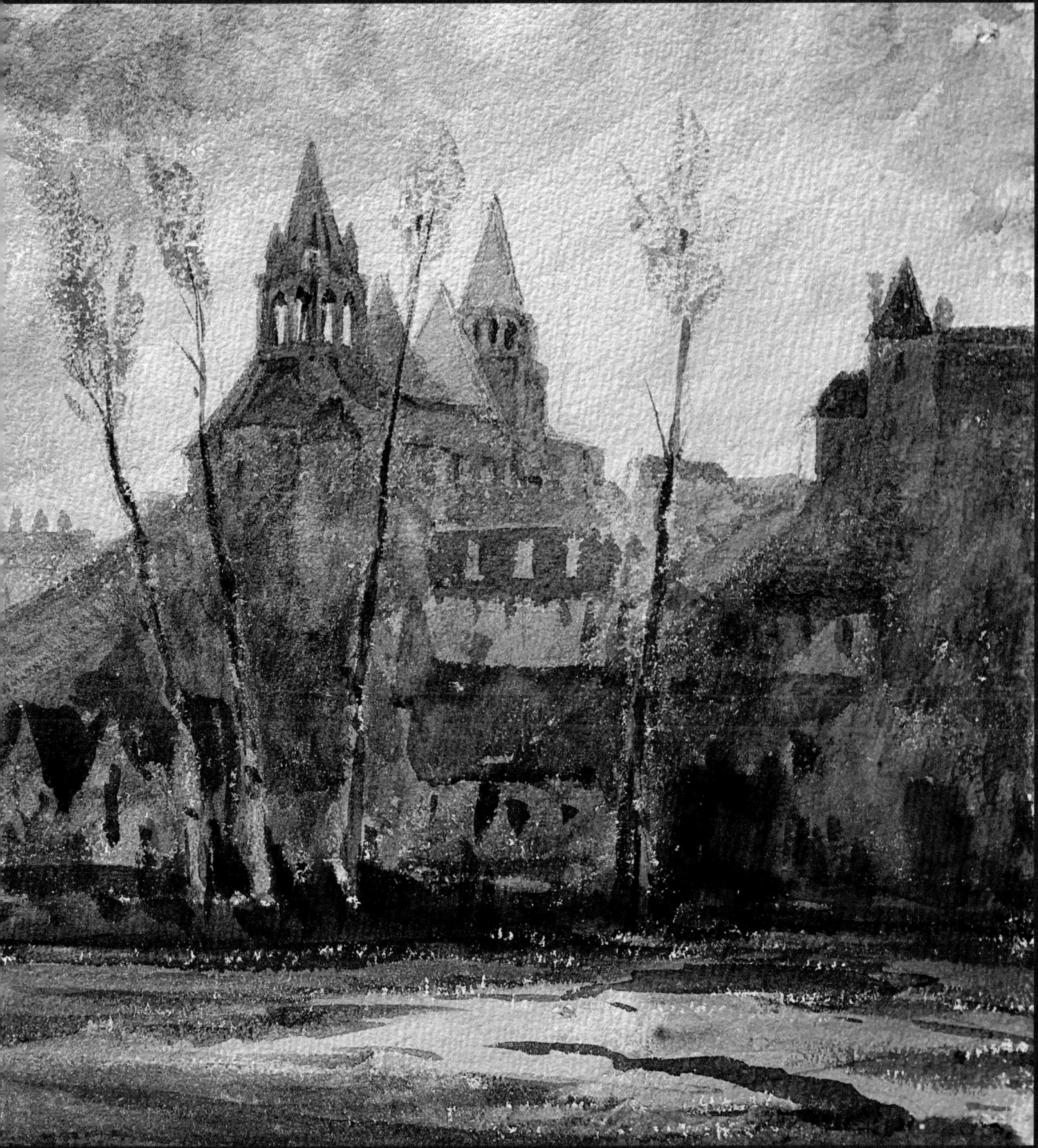

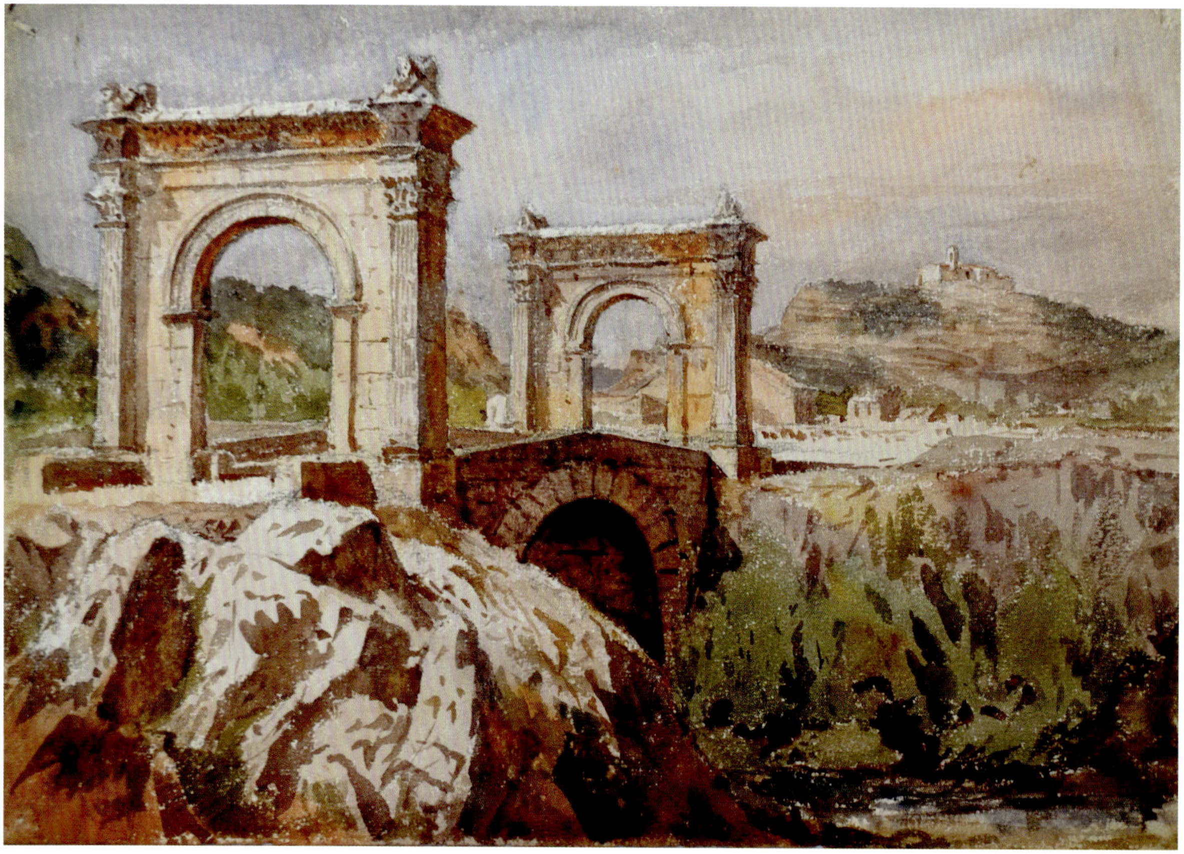

72. *Bridge at Saint-Chamas*, 1854
73. Opposite page: *Near Wolverhampton*, 1852-3

Architectural Studies

Petit is known for his studies of medieval churches, however he continued to paint other architecturally interesting subjects. Bridges - both old and new - retained a fascination for him. Some of the old Roman bridges displayed power and grandeur which he felt was missing from modern ecclesiastical architecture (see opposite).

Petit also continued to paint factories, and returned to the one near Wolverhampton to repaint it more starkly (compare with 50 previously) to convey its architectural impact in a lecture in 1856 *On Utilitarianism in Architecture.*

More broadly there are occasional town scenes where the church is not the primary focus, such as the square at Ypres (74), and he visited the Crystal Palace to capture it in his way, often working alongside Philip Delamotte, so that both could see the advantages and disadvantages of each medium. Delamotte was a pioneer of photography and made an important series of photographs of the Crystal Palace.

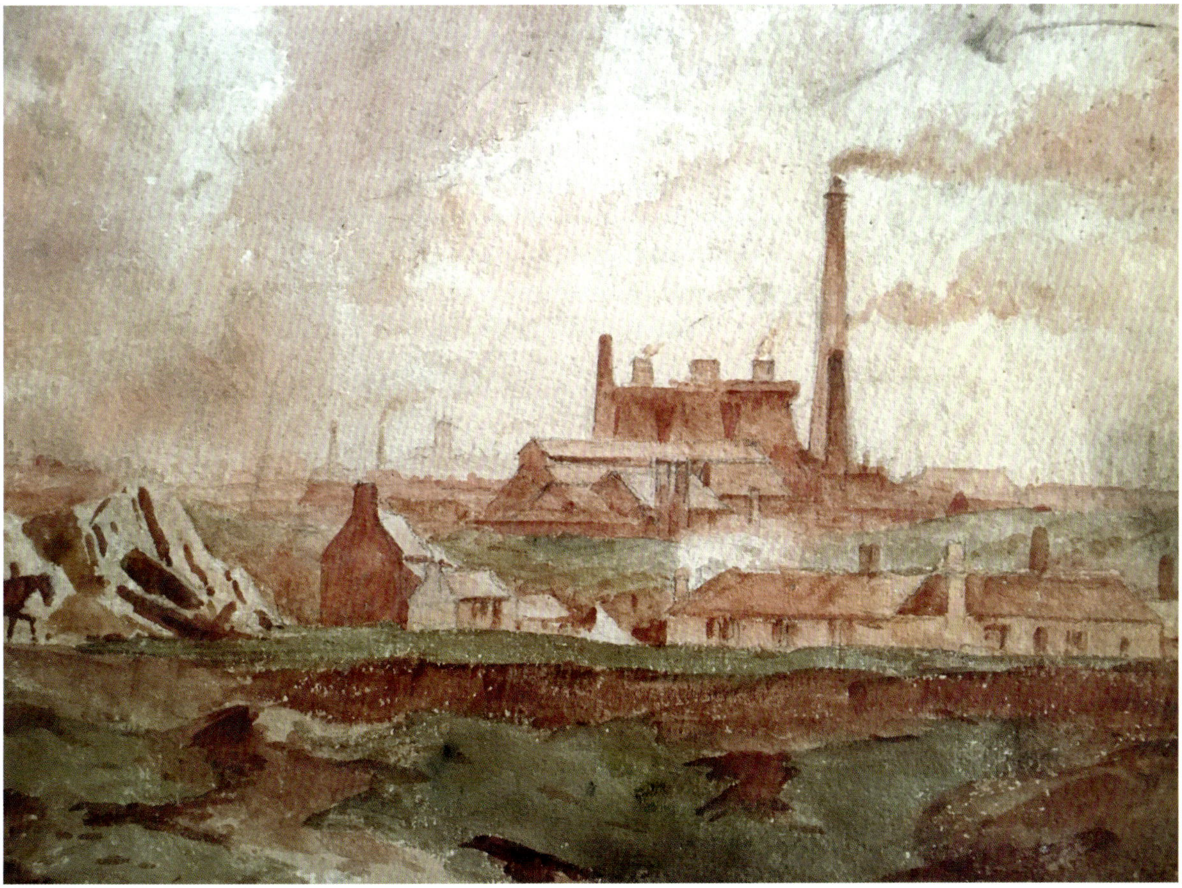

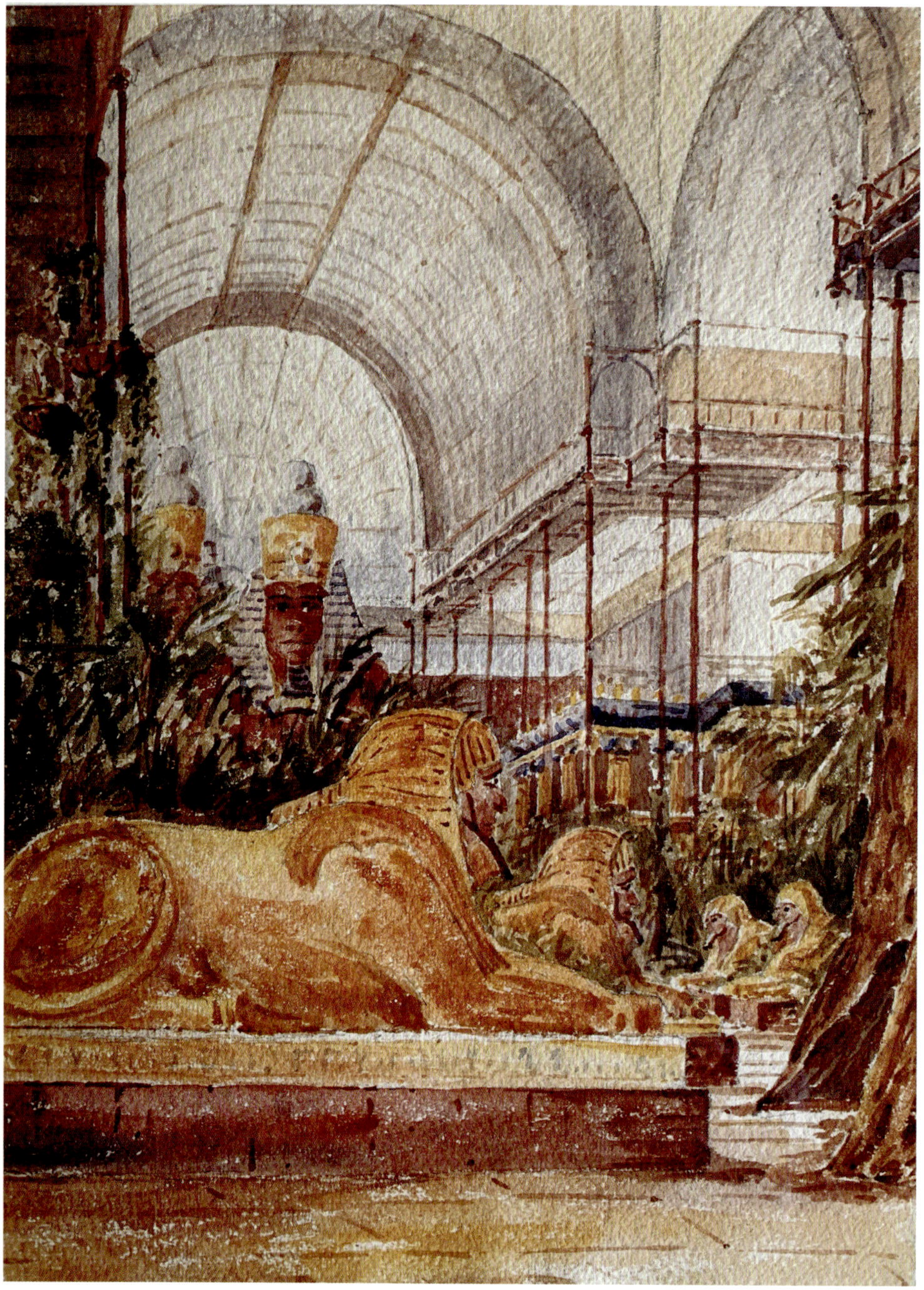

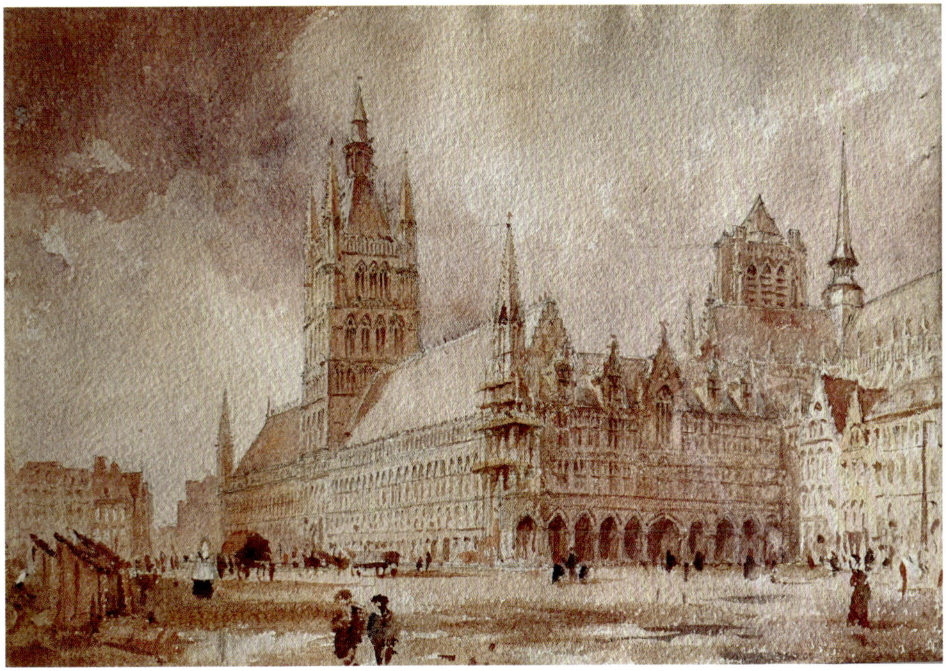

74. *The town square, Ypres,* date unknown, 1850s or 1860s
75. Opposite page: *The interior, Crystal Palace,* date unknown, 1853 or 1867

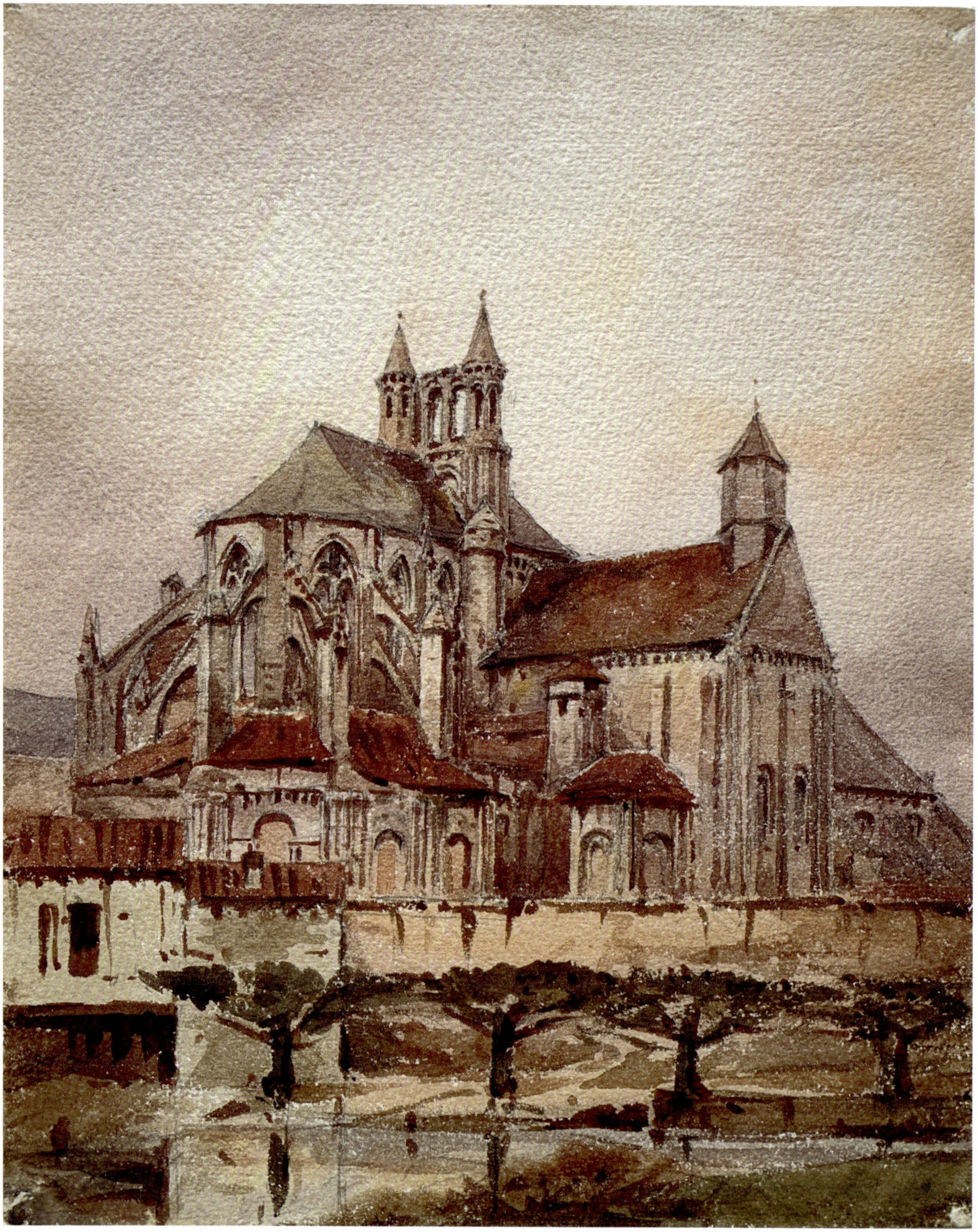

Church Architectural Studies

After 1848 art is no longer stuck into albums and the works often carry small exhibition labels hanging on the back. For the rest of his life Petit painted incessantly, from 100 to over 500 sketches each year, all *en plein air,* plus drawings for published illustrations. The majority of this output was sketches of churches, although this book concentrates more on the significance of his wider landscapes. However, Petit can claim to be Britain's, perhaps even Europe's, greatest artist of churches, both in volume and in capturing their character, from simple parish churches to grand cathedrals. As Petit wrote:

'In every country the temples devoted to worship are the richest, the most durable, and the most beautiful, among the structures remaining to us.'[32]

The closest view, an architectural sketch, like a portrait of a person's head, was intended to convey both an accurate likeness and character (see 77 opposite, and 79 next page). Often such portraits have minimal foreground, background or sky, and a limited colour range, again similar to portraits of people. Mostly such views are in Petit's traditional reddish palette and were completed on the spot. Occasionally there are grisaille studies (see below) which might have been copies specifically for exhibiting.

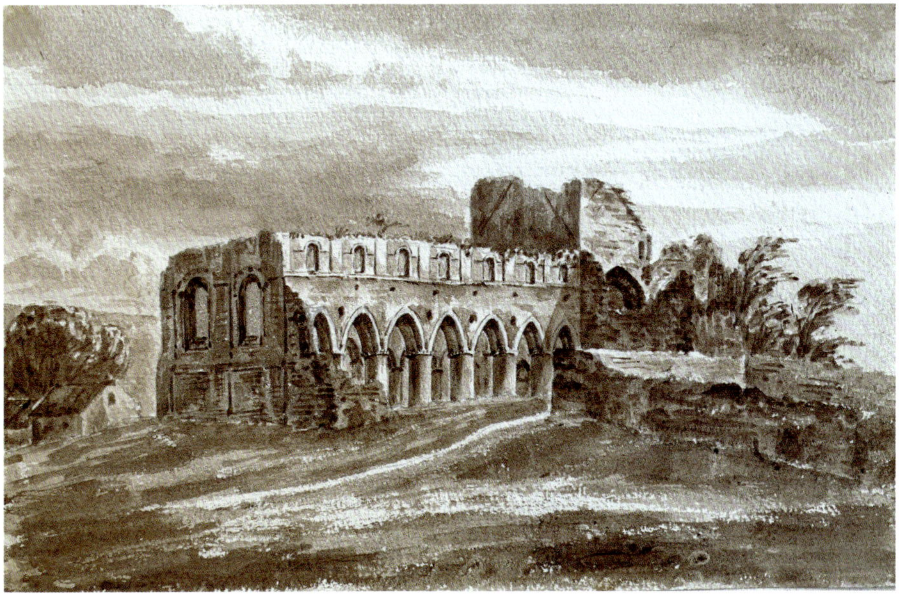

76. *Buildwas Abbey,* date unknown
77. Opposite page: *Montierneuf,* 1851-2, reproduced in *Architectural Studies in France,* p. 102

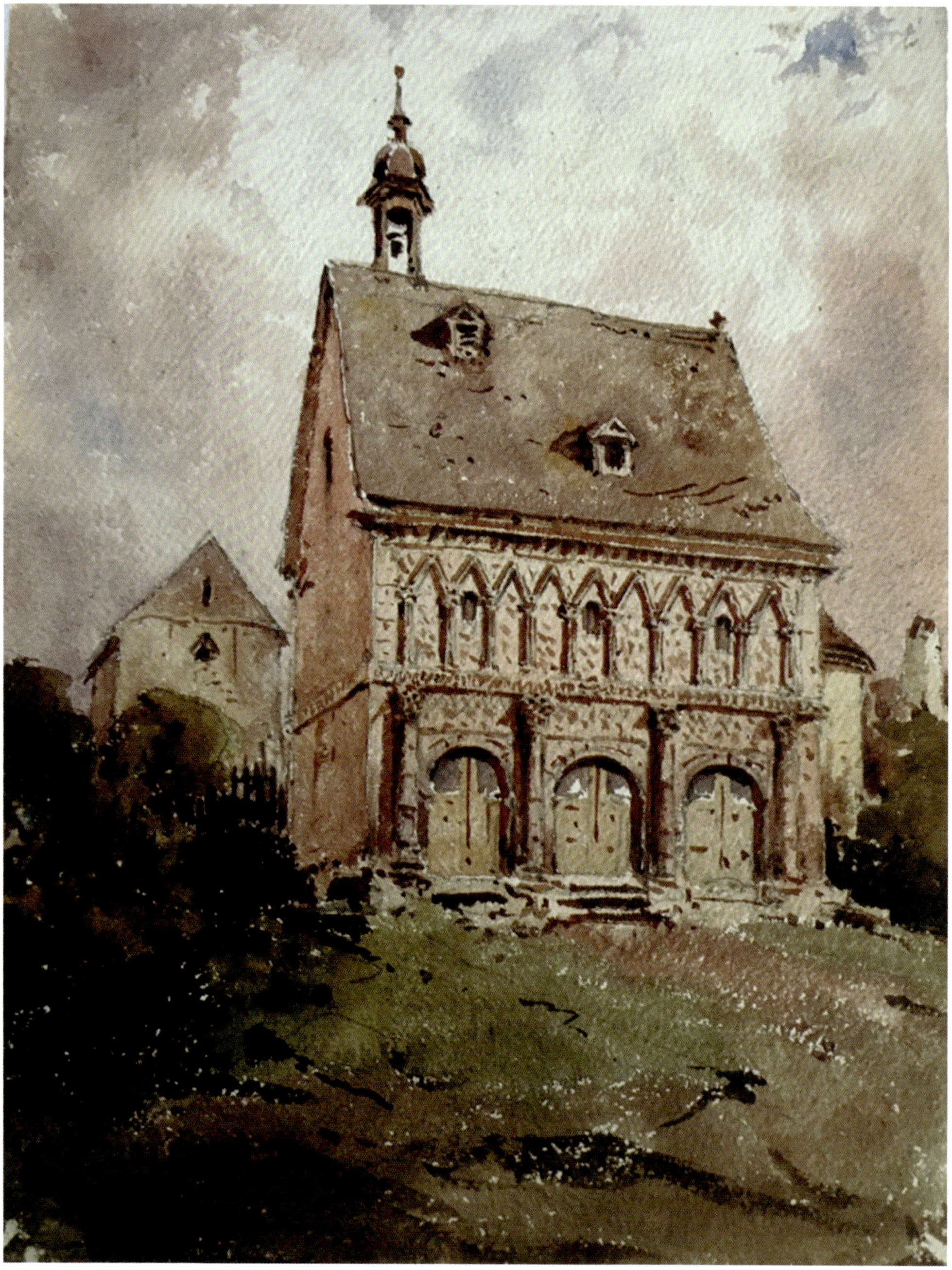

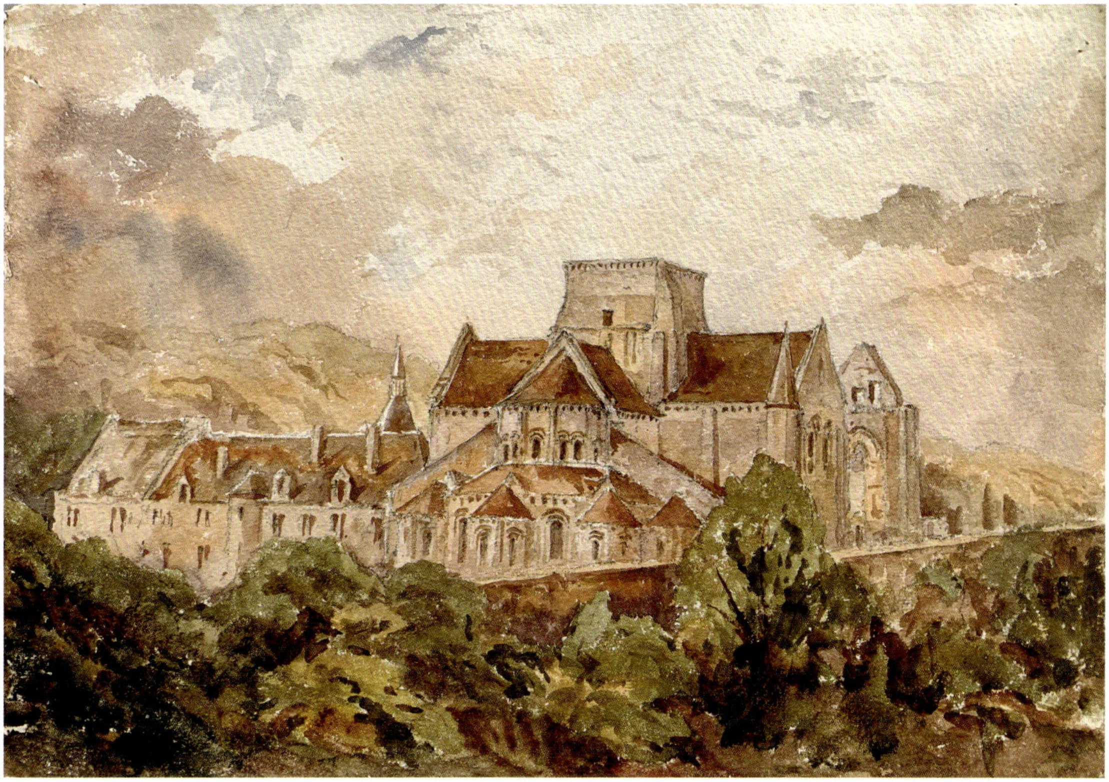

78. *'Fontgombaud'*, 30 September 1858
79. Opposite page: *Lorsch*, 16 October 1855

Slightly further back, middle distance views such as *Fontgombault Abbey* (above), contain some setting while still showing the main architectural details. A little further away and they gradually shade into full landscapes such as *Loches* (p. 72) where it is 'effect' i.e. impression, not detail, which is important.

The hastiest sketches are very plain, just notes for his records. The ones on which he devoted more attention can make beautiful pictures. It is not unusual to find a variety of views of each location, especially of those churches or ruins that occur in his writing. The oldest Byzantine church in Corfu (83) was used as a basis for designs shown to RIBA and the Architectural Exhibition, and several views exist.

Petit adopted photography very early on to capture detail. This miraculous technique could convey facts but not 'effect', especially at the middle distance. Petit explained: *'It is as necessary to know the effect of a building, as the means by which the effect is produced. Plans and drawings show the means, a sketch shows the result.'*[33]

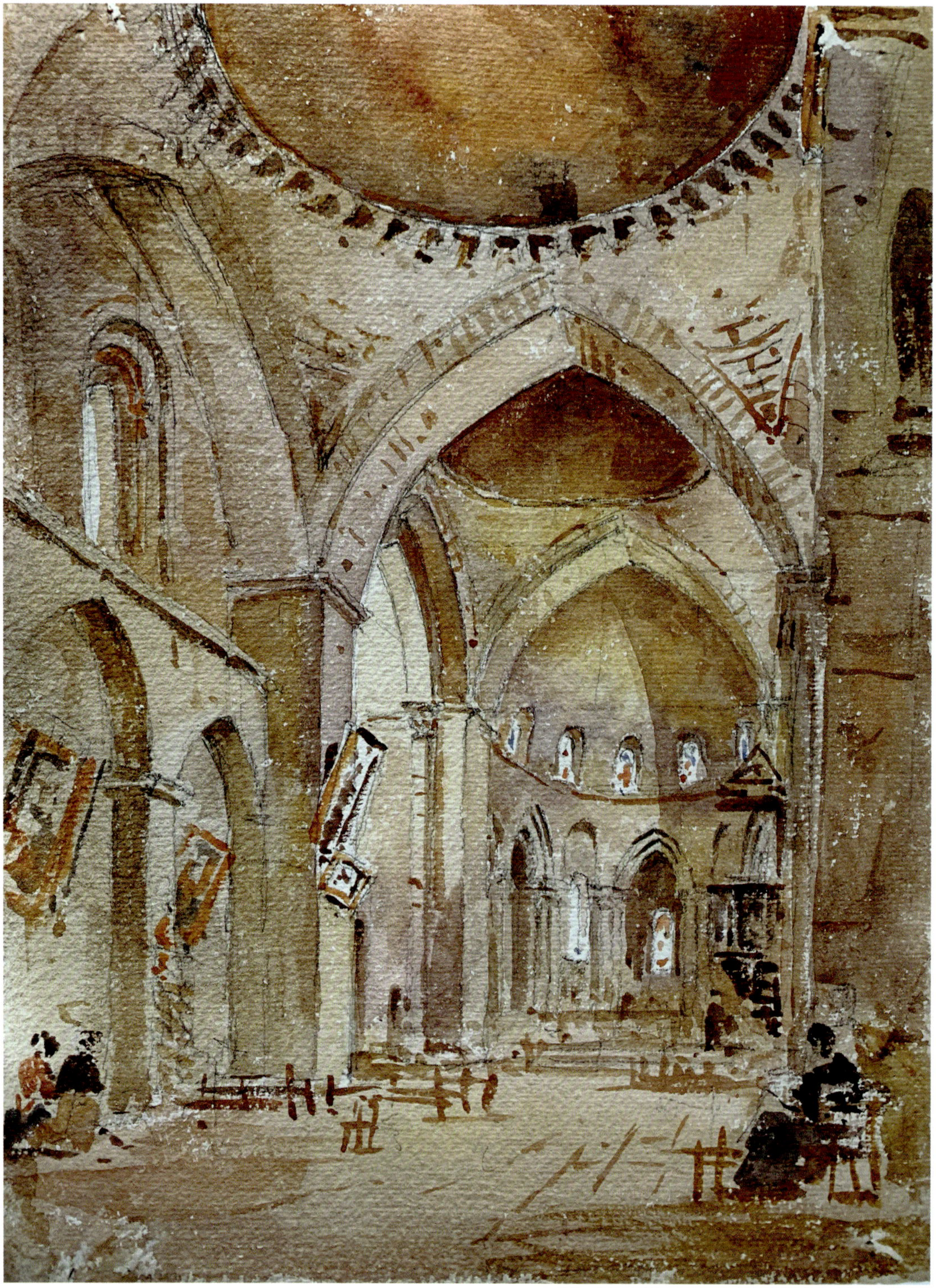

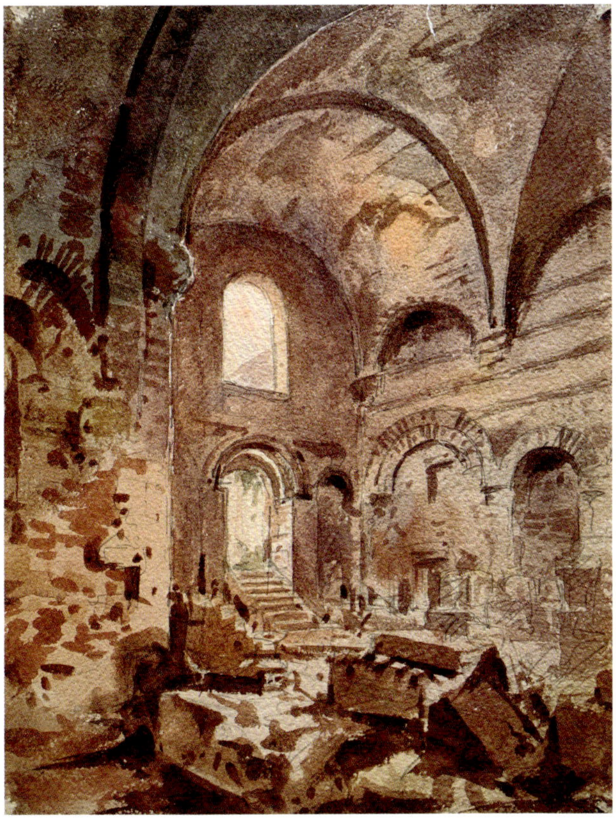

80. Bottom right: Emma Petit, *Angoulême Cathedral*, 7 October 1858
81. Left: *Hôtel de Cluny, Paris*, 1851, reproduced in *Architectural Studies in France* p. 166
82. Opposite page: *Souillac*, 15 October 1858, possibly his sister shown sketching

An important group is from 1851–2, when Petit embarked upon his research for his last book, *Architectural Studies in France*, producing some five folios of 80 to 100 pictures each, mainly in western France, especially around Tours. They are almost entirely simple architectural sketches such as *Montierneuf* (77). On most other trips, he produced a mixture of architectural sketches and landscapes.

From 1854 Petit ventured abroad at least once each year, accompanied by one or more of his sisters. Petit's most frequent companion was Emma Gentille Petit, who worked closely with him. However, three other sisters, and his sister-in-law Amelia Reid, occasionally accompanied Petit and also emulated his style. During the 1850s their pictures did not match the quality of their brother's work; their brush strokes are sometimes unconvincing (see 80 right). They continued to paint after Petit had died.

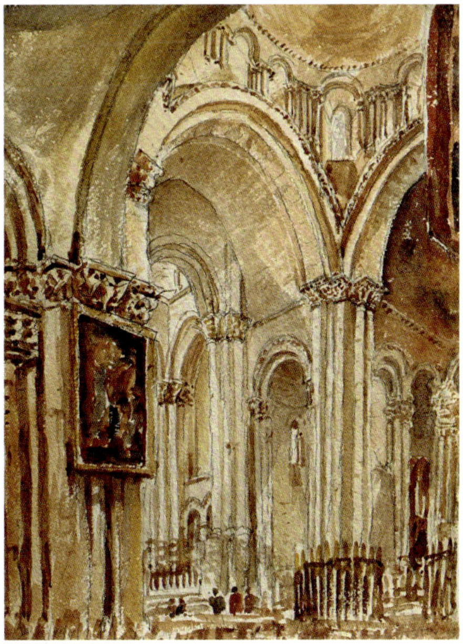

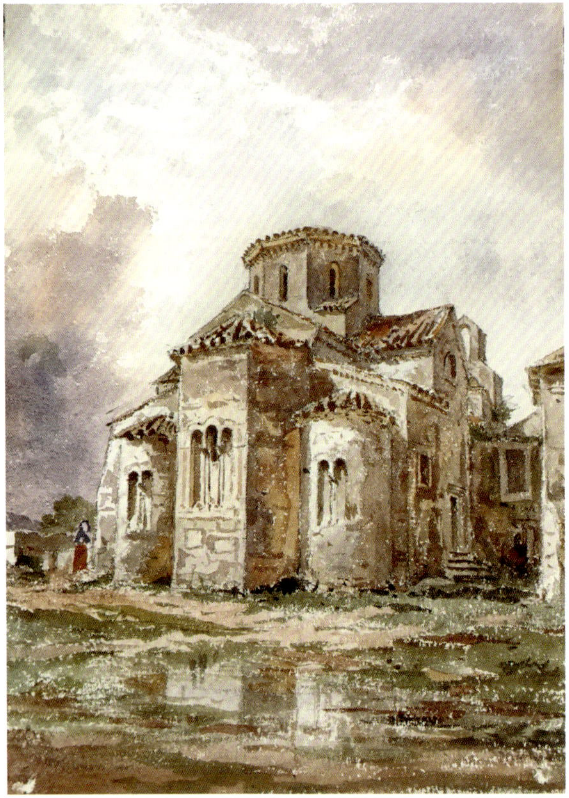

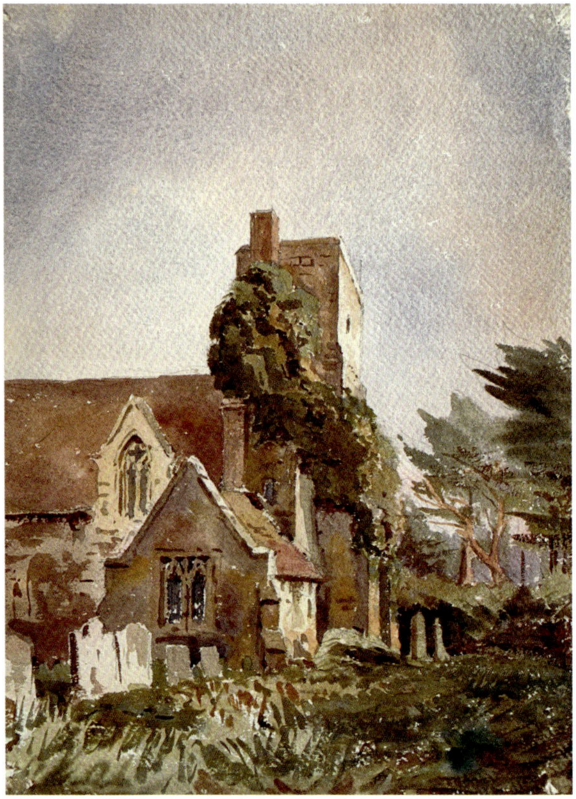

83. Above: *Saints Jason and Sosipater,* Corfu, 16 October 1857
84. Above right: *Ore, East Sussex,* 4 September 1868.
    A rare coloured church sketch
85. Opposite page top: *Soignier,* 1851

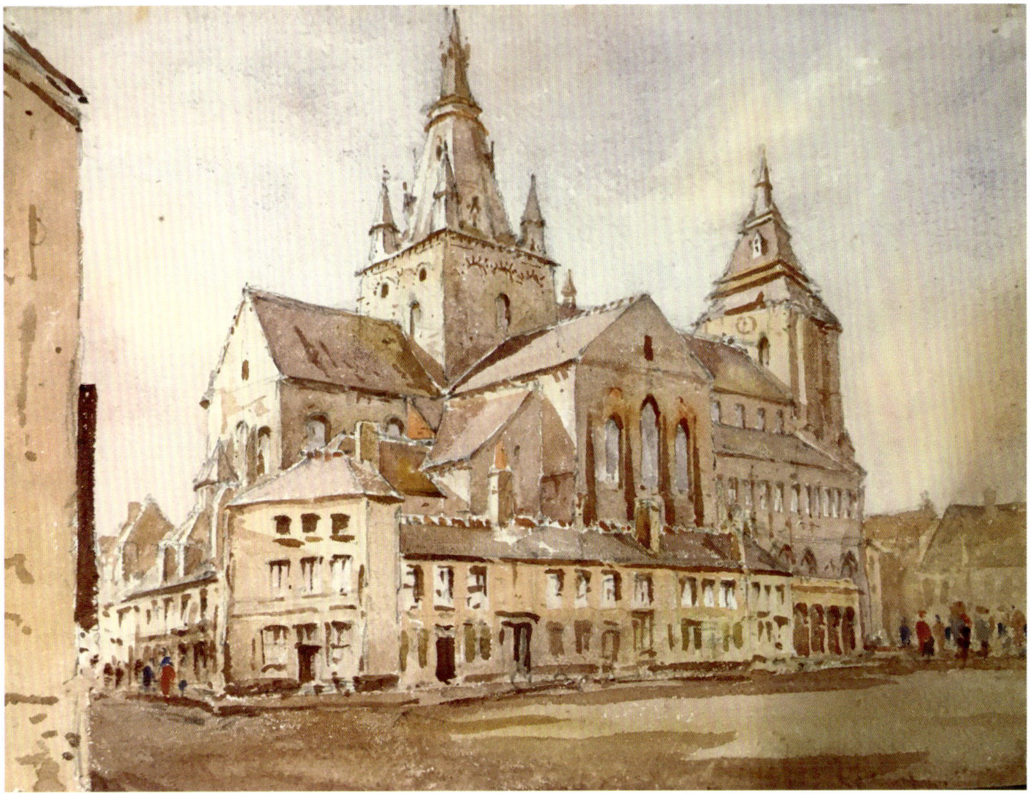

The main trips were: France (1851-52); Italy, via France (1854); Germany as far east as Prague (1856); the Adriatic, Corfu, Greece and Constantinople (1857); Spain and Morocco (1858); Ireland (1862); and Egypt and Syria (1864–5). Petit visited or passed through France almost every year, and also travelled and painted around Britain for lectures each year. So pictures from Britain and France are the most common. It is also in Britain and France that Petit seems to have taken the time to paint landscapes most frequently.

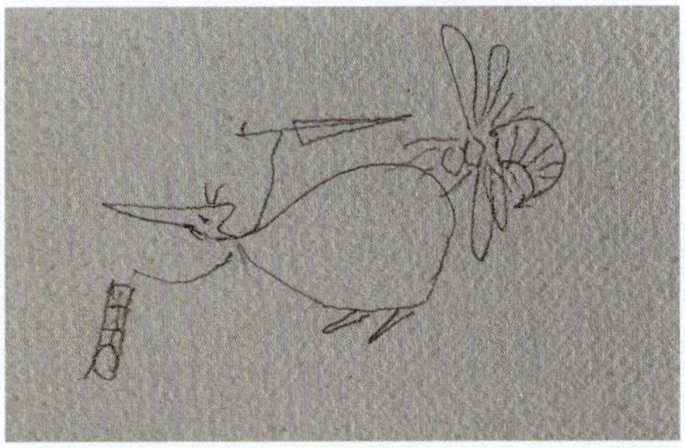

The Doodles

D6. Emma stung by a wasp, at old St Helen's church Ore, East Sussex, 4 September 1868. In three months Petit would be dead. The following year Ore church was pulled down

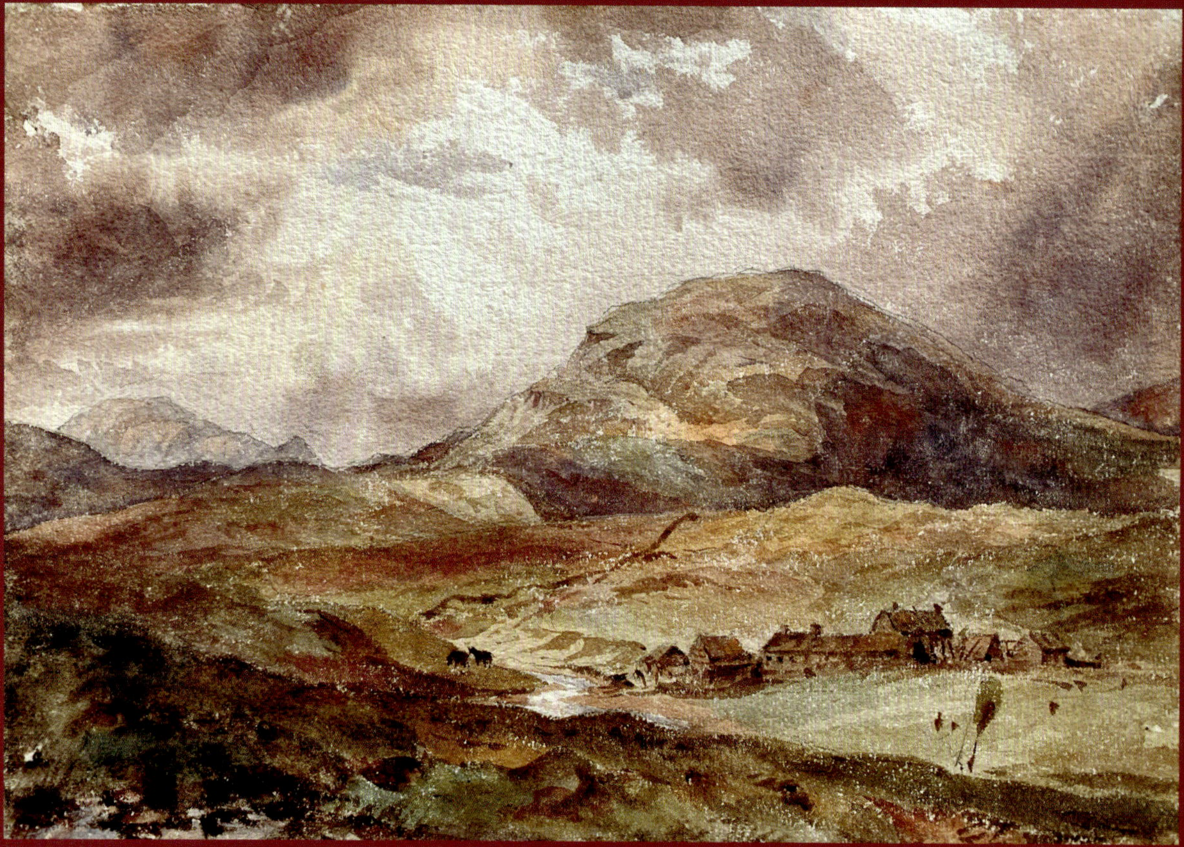

86. *Finnart, 3* September 1860
87. Opposite page: *Saumur,* 20 April 1854
Courtesy The Ian Cooke Collection, National Library of Wales

Later Landscapes

About one third of Petit's later works were landscapes. Exhibited alongside the architectural sketches at his lectures, they are much more varied. Harbour and river scenes capture contemporary life (see 87 below and 114), others show Petit often experimenting with how to communicate his vision. His long poem, published by his sister, Emma, in 1869, *The Lesser and the Greater Light,* provides many clues as to what underlies Petit's landscape art. We highlight five groups, which are by no means all that could be described.

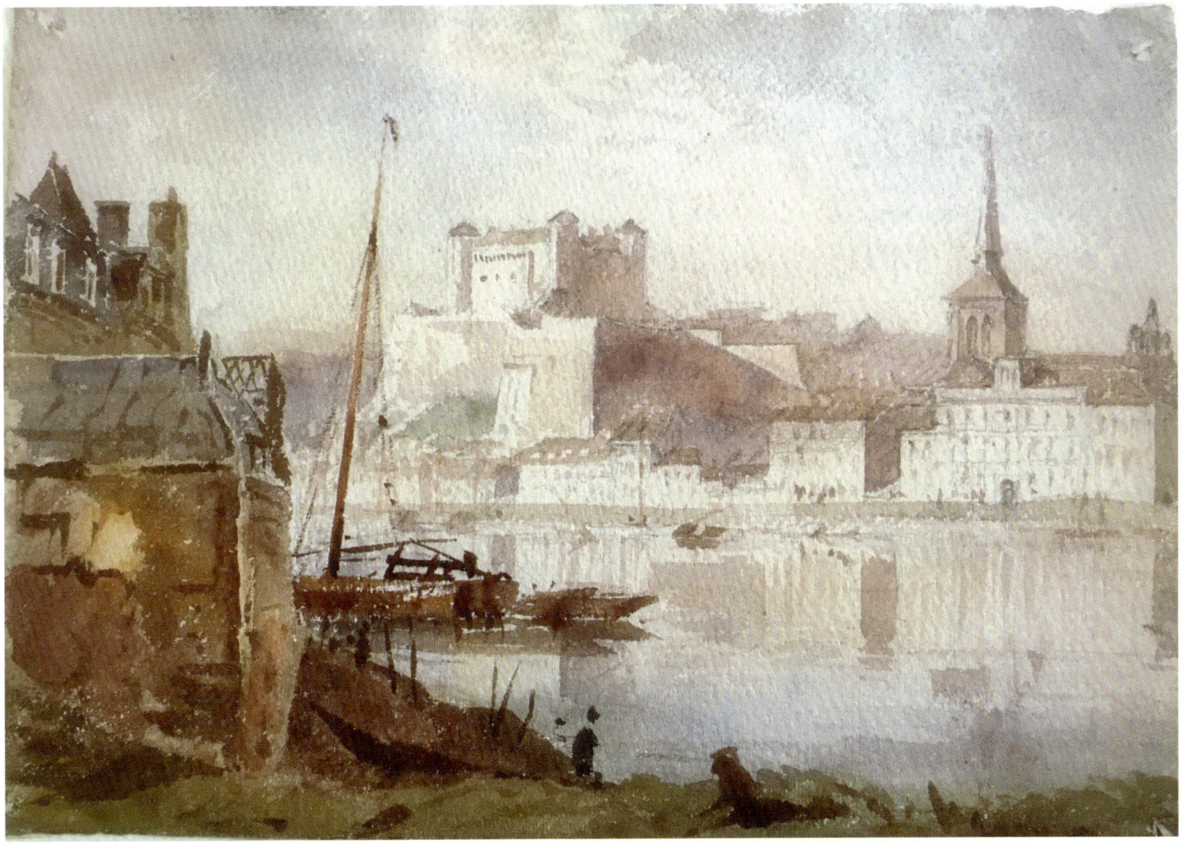

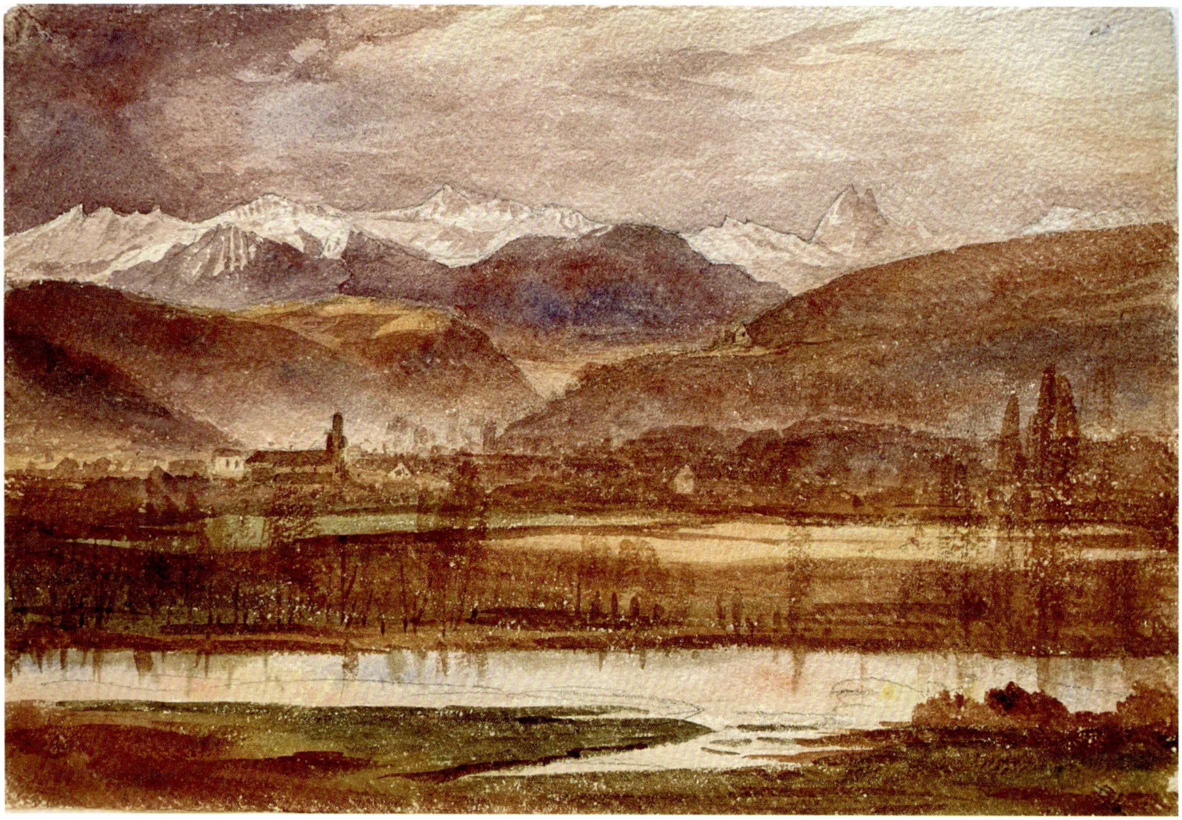

88. *Near Pau*, 1852
89. Opposite page: *Langenschwalbach*, 7 September 1854

The Distant Church

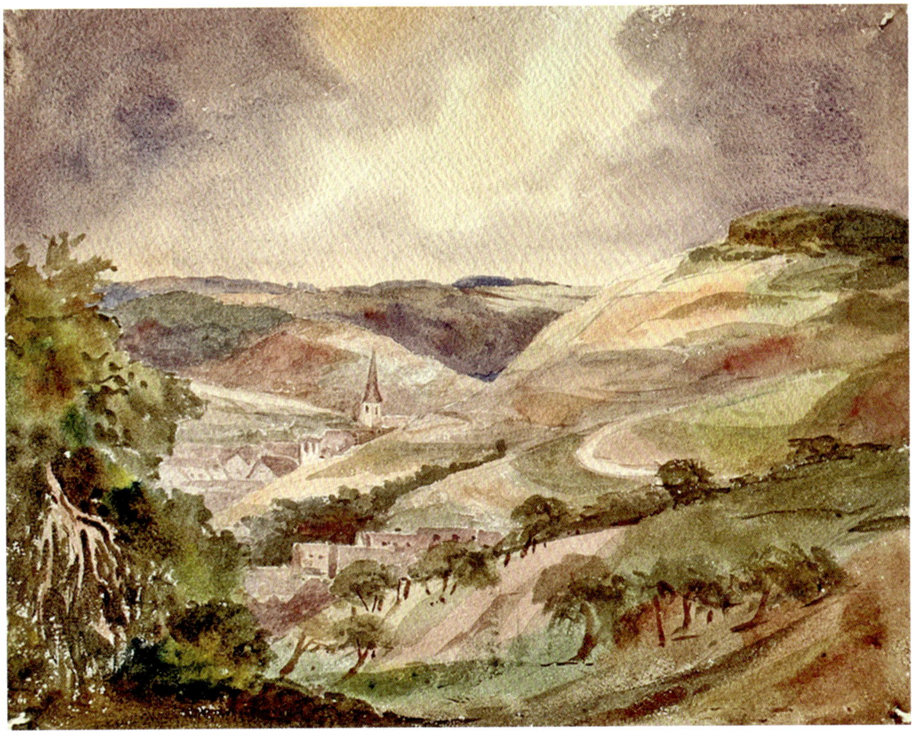

Often in a Petit landscape there is a church in the middle or far distance. The focus is not the architectural detail but the church in the landscape, natural or urban. There can be little doubt of Petit's intention in these pictures.

'Far o'er the waste his hospitable light
Gleams not to warn or threaten, but invite;
His call is heard, to welcome and to press
The weary stranger from the wilderness.'[34]

Ruskin similarly believed that art should neither exclude, nor focus solely on, man and his affairs. The combining of the church with nature or town is one of the ways in which Petit balances and locates man and his works in the wider natural world, while at the same time forming an aspect of his study of church architecture. Mountain pictures (88 and 89) especially point to the relative proportions of man's versus God's works.

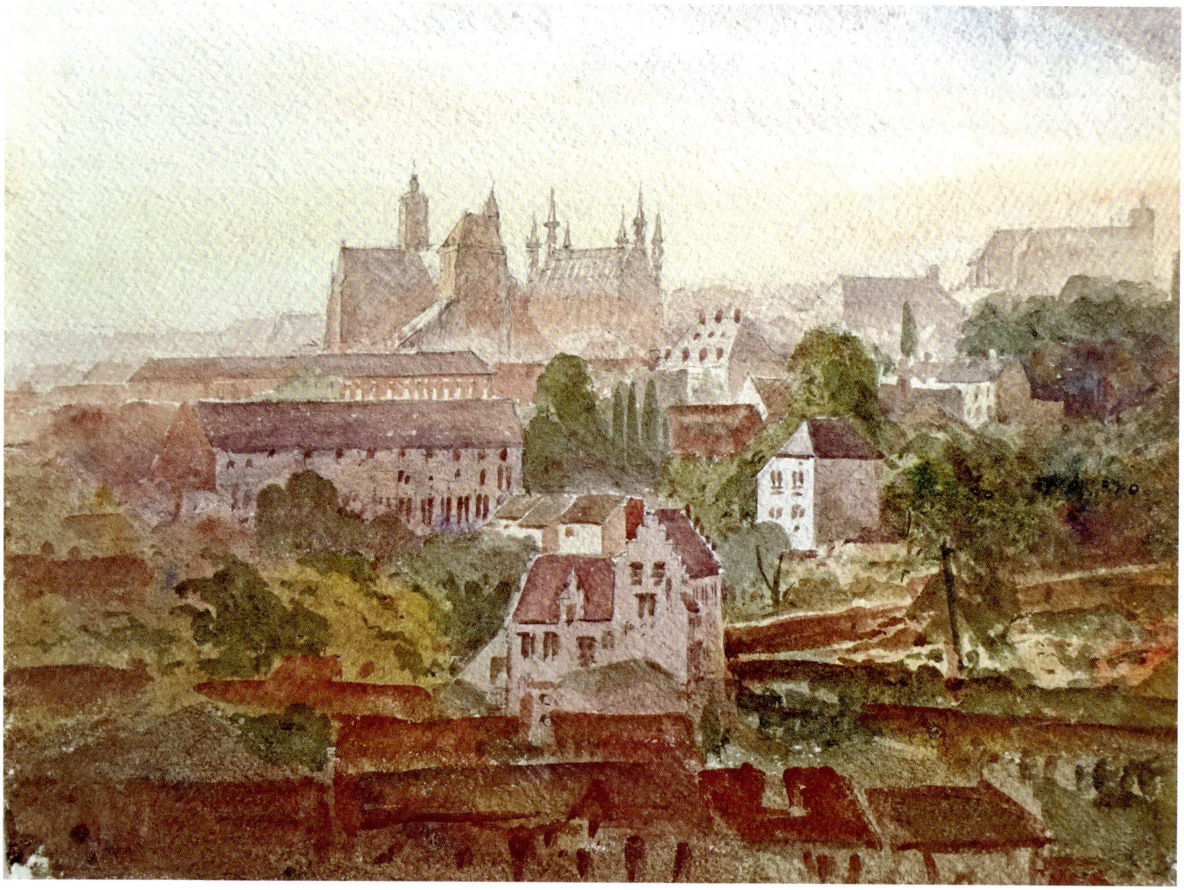

90. *Louvain,* Belgium 21 September 1854
91. Opposite page: *Outside Rheims,* 1855
Courtesy The Ian Cooke Collection, National Library of Wales

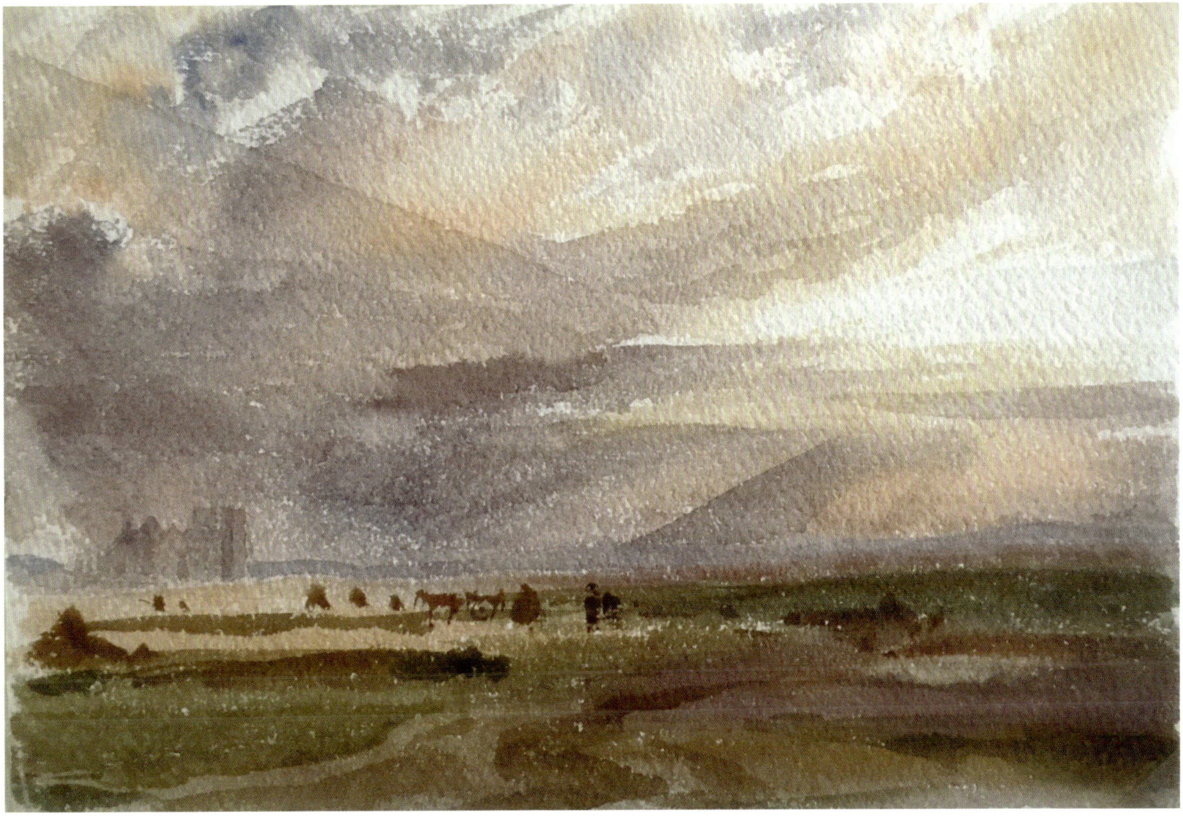

The town scenes (90 opposite) still have the same objective of showing the 'effect' of the church in its context. Here the contrast is more between man's spiritual and less spiritual works. Effect was the word Petit used frequently where we might say impression or impact. The four together show a range of different palettes. The absence of colour in the first (88) shows his most serious style and was used frequently. The second (89), has blocks of harmonising colours anticipating more modern landscape work, while the third and fourth, opposite and above are more conventionally atmospheric.

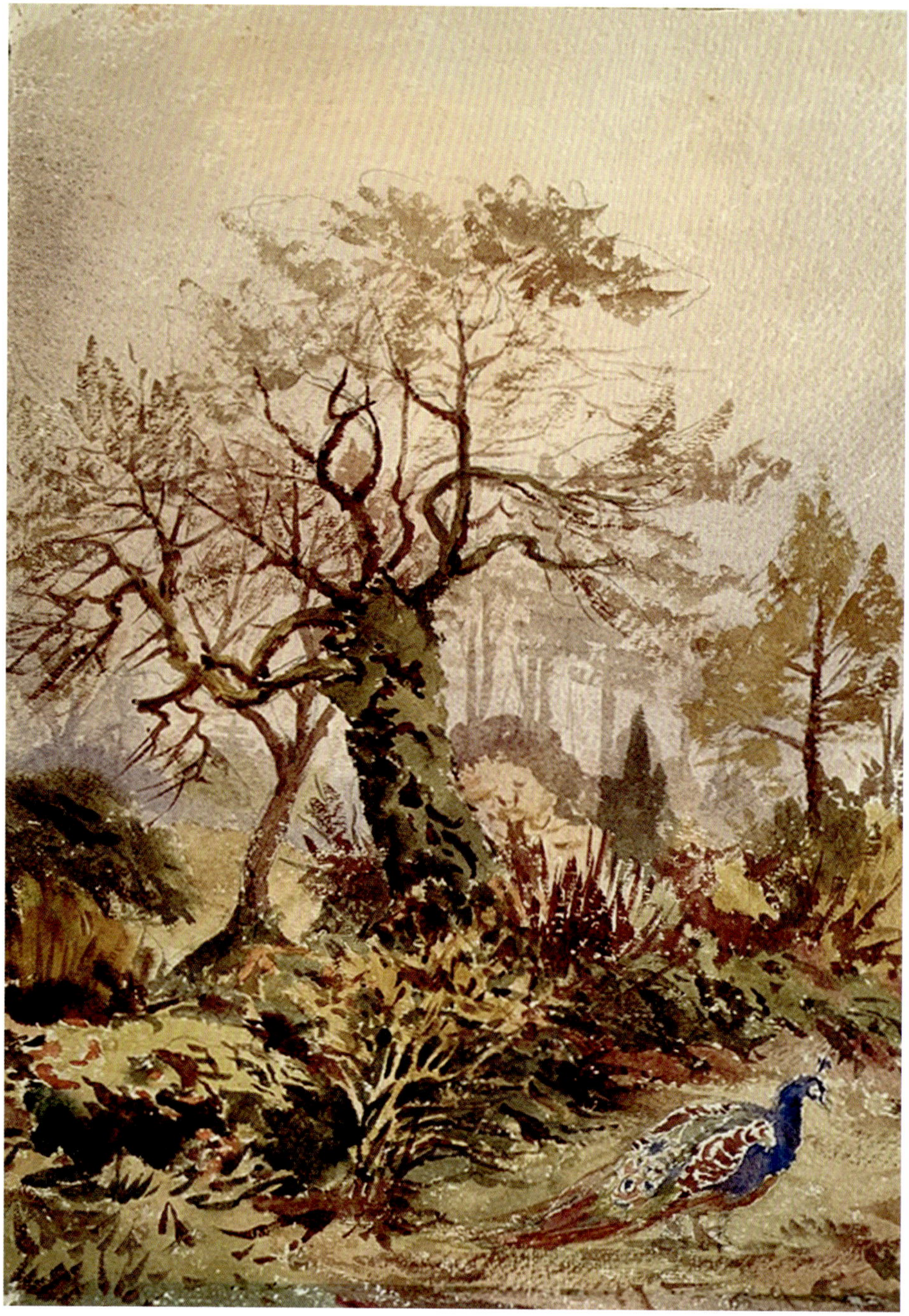

92. *Upper Longdon*, 14 November 1867
93. Opposite page: *Near Rovereto*, 12 August 1854

Nature, Mountains and Rock Studies

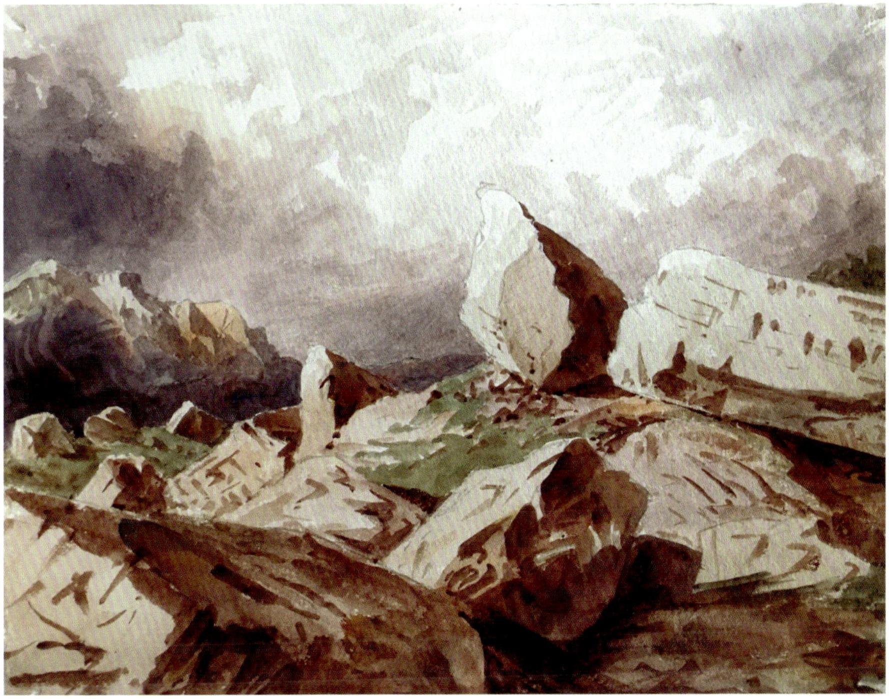

Mountain pictures where there is no church to be seen are often equally serious and spiritual. Rock studies are no less contemplative, capturing the depths of nature, and the weight of the rocks, with a few brush strokes. Petit's poem leaves little doubt as to his thoughts on the wonders of nature, be it the mountains of the Pyrenees or Wales, or individual rocks.

'Earth's fleeting gems in wild profusion thrown
Outshine the pomp of Israel's richest throne
...a truth, which dwells at hand
In every flower, each leaf, each grain of sand'[35]

There are fewer shipping and tree studies than in the 1830s.

Nature as God's work chimes with our realisation, almost too late, of the fragility of the natural world. For Petit, Ruskin and others, the challenge was different: to reconcile the discoveries of science, and especially Darwin's theories of evolution, with what they had been taught and believed in – God's ultimate role in creation.

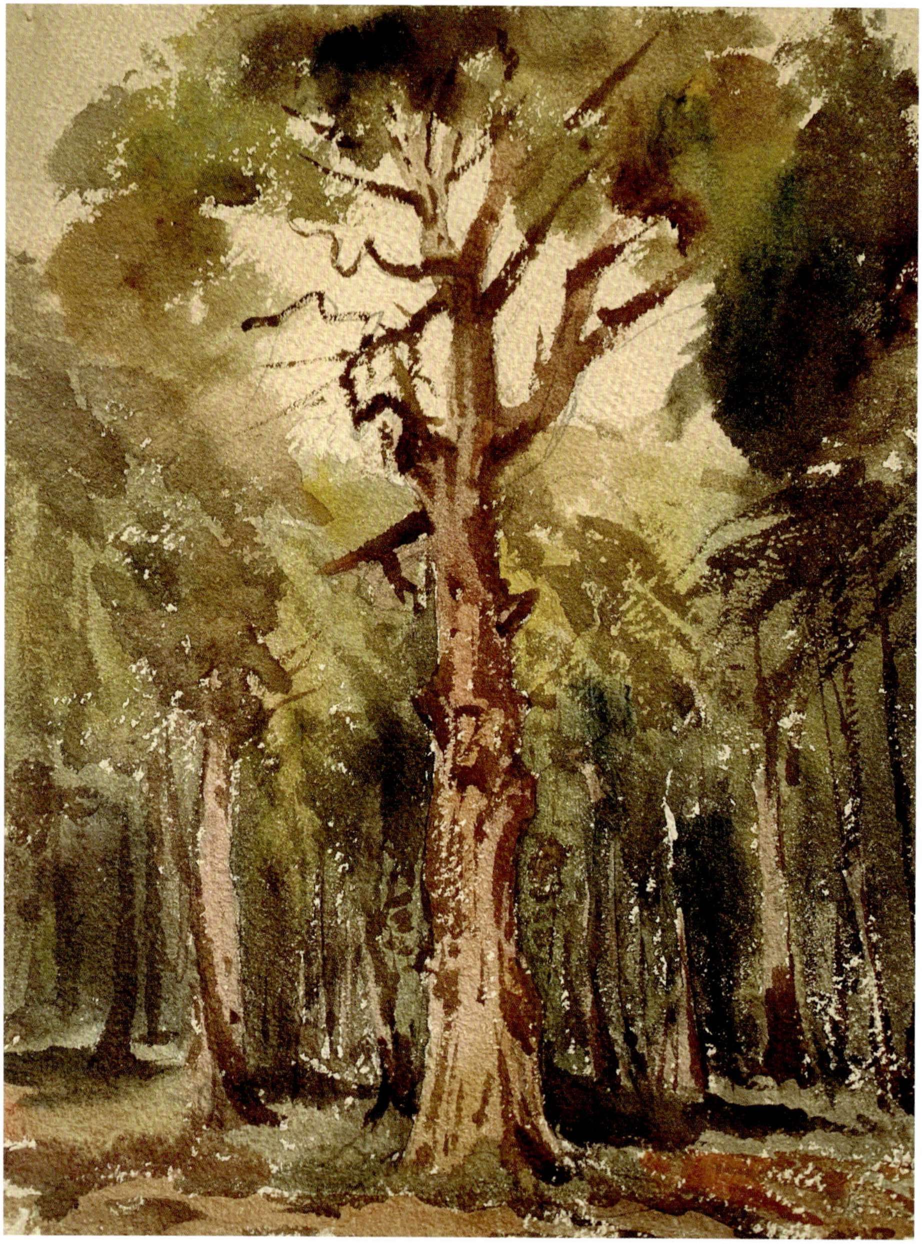

94. *Fontainebleau,* 12 October 1855
95. Opposite page: *Tintagel,* Cornwall, 16 May 1862

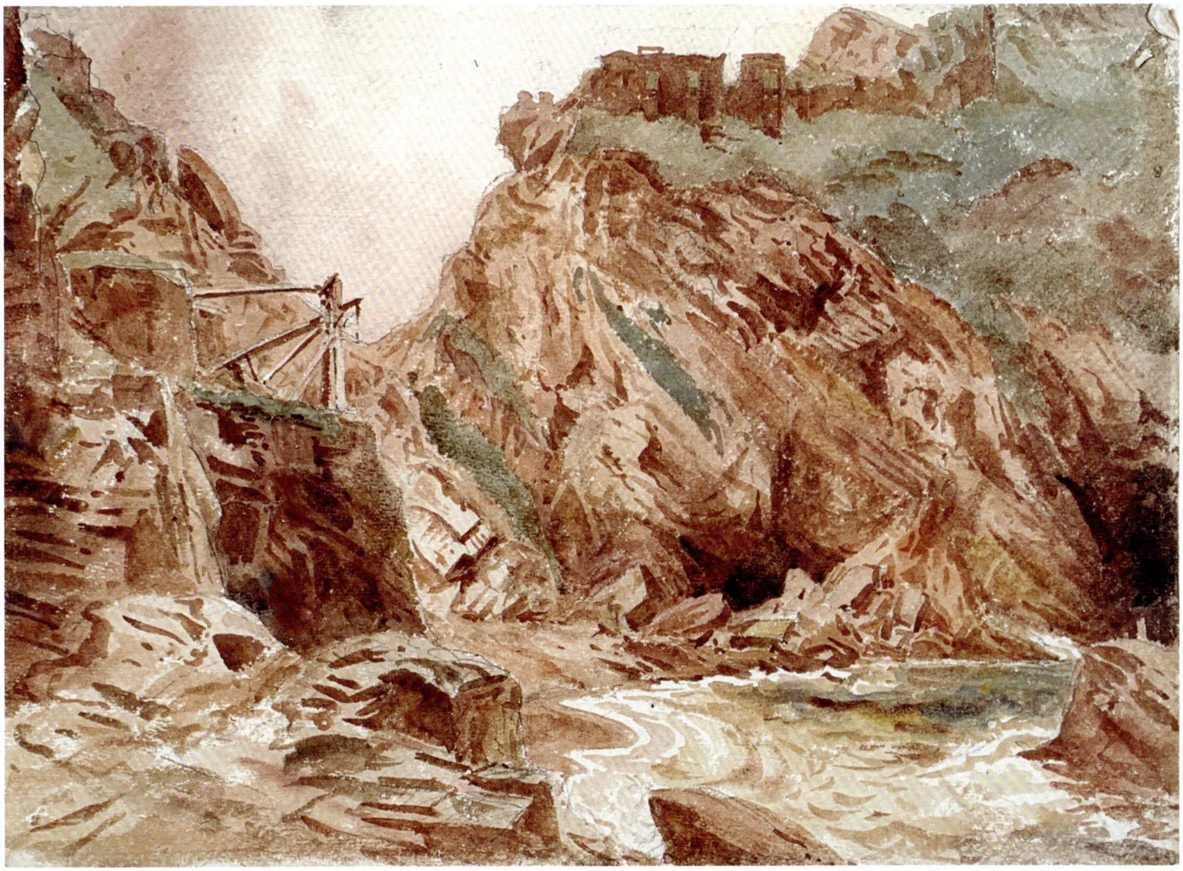

For Petit, reason and scientific discovery are the Lesser Light which helps explain the natural world, but not its existence, nor its harmony and beauty. Ruskin likened the artist to the preacher, the role of both being to point the way to a deeper understanding and appreciation of the natural world and how we should treat it.

The rock and cliff studies experiment with capturing form and solidity with light and shade (95 and 96). These works were passed over by his family in favour of famous locations, and can probably be appreciated more nowadays, after later and more modern artists, especially Cézanne, brought such pictures into the mainstream.

There is an immediacy in Petit's natural landscapes. The compositions never seem artificial or posed. Ruskin explained: *'The skill of the artist, and the perfection of his art, are never proved until both are forgotten. The artist has done nothing until he has concealed himself, – the art is imperfect which is visible.'*[36]

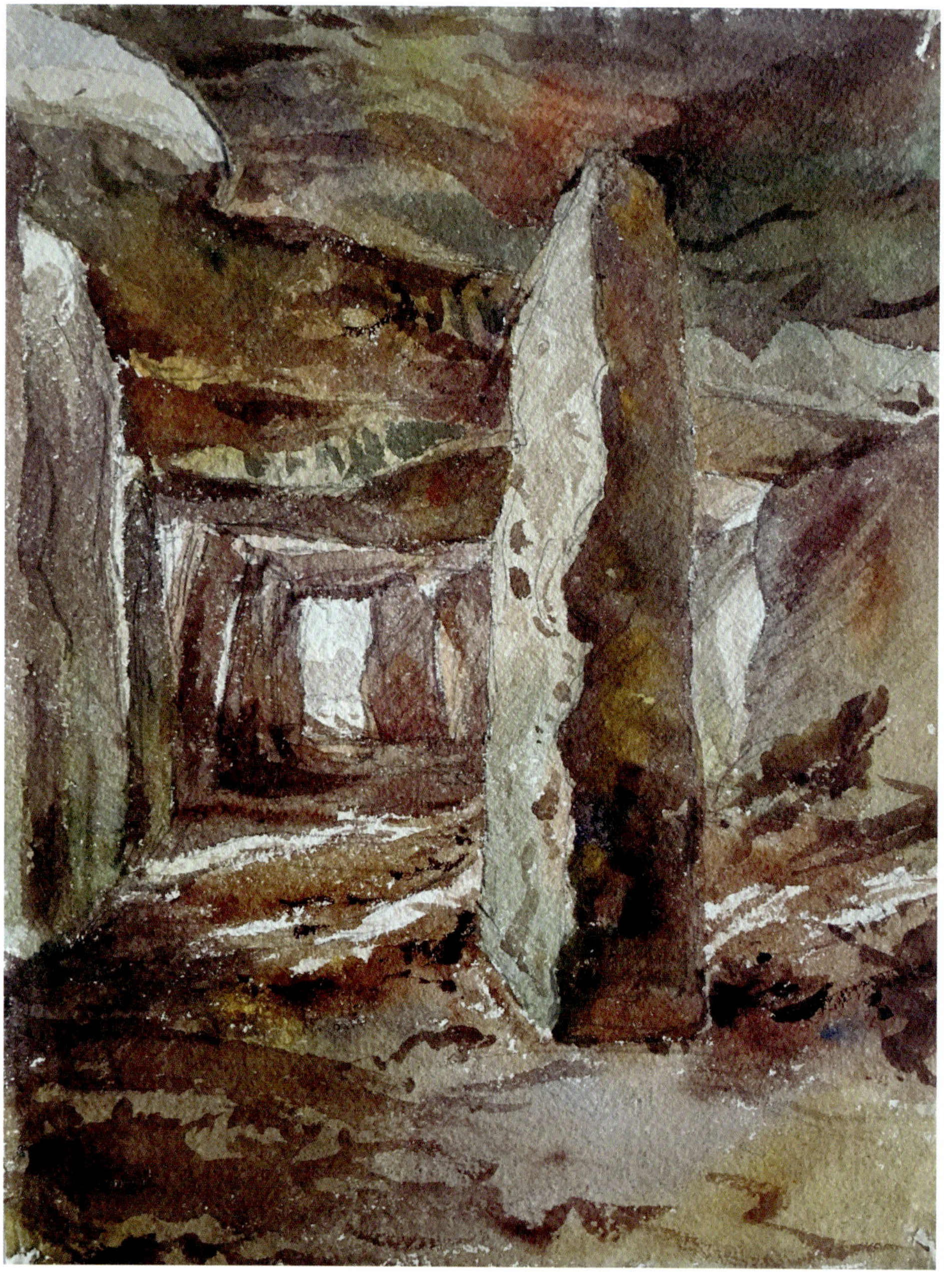

96. *Allée Couverte, Saumur,* 30 March 1854

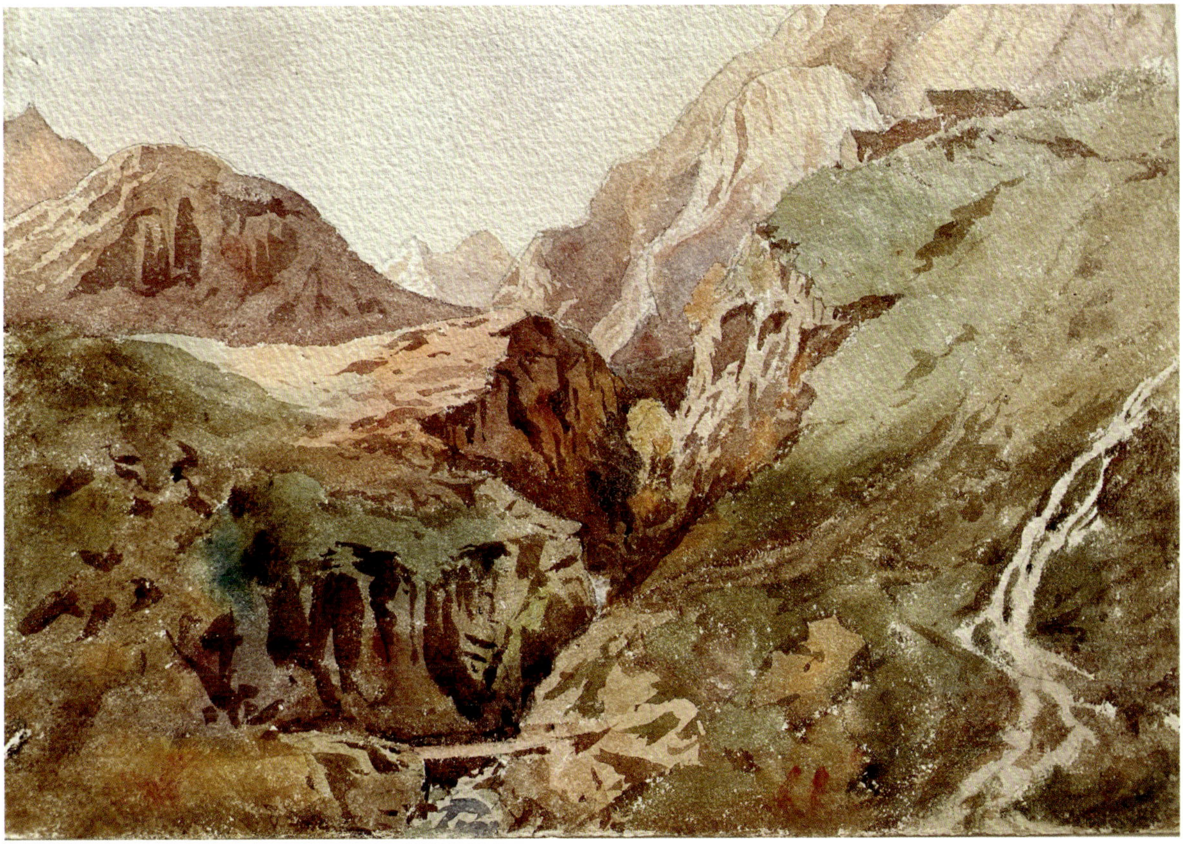

97. *Nr Gavarnie,* November 1858

Later Landscapes: Lichfield

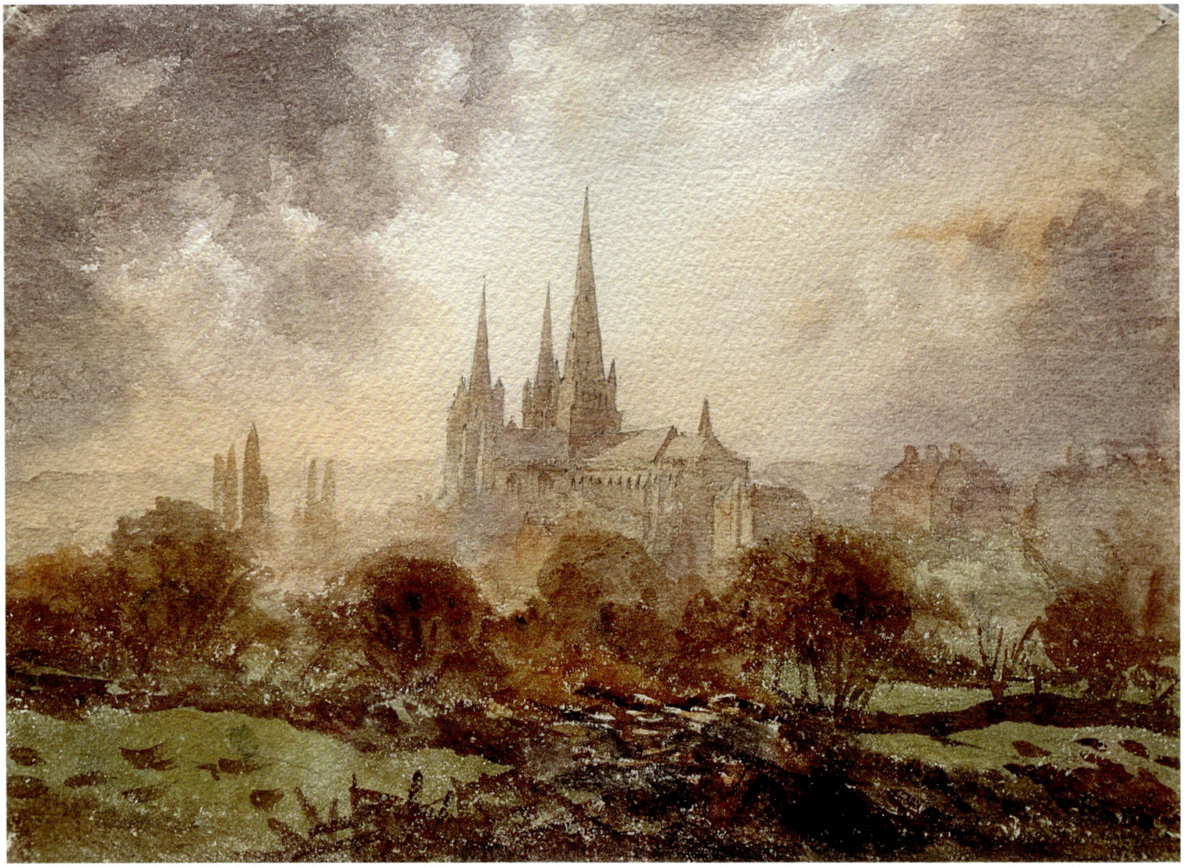

98. *Lichfield,* 26 January 1857

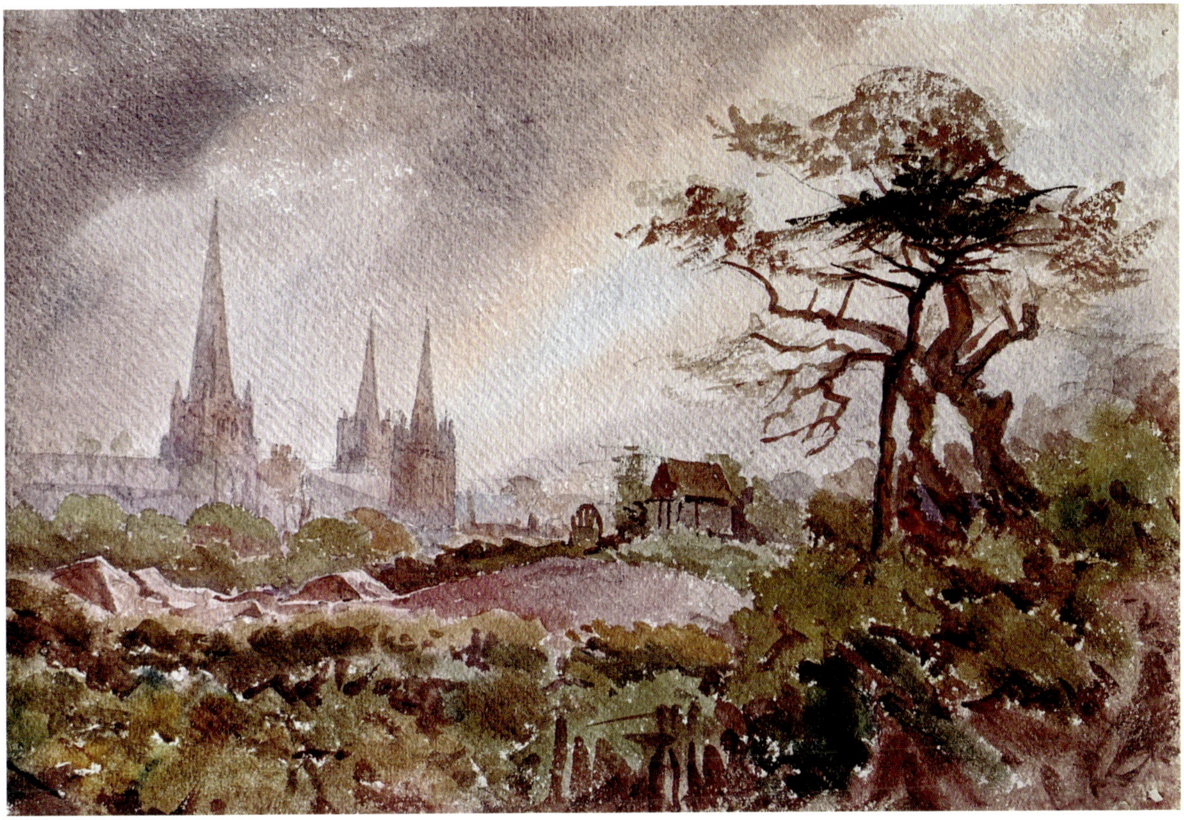

99. *Lichfield,* 27 April 1868

Lichfield was Petit's home base, and when there he constantly went out to paint watercolours of the cathedral from every angle, in every season and weather condition. This was his practice ground. Over 150 Lichfield pictures are known to have been completed from the third of folios for which we have a record, so there will have been many more.[37]

Many were chosen by his relatives on his death, or removed from the hoard later. For example there were four folios completed in 1857, the last three during his trip abroad through Europe to Constantinople. The first covers the first seven months of that year in Britain. The record for this folio, which survives, lists 18 pictures of Lichfield, of which five were given away on Petit's death and a further eight removed, leaving only five when the hoard was sold off. Pictures 98 and 99 are two of these survivors, not previously removed. Nevertheless there will be many other Lichfield pictures yet to be traced.

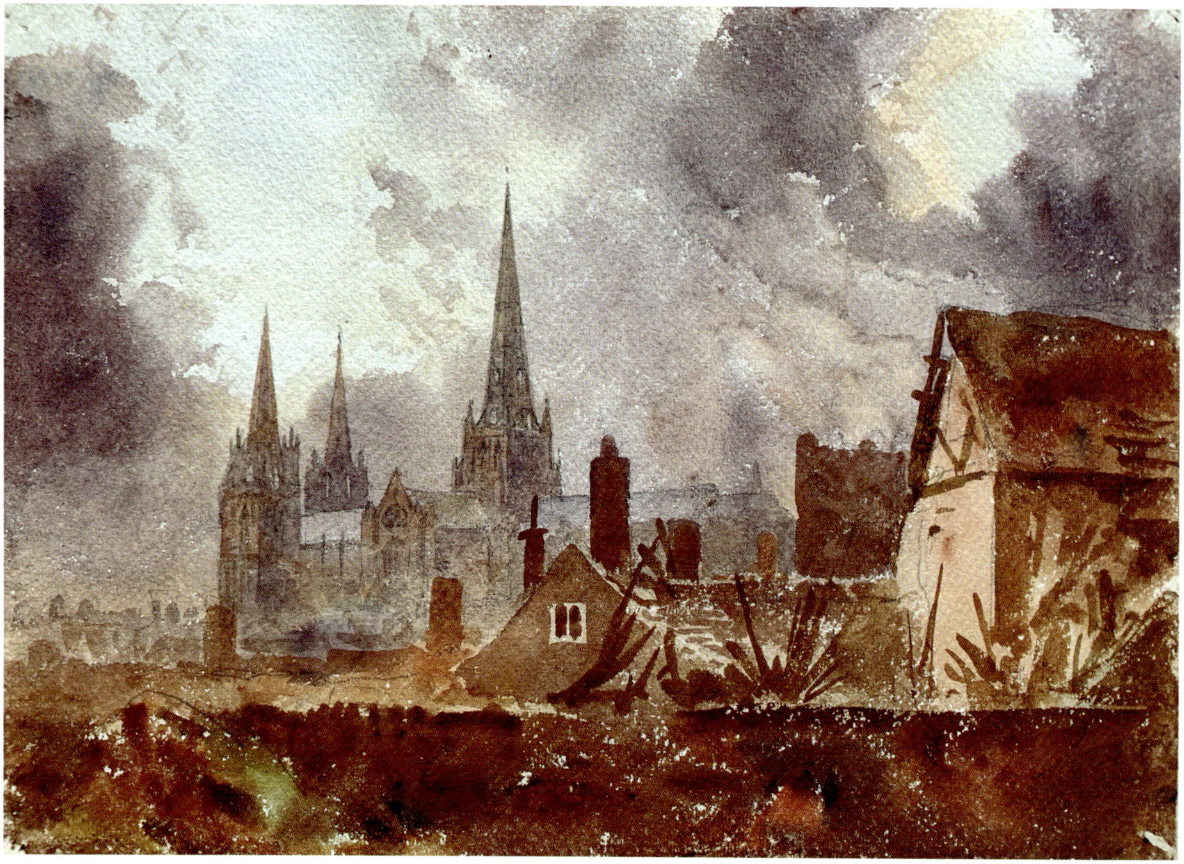

100. *Lichfield,* Cathedral, 9 April 1857

The Lichfield pictures are important as, in just the twenty unspoilt ones that are currently known,[38] they suggest the most varied artistic interpretation of the cathedral, or indeed of any English cathedral. Other impressionistic watercolourists painted the same scene many times, such as David Cox at Morecombe Bay thirty years earlier. Pre-Raphaelite artists dwelt on one subject or a particular female model. Monet painted several profound series to capture light effects: including that of Rouen Cathedral, a generation later. But even against these examples Petit's was an extraordinarily intensive study, especially during the last 12 years of his life when it appears to have been consciously exploratory.

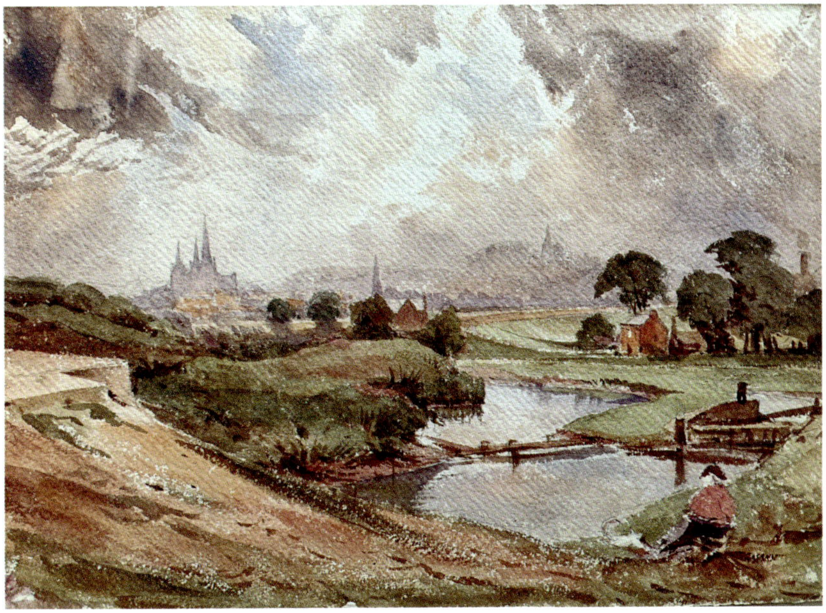

101. Above: *Lichfield,* Cathedral, 12 August 1867

102. Below: Elizabeth Haig (née Petit) *Lichfield,* 5 September 1867. The J. L. Petit picture above shows one of his sisters painting. This shows Petit painting a slightly different view

In a speech in 1852 Petit discussed the cathedral's unique architectural and artistic characteristics:

> *'In [Lichfield Cathedral] everything is so accurately adjusted, as to give an air of compactness and unity. I doubt if even an alteration of scale would not be prejudicial. For grandeur is not intended to be its characteristic so much as beauty of outline. [...] The cathedral is not a large one, and perhaps the excellence of its proportions may make it appear smaller than it really is. I have rarely seen a satisfactory drawing of this cathedral, and I believe it to be a very difficult subject for the artist.'*[39]

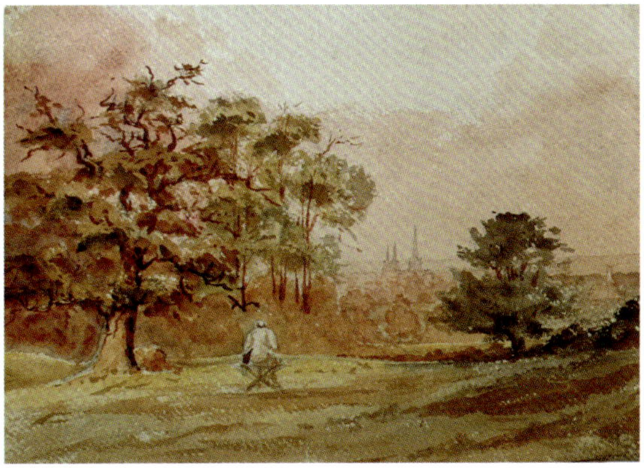

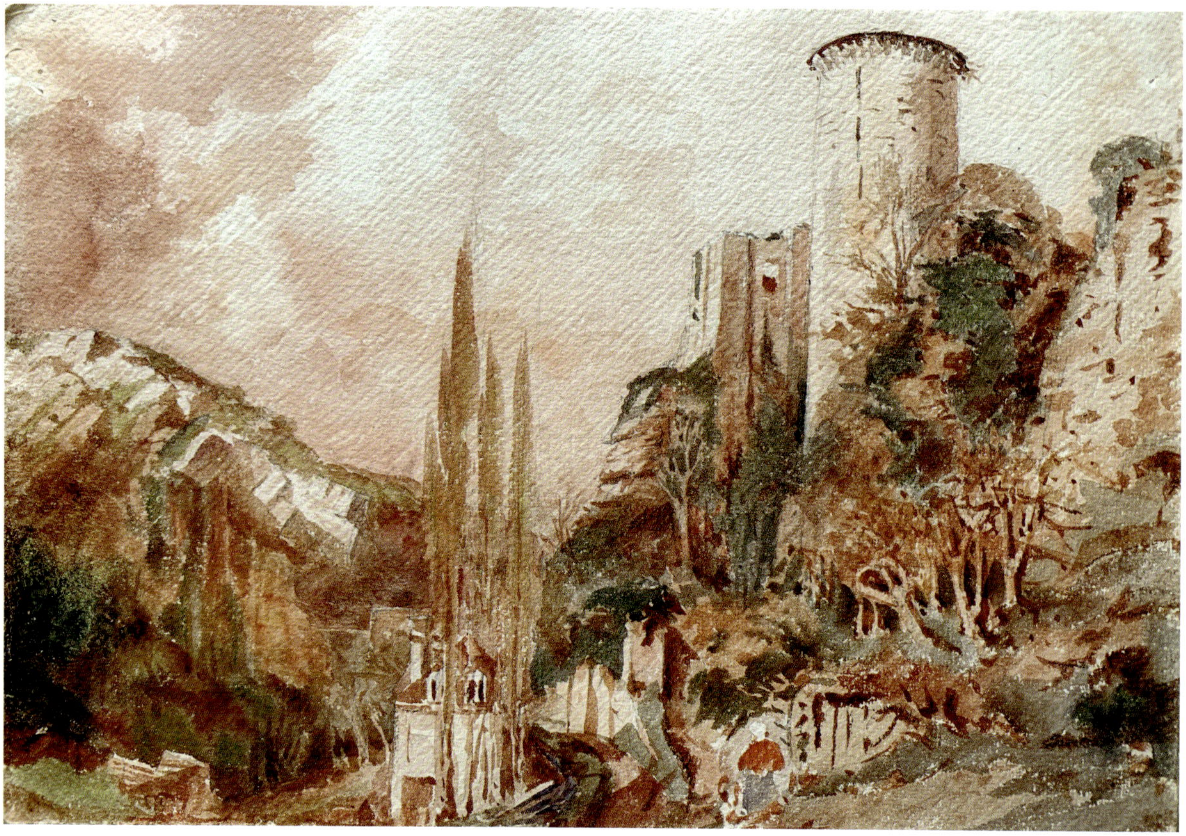

103. *Falaise Castle,* Normandy, November 1859
104. Opposite page: *Askeaton,* 14 October 1862

Landscape and Petit's Colour

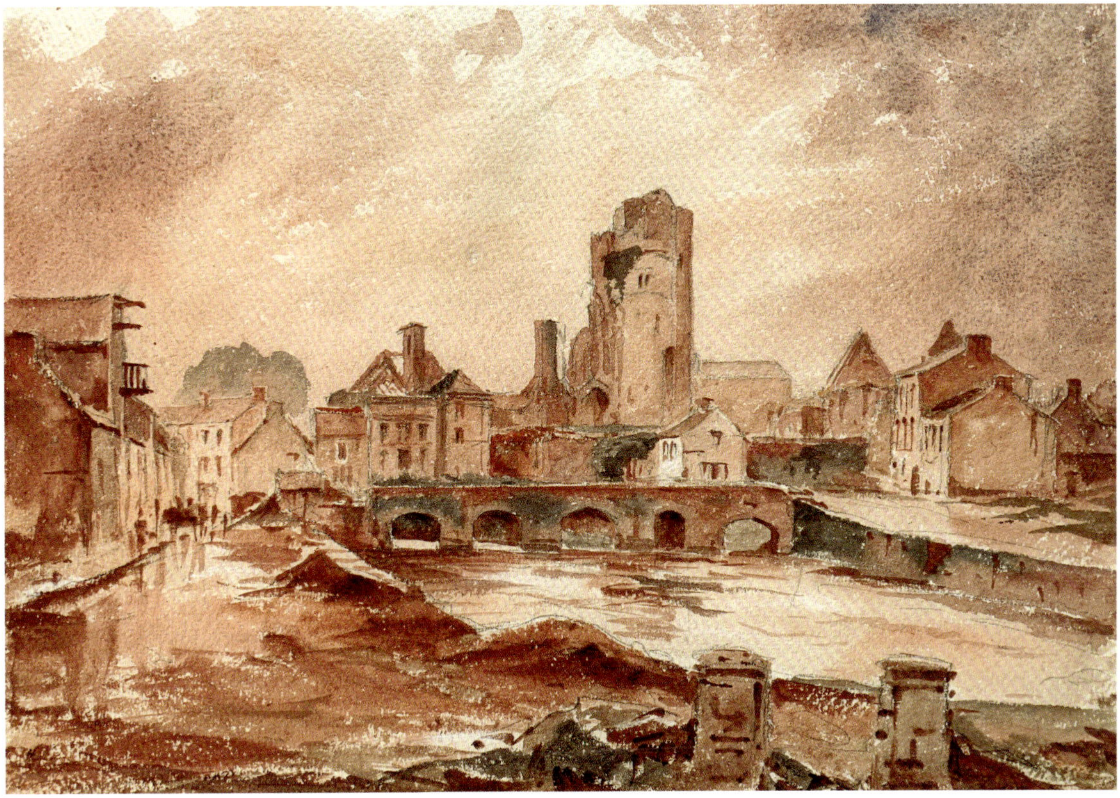

The majority of Petit's later works have a reddish cast, which can be disconcerting when encountered for the first time. On closer acquaintance this contributes to Petit's originality and power. It foreshadows a more modern approach to landscape where colour is not to be copied, as in a photograph, but is used as an instrument for the artist's purpose.

This palette, or something approaching it, seems to have been first used around 1843 (see pages 70-71) when Petit retreated from the exuberant style he had adopted just before publication of *Remarks*. Possibly this was in reaction to comments about the prettiness of its illustrations. Perhaps as his reputation grew as an architectural commentator, his art had to reflect the seriousness of that endeavour. Or the intention could have been to stand apart from the purely decorative art of earlier watercolourists, classical artists and the later Pre-Raphaelite and Aesthetic art of the 1850s and 1860s and communicate a more spiritual message (see also *Artix*, inside front cover). Most likely it was a combination of these reasons, and even convenience too.

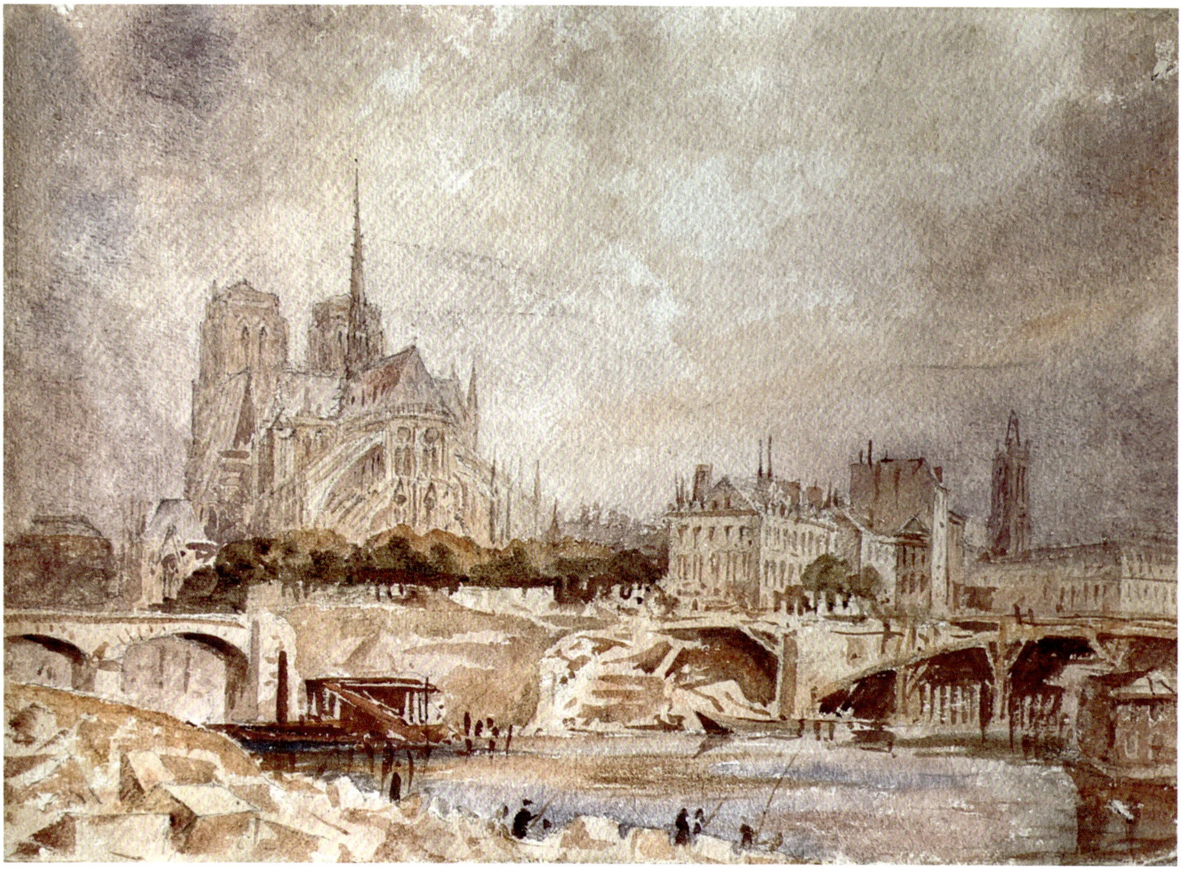

105. *Notre-Dame, Paris,* 10 September 1861

One can at least be sure that it was deliberate. A few pictures were given a more typical colouring throughout the same period – as we have seen. Also, Petit returned to paint using bright colours during his trip down the Nile and then across Syria in 1865 shown in the next section.

Askeaton (104) and *Near Pau* shown opposite are among the most severe. In *Notre-Dame* (above), the contrast between the cathedral and the grubby banks of the Seine would have made this picture discordant in the 19th century, both in England and France.

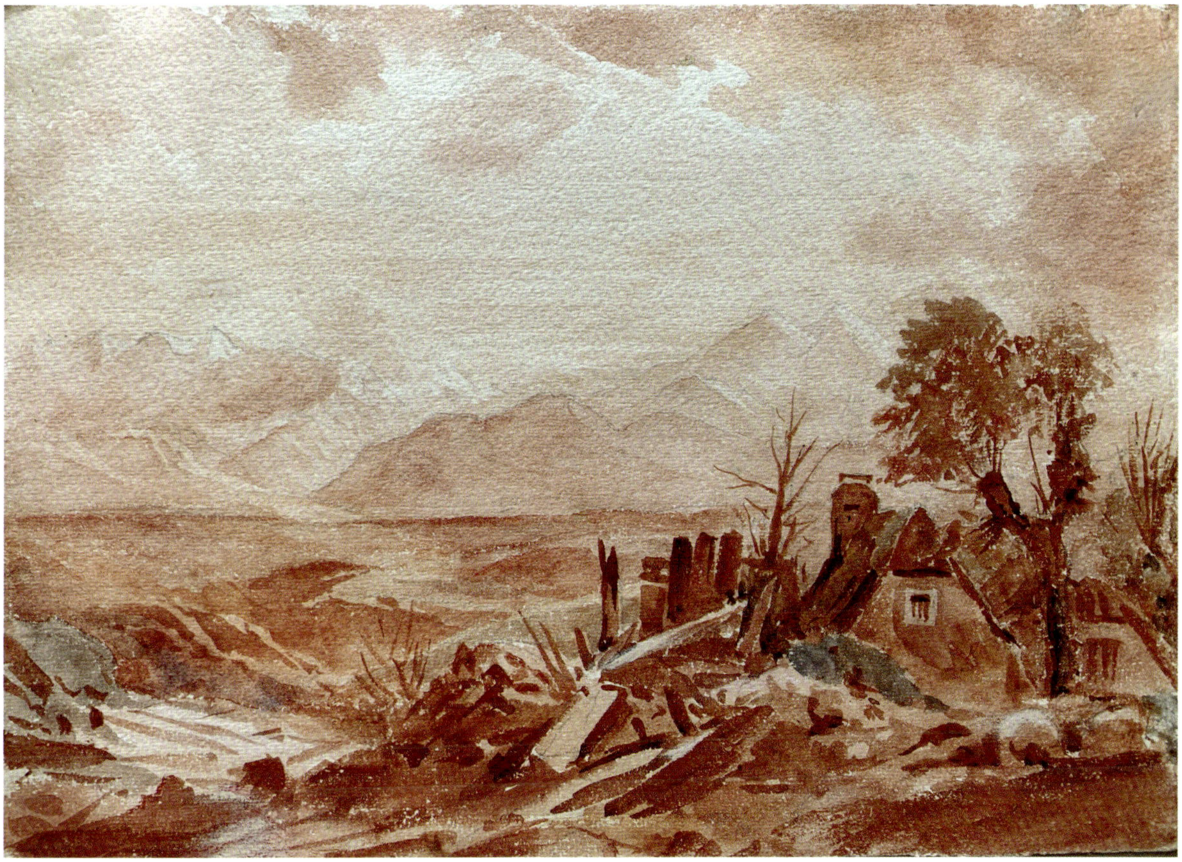

106. *Near Pau,* Pyrenees, 3 December 1859

Yet in none is the colour uniform: there are many subtle changes of shade, dashes of other colours and a clear sense of light and shadow. Exhibition labels on the backs indicate that such pictures were exhibited. Sir George Gilbert Scott described Petit as a 'most original artist' (see p. 35) and these are among the most original of Petit's works.

As Ruskin said:

> *'...it is possible that such means may be singular, and then it will be said that [the artist's] style is strange; but it is not a style at all, it is the saying of a particular thing in the only way in which it possibly can be said.'*[40]

The Middle East 1865: Egypt and Syria

We end our brief introduction with Petit's trip to the Middle East, because there, in 1865, near the end of his life, for a few months he recaptured that remarkable exuberance of colour shown in 1828 and in 1839.

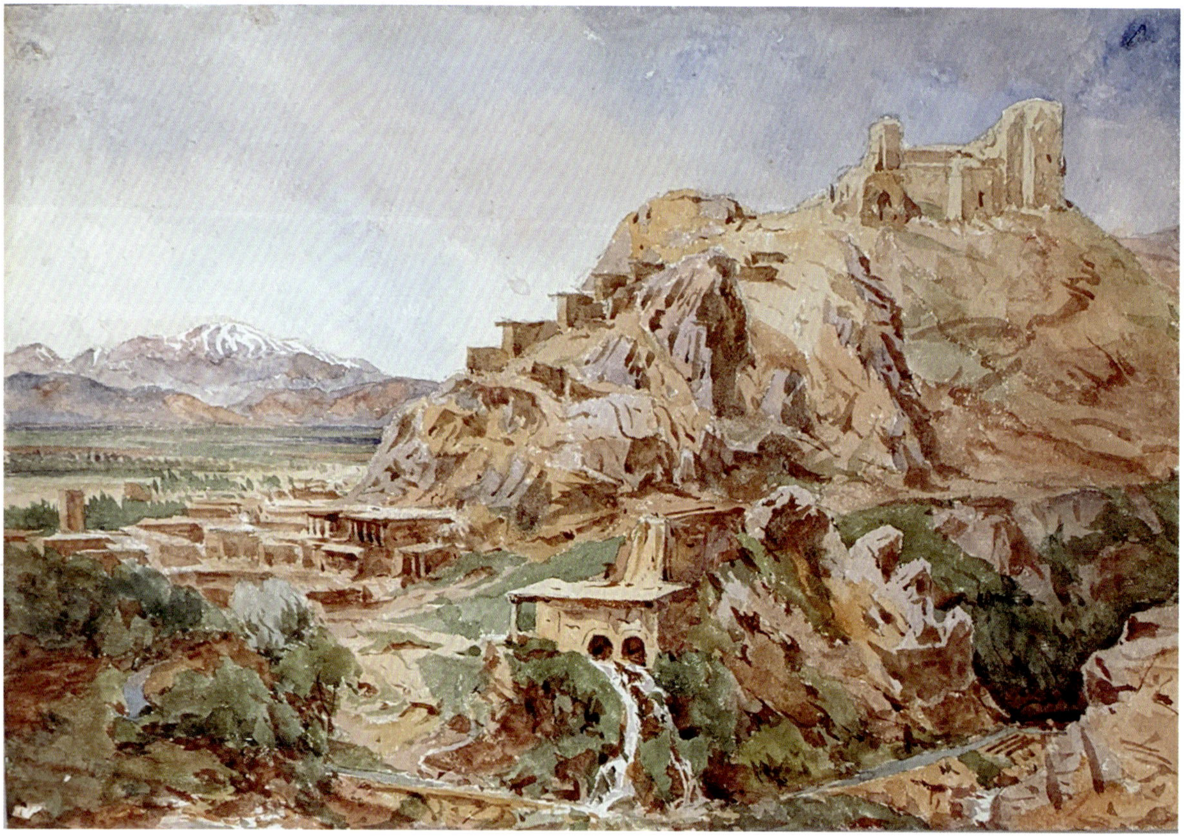

107. *Kubb Elias* (Qabb Ilyas), 7 June 1865

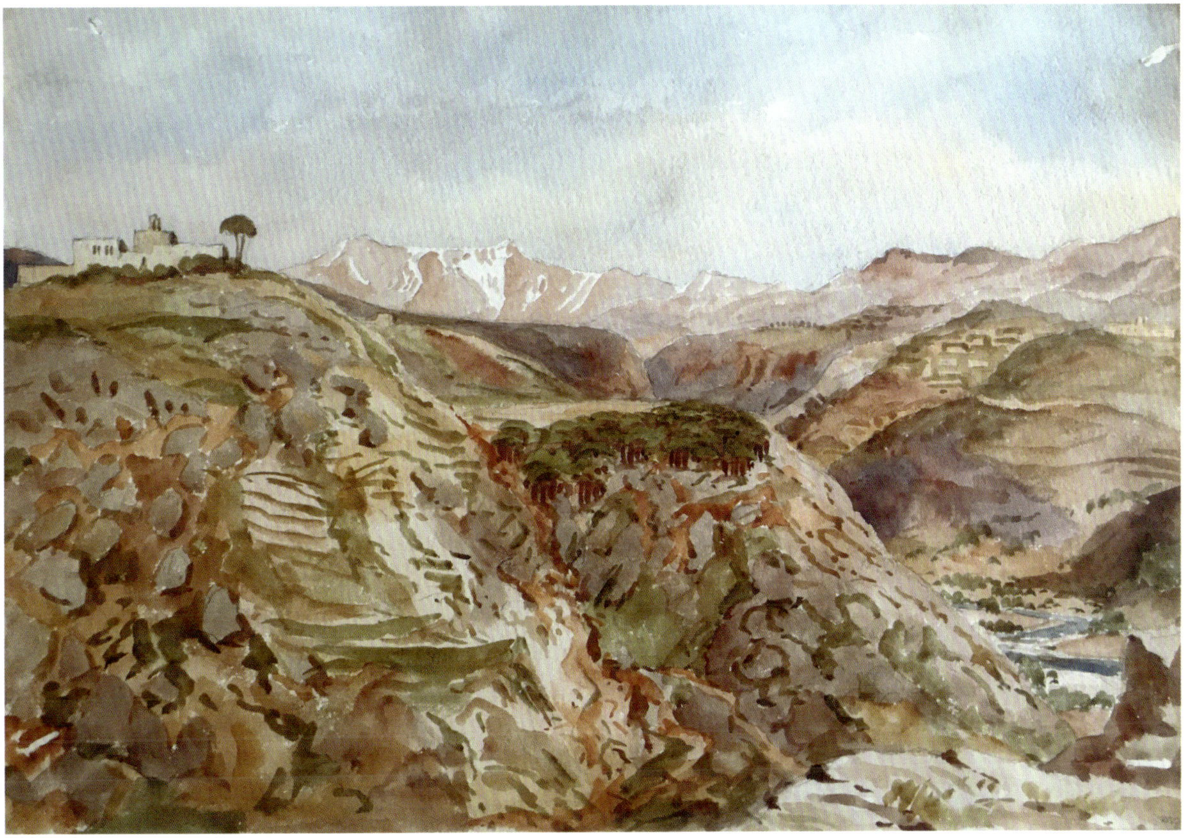

108. *Maronite Convent*, Lebanon, 23 May 1865

The trip was in two halves: first, a leisurely four to five months with several family companions travelling by hired boat down the Nile, visiting the sights in Egypt in reach of the river. This had become a fairly well-established holiday itinerary for wealthy Europeans.[41] Secondly, it was followed by a more typical rapid Petit dash through Syria, Palestine and Lebanon, accompanied probably only by his closest sister, Emma. Some architectural aspects of the trip were written up later in the form of a double article for the *Archaeological Journal*, and a public speech at the Architectural Exhibition in 1866.

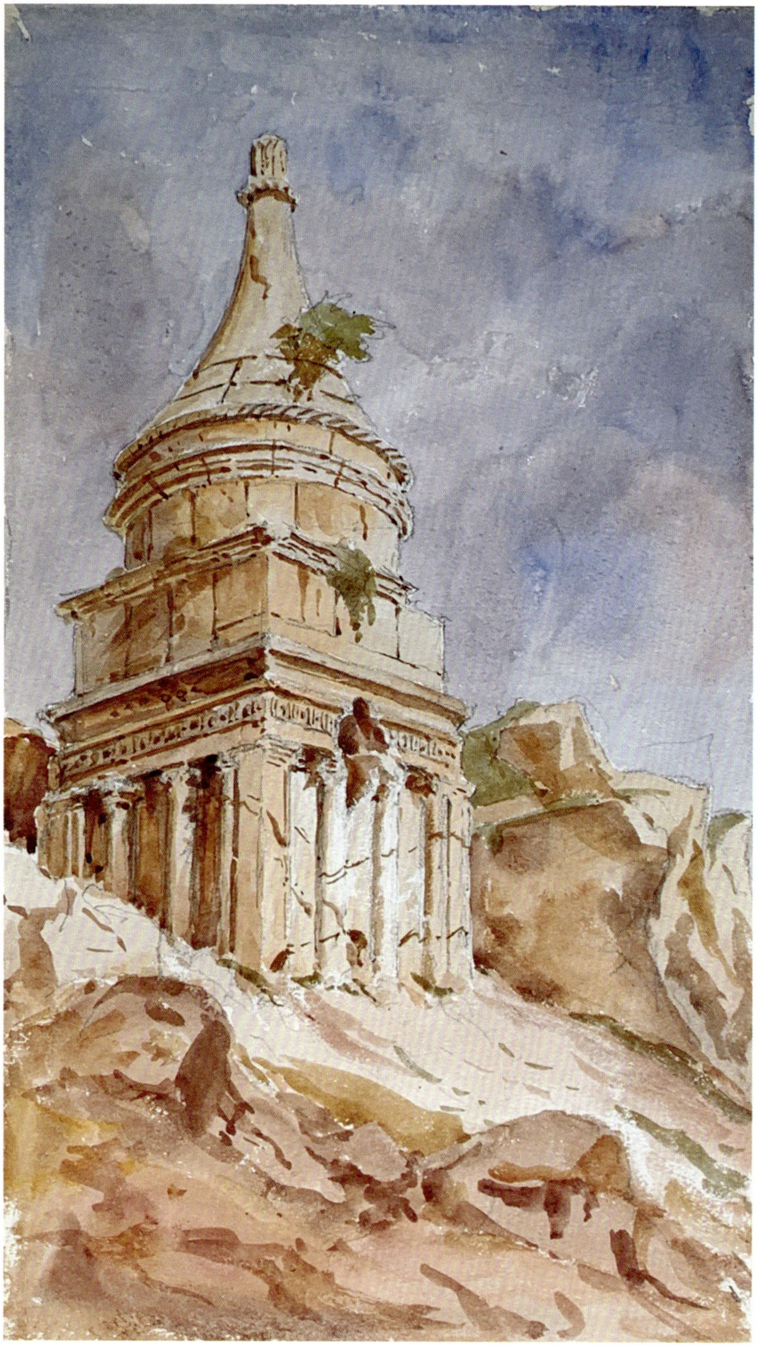

109. *Absalom's Tomb*, 10 May 1865

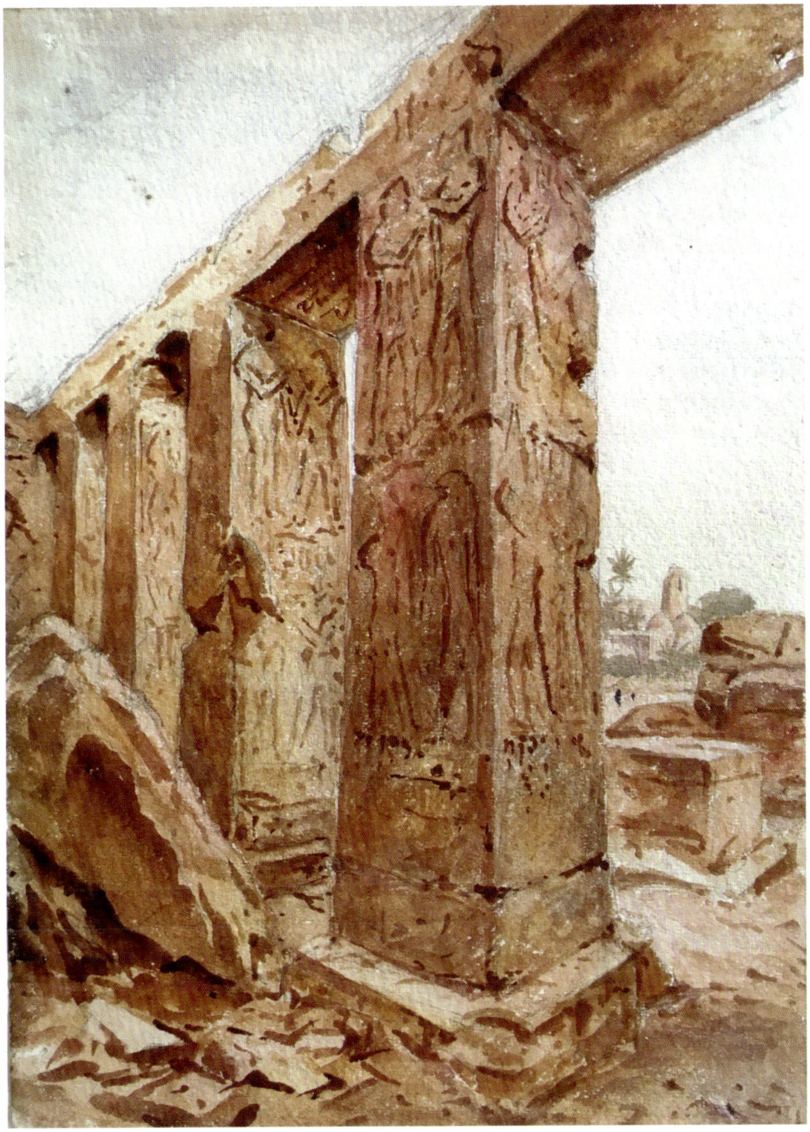

110. *Derr,* 2 Feb 1865 The Temple of Derr was relocated in 1964

While many Middle Eastern pictures emerged in the auctions at the end of the twentieth century, most were by Emma, or by other family members in Egypt. Petit completed three folios – around 300 pictures – on this trip but relatively few genuine J. L. Petits have been located. They may have been among the most sought after by his relatives on his death or those most raided by descendants afterwards. Abbott and Holder dispersed most others. The ones shown here are some of the few survivors of mice and damp not taken by relatives, descendants, or the dealer's other customers.

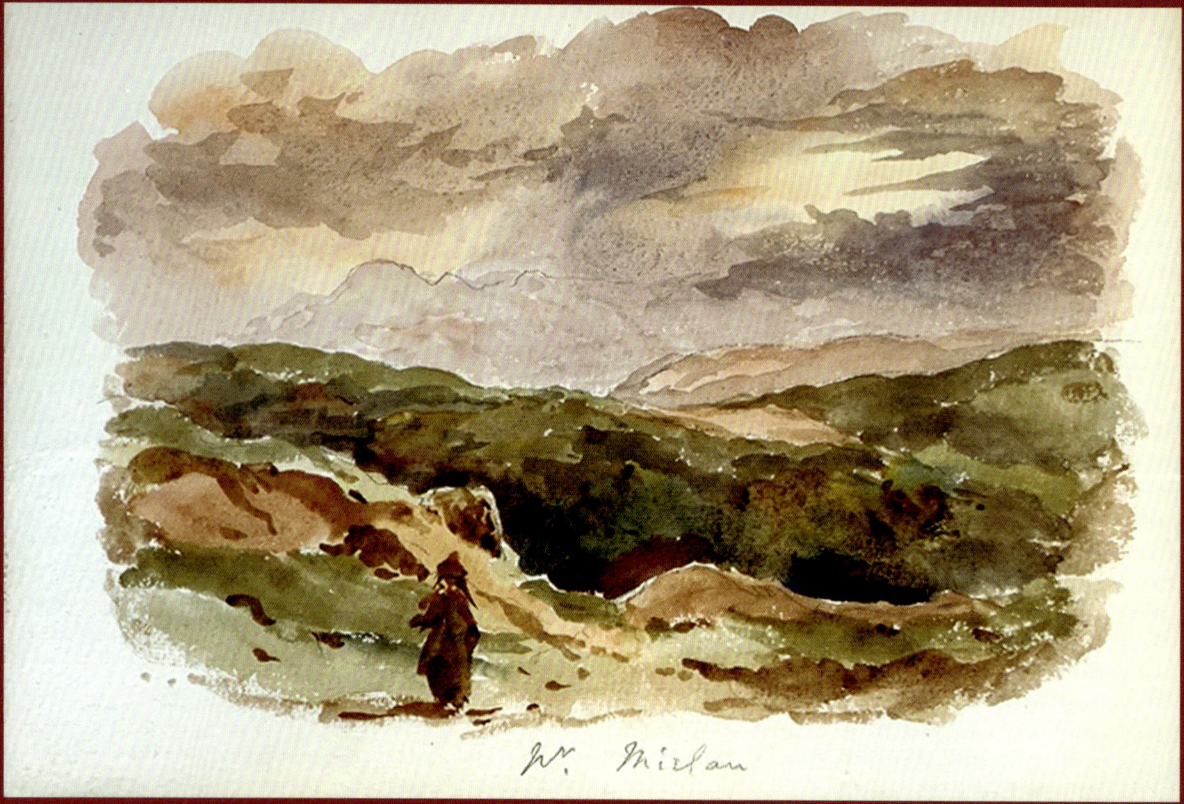

111. *Near Miélan,* southwestern France, 1858

Postscript

That then which I would have the reader inquire respecting every work of art of undetermined merit submitted to his judgement, is not whether it be a work of especial grandeur, importance or power; but whether it have any virtue or substance as a link in this chain of truth, whether it have recorded or interpreted anything before unknown, whether it have added one single stone to our heaven pointed pyramid, cut away one dark bough, or levelled one rugged hillock in our path.

J. Ruskin, *Modern Painters vol I*[42]

Petit's historical significance may be that he occupies a position unlike any of his contemporaries: unusual, for the mid-nineteenth century, for his choice of subject, his technique, his disdain of finish, and his immediacy in capturing an impression. Never oriented towards a market, Petit was just as highly motivated to communicate the beauty he saw - in factories and towns, and in sacred spaces, whether man or God-made.

As Petit wrote to a collector, Elias Magoon, from the USA, who had asked for a gift of several watercolours for his collection:[43]

> *'I have always been accustomed to sketch in a rough manner, and I don't suppose I should succeed if I attempted any other, and I do not touch my drawings, except to correct palpable errors, after I have finished working at them on the spot – Such as they are I hope you will accept them.'*

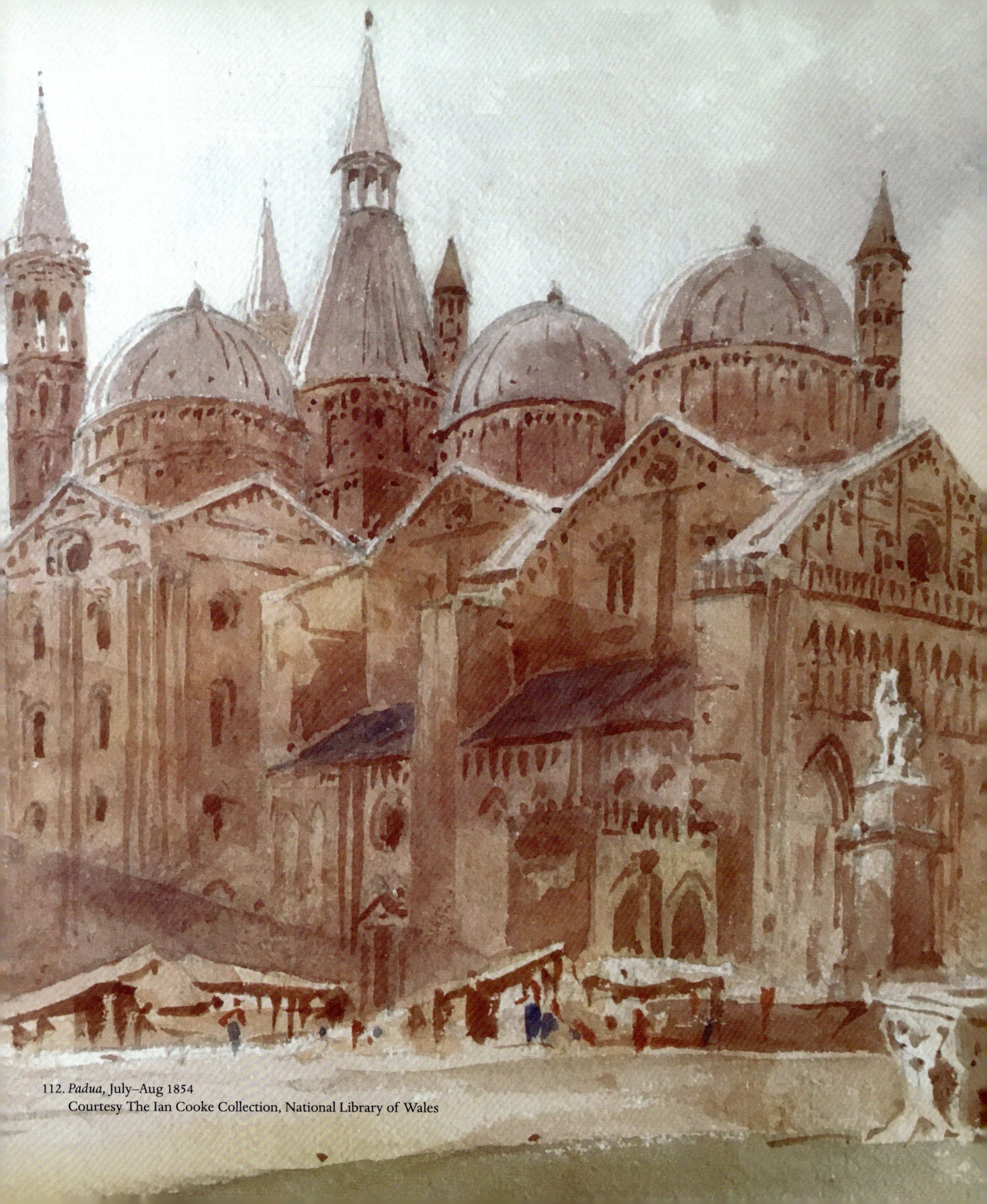

112. *Padua*, July–Aug 1854
Courtesy The Ian Cooke Collection, National Library of Wales

J. L. Petit Key Dates

Biographical

1801	J. L. Petit born to Rev. John Hayes Petit, vicar of Shareshill, and Harriet (née Astley)
1822–6	BA, MA Cambridge, Trinity College; Holy Orders Diocese of Lichfield
1826–8	Assistant curate, St Michael's, Lichfield
1828	Married Louisa Reid at Wye, Kent. No children
1828–34	Curate Bradfield and Mistley, Essex (on Stour near Harwich)
1834–c. 1849	Lived at Shifnal, Shropshire and Hastings, Sussex (at least 1839-42)
1849–68	Lived in Lichfield, London and small summer house at Upper Longdon, Staffs
1868	Died in Lichfield; buried in St Michael's churchyard, Lichfield

Writing and Public Career

1841	First major book: *Remarks on Church Architecture*
1841	Dispute with Gilbert Scott re. St Mary's, Stafford
1845	Second book: *Remarks on Architectural Character*
1845–80	Articles (17) and papers delivered for the Archaeological Institute (3 posthumous)
	Four booklets of speeches
1848–60	Fellow RIBA; FSA; honorary degree Oxford
1854	Third book: *Architectural Studies in France*
1856–66	Exhibited and lectured at annual Architectural Exhibition, London
1869	Exhibition of over 300 Petit pictures at the last Architectural Exhibition
1869	Publication (by Emma G. Petit, sister) of poem *The Lesser and the Greater Light*

Main Painting Tours *(excludes frequent travel around Britain and France)*

1832–4	First known painting trip abroad – Low Countries
1839	Germany, Switzerland, Italy and France for *Remarks*
c.1843	Isle of Man, also in 1845 and one or two other occasions
1851–2	Intensive trip through western France for *Architectural Studies*
1854	Six-month trip through France, Italy and Germany, with two sisters
1856	Through Germany to Prague with Emma and Sarah Salt
1857	First trip to East: Adriatic, Corfu, Athens and Constantinople
1858	Southern France, Spain and North Africa (pictures not traced)
1861–2	Supervised building of church at Caerdeon, near Barmouth, Wales
1862	Main Ireland trip. Others in 1867 and possibly 1830s
1864–5	Six-month trip to Egypt and Syria (including Lebanon and Jerusalem)

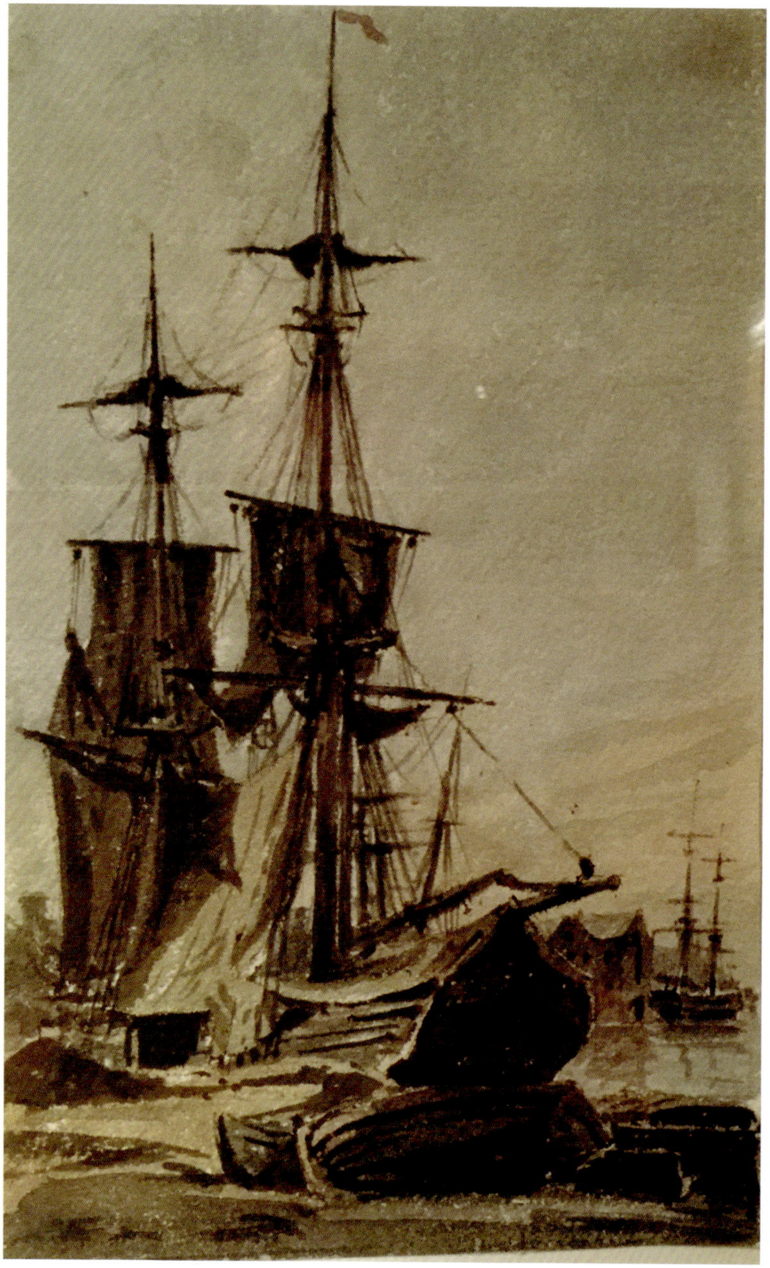

113. *The Brig*, Harwich, 1830-34

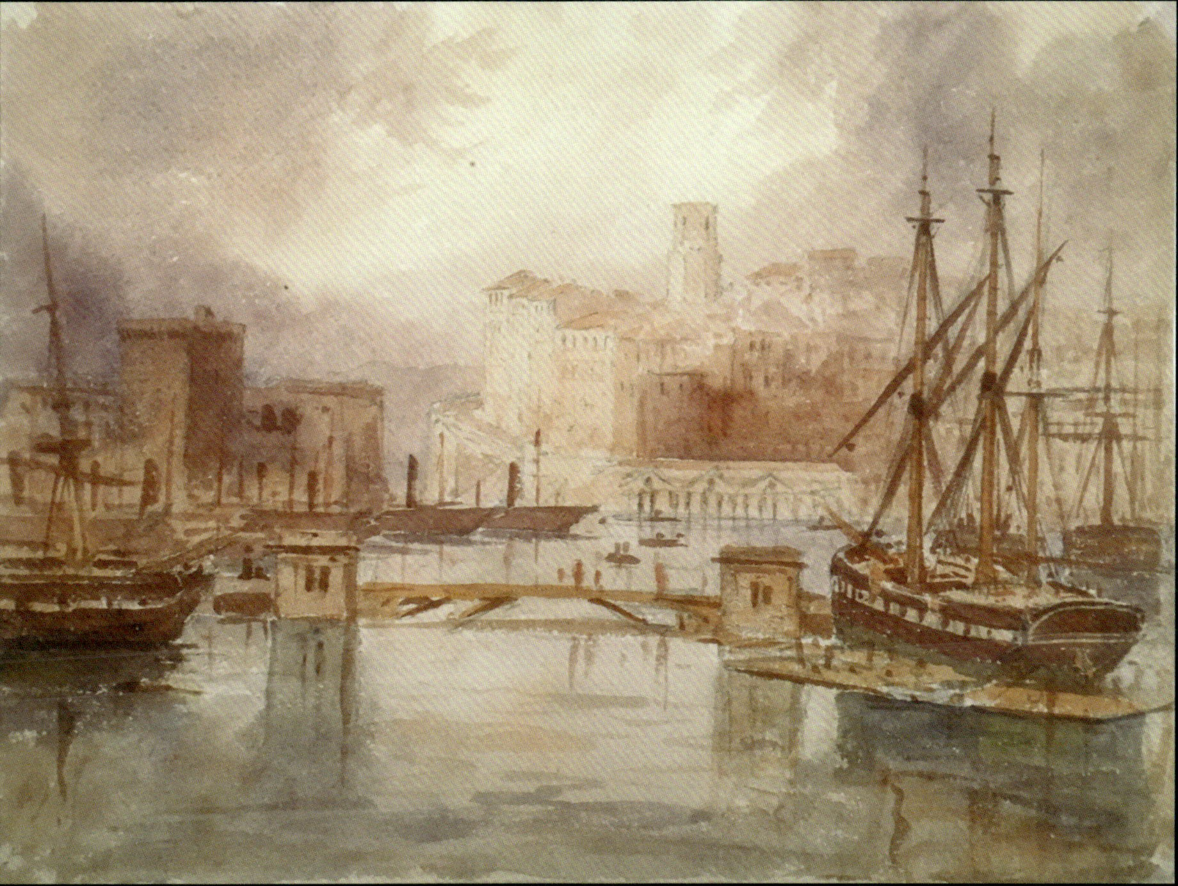

114. *Marseilles,* 20 April 1854
Courtesy The Ian Cooke Collection, National Library of Wales

List of Illustrations

All watercolours with pencil by J. L. Petit except where stated, measurements in cm (height x width)

Petit Pictures - Places Depicted

Petit pictures by country, location and date.
Petit's title italicised

Footnotes

1. Starting in 1850 purely as an exhibition in response to the declining emphasis on architecture in the Royal Academy exhibitions. A lecture series was added in 1855. For the next 13 years they were major events. The last exhibition was in 1869, the occasion of the large Petit exhibition, where there were no lectures.
2. A catalogue listing the pictures is held in the National Art Library at the V&A.
3. John Ruskin, *Modern Painters,* Vol. III, p. 42. Page numbers are from The Library Edition (1912) online edition hosted by Lancaster University.
4. For a biography, see www.revpetit.com, or the biographical chapter in *Petit's Tours of Old Staffordshire* (RPS Publications 2019). 'Noble-hearted' is from Sir George Gilbert Scott (*Recollections,* 2005 ed, pp. 297-8).
5. For example, Edward Freeman, a leading authority, wrote in his own 1849 book, *History of Architecture,* that he put two authors head and shoulders above the rest. One was Petit; the other, Thomas Hope, who had died nearly twenty years before. Other books, according to Freeman, had not been so wide-ranging, insightful and fact-based.
6. *The Lesser and the Greater Light* was published, unfinished, after his death by his sister, Emma Petit, who organised most of his work and painted with him on many occasions. The poem confirms Petit's combination of forward thinking and traditional, albeit liberal, sincere belief. These are stanzas 79 and 83.
7. This particular passage comes from the preface written in 1842, Vol. I, p. 22. However, the comparisons run through Ruskin's *Modern Painters,* despite Ruskin not referring to Petit directly in any volume.
8. J. L. Petit, 'Utilitarianism in Architecture', speech to the 1856 Architectural Exhibition published in *The Builder,* 26 January 1856.
9. J. L. Petit, 'On Architectural Refinement', 16 March 1859, speech to the Architectural Museum, South Kensington, published in *The Builder.*
10. The substance of this section was first published in the *British Art Journal* 2021, and is summarised here with kind permission of the editor.
11. J. L. Petit, 'On Architectural Refinement', March 1859.
12. John Abbott of Abbott and Holder used this term in introducing Petit in 1984. At that stage they had many of his early works but not his later works.
13. J. L. Petit, *Remarks on Church Architecture* (1841), Vol. II, p. 163.
14. Ruskin first criticised Pre-Raphaelite landscapes in Vol. IV (1855), p. 30, and then repeated his disillusion at length in Vol. V in 1860, p. 233. It was not one isolated comment, but one he reiterated with intense regret.
15. J. Ruskin, *Modern Painters,* Vol. I, p. 176.
16. Dante Gabriel Rossetti is quoted as saying this about his *Monna Vanna* (1866), in the catalogue description on the Tate website (2021).
17. John Ruskin, *Modern Painters,* Vol. III, p. 186.
18. J. L. Petit, 'Remarks on Byzantine Churches', *RIBA Transactions,* 8 March 1858, p. 132.
19. J. L. Petit, 'On the Revival of Styles', speech to the Architectural Exhibition published in *The Builder,* 25 May 1859.
20. One of Petit's nephews, Sir Thomas Salt, acquired most of those that had been exhibited in 1869 and built a large gallery under a glass roof to display them in.
21. For two examples of Petit's sisters' works see numbers 80 and 102 on p. 83 and p. 101; more are at www.revpetit.com/circle. They vary from the obviously weaker to ones that are hard to distinguish. Until 2017 all were sold as J. L. Petit.
22. Sir George Gilbert Scott, *Recollections,* edited by Gavin Stamp (2005), p. 297–8.
23. *The Lesser and the Greater Light* stanzas 429-430
24. J. L. Petit, 'Utilitarianism in Architecture', 1856.
25. J. L. Petit, *Remarks,* Vol. 2, p. 209.
26. J. L. Petit, *Remarks,* preface, p. vi.
27. Jonathan Richardson the Elder, *An Essay on the Theory of Painting* (London 1715).
28. J. L. Petit, *Architectural Studies in France,* (1854) concluding chapter p. 170.
29. J. L. Petit, 'On Architectural Refinement', March 1859.
30. See *Clarke, Petit and St Mark's – A 19th Century Journey on the Isle of Man* (RPS publications, 2022).
31. Petit's mother had had an accident and stayed at Thirsk for several months; Petit stayed with her.
32. J. L. Petit, *Remarks,* Vol. 1, p. 2.
33. J. L. Petit, 'Utilitarianism in Architecture', *op. cit.* at no. 8.
34. *The Lesser and the Greater Light,* lines 1062-65.
35. *The Lesser and the Greater Light,* lines 730–31.
36. J. Ruskin, *Modern Painters,* Vol. I, p. 22.
37. Judging by the labels on the back of pictures, there were over 60 folios of later work. Only 21 lists of their contents have been found. Many pictures are thought to have been destroyed by damp.
38. See *Petit's Tours of Old Staffordshire* where twelve are illustrated.
39. J. L. Petit, 'On Architectural Principles and Prejudices', speech to the Northampton Mechanics Institute, 21 December 1853, Northampton 1854.
40. J. Ruskin, *Modern Painters,* Vol. 1, p. 194.
41. See a description, from a trip in the same year, by Rev. Alfred Smith in *The Nile and Its Banks* (London 1868).
42. J. Ruskin, *Modern Painters,* Vol I, p. 173.
43. J. L. Petit to Rev. Elias Magoon, 27 February 1856, item 5.41 Artistic Autographs, box 5, Magoon Papers, Special Collections, Vassar College, NY, who also hold the pictures.

General Index

(q) indicates the entry may be a quote

Acknowledgements

I am grateful to Robin Simon, Andrew Graham-Dixon and Trevor James for their endorsements. Jenny Gaschke, senior curator at Bristol Museum, David Blayney Brown, formerly of Tate, and Wojtek Szatkowski read the text and suggested many useful changes. My thanks also to the Lichfield Conduit Lands Trust and the Paul Mellon Centre for British Art who awarded grants to the Petit Society which facilitated the production of this book.

Thanks also to the following dealers who assisted with research above and beyond normal commercial considerations: Abbott and Holder, Chris Beetles, Jacob Boston, Cliff Evans, Greg Page-Turner, Guy Peppiatt, John Robertson, and Jeremy Wood.

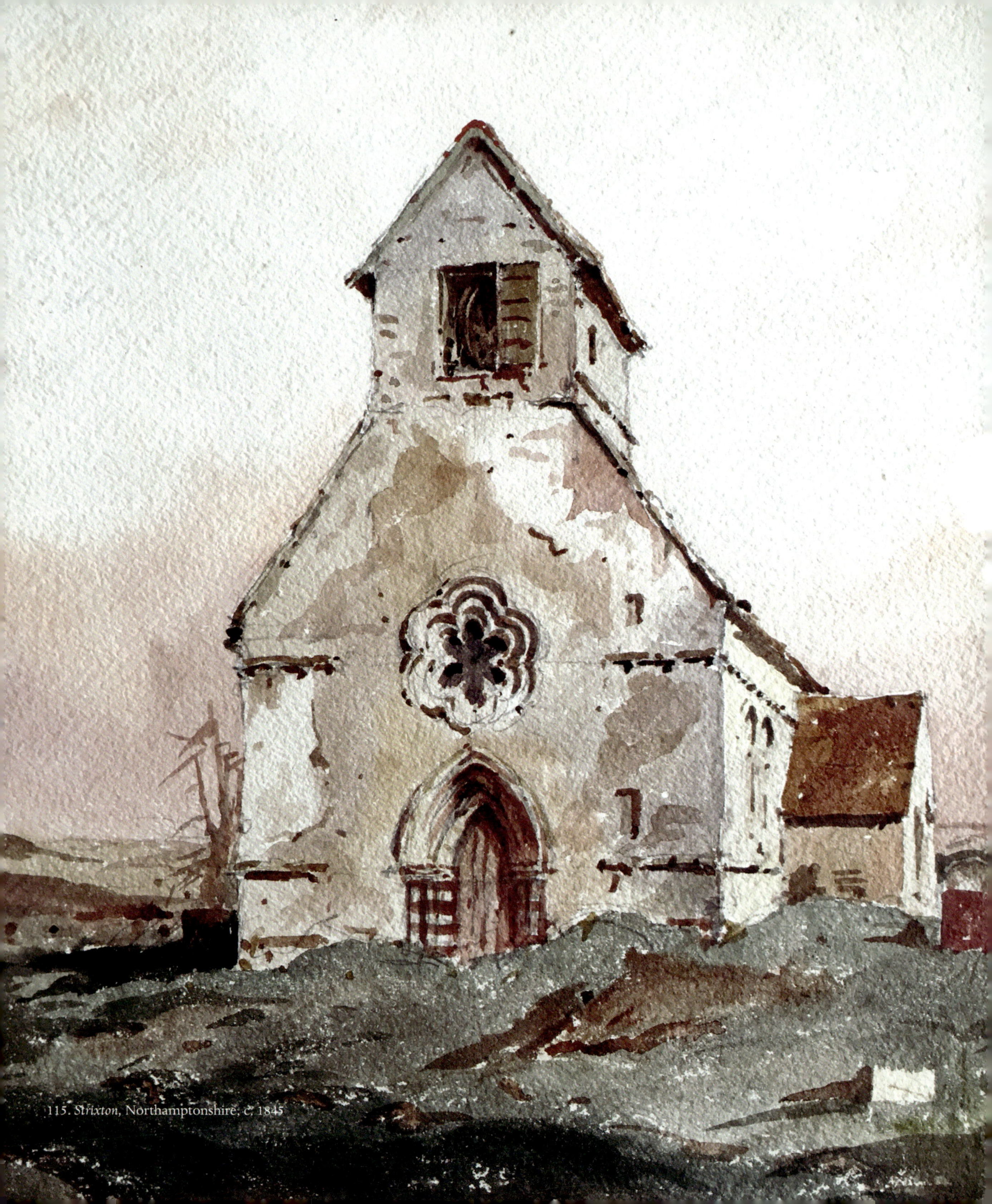

115. *Strixton*, Northamptonshire, c. 1845